Among Equals

Among Equals

The Causes of Effective Corruption Prosecution in Italy

Lucia Manzi

LEXINGTON BOOKS
Lanham • Boulder • New York • London

Published by Lexington Books
An imprint of The Rowman & Littlefield Publishing Group, Inc.
4501 Forbes Boulevard, Suite 200, Lanham, Maryland 20706
www.rowman.com

86-90 Paul Street, London EC2A 4NE

British Library Cataloguing in Publication Information Available

Library of Congress Cataloging-in-Publication Data

Names: Manzi, Lucia, author.
Title: Among equals : the causes of effective corruption prosecution in Italy / Lucia Manzi.
Description: Lanham : Lexington Books, 2023. | Includes bibliographical references and index. | Contents: Introduction : the long failure of corruption prosecutions and the Mani Pulite operation's breakthrough — From hierarchical to egalitarian : the root causes of prosecutorial independence and effectiveness against systemic corruption — A more democratic judiciary : the transformation of Italian judicial and prosecutorial institutions — All investigations lead to Rome : the Roman Prosecutor's Office — A new model of criminal justice : the Milan Prosecutor's Office — Tackling Omertà : the Prosecutors' Offices in Palermo and Reggio Calabria — Conclusion-lessons for prosecutorial success against corruption. | Summary: "Through a study of the Italian Clean Hands operation, the author shows that the introduction of egalitarian decision-making within local prosecutors' offices is a crucial condition for the effective prosecution of systemic corruption"—Provided by publisher.
Identifiers: LCCN 2023039049 (print) | LCCN 2023039050 (ebook) | ISBN 9781666938487 (cloth) | ISBN 9781666938494 (epub)
Subjects: LCSH: Corruption—Law and legislation—Italy. | Misconduct in office—Law and legislation—Italy. | Prosecution—Italy. | Special prosecutors—Italy. | Corruption—Italy—Prevention. | Equality before the law—Italy. | Criminal justice, Administration of—Italy.
Classification: LCC KKH4516 .M36 2023 (print) | LCC KKH4516 (ebook) | DDC 345.45/02323—dc23/eng/20230929
LC record available at https://lccn.loc.gov/2023039049
LC ebook record available at https://lccn.loc.gov/2023039050

Contents

List of Figures

List of Tables

Acknowledgments

It is one of my firm beliefs that sometimes the research projects we choose to work on have deep ties to our own identity and sense of self. The way I landed on the topic for this book feels deeply personal, even though, when I chose the topic of my dissertation, I did not immediately realize the relevance it held for me. As an Italian abroad, I am particularly proud of the efforts and stories of Italian judicial professionals who devoted their whole careers, and sometimes sacrificed their lives, in the pursuit of the democratic rule of law. I am happy that the research in this book also gave me a chance to discuss and present some of these stories, such as the impressive ethical commitment of Guido Galli, the genius and bravery of Giovanni Falcone and Paolo Borsellino, and many other stories of devotion to the rule of law. I hope this book is also, in a very small way, an attempt to honor these judicial professionals' efforts.

This book has been a long time in the making, and it would not have been possible without the intellectual, professional, and personal support of a lot of people to whom I am immensely grateful. First of all, I owe a huge debt of gratitude to my dissertation committee, above all my advisor Scott Mainwaring, whose knowledge and support made this research possible. This research would also not have come to fruition without the expert guidance of my co-advisor, Andy Gould, and my committee members, Emilia Powell and Paolo Carozza. I also wish to thank Sandra Botero, whose feedback, guidance, and support over the years were indispensable, and Ezequiel González-Ocantos, whose brilliant insights helped me give shape to this research and whose support for this project has been fundamental. I also owe immense gratitude to Lisa Hilbink for her continuous support and encouragement, her helpful feedback, and incredible generosity. Furthermore, I wish to thank Laura Gamboa and Ana Petrova for helping me think through several parts of this project.

I am also immensely grateful to Barbara J. Denison for all her guidance and help over the years. I also owe debt of gratitude to Rocco D'Ambrosio, who always encouraged me in my research efforts. I am grateful for the editorial support I received at Lexington from Sara Noakes and Becca Beurer. I am also thankful to the anonymous reviewers who provided comments and feedback on this project at different stages of its development.

Over the last years, I have had a chance to present different parts of this book at several workshops and conferences. I am especially grateful to Maria Popova and Manuel Balán for inviting me to participate in the workshop on the politics of corruption prosecutions at McGill University. I am also thankful to Matthew M. Taylor and Luciano Da Ros for their comments on my paper. I am also grateful to Emily Bacchus and Tiffany Barnes for inviting me to present my work at a panel on corruption and democracy at the International Studies Association annual conference. Special thanks also go to Yasser Kureshi for inviting me, along with Lisa Hilbink, to participate in a workshop on judicial populism. I also wish to thank the other workshop participants: Anuj Bhuwania, Rafael Mafei Rabelo Queiroz, Rohit De, and Fabio Costa Morais de Sa E Silva. Finally, I am grateful to Diana Kapiszewski and Sebastian Karcher for inviting me to present my work at a special workshop on ATI. In the context of the latter workshop, I am grateful to Anne Holthoefer, Katarina Sipulova, Gregory Michener, and Brad Epperly for their feedback. I am immensely grateful to Tommaso Pavone for his insightful feedback on this project and precious advice. Finally, I am thankful to Richard Ashby Wilson for his helpful feedback on a paper related to this project, which I presented at the Law and Society Association's annual conference. My thanks also go to my department colleagues at SUNY Plattsburgh for their unending support: Dan Lake, Ray Carman, John McMahon, and Harvey Schantz.

Parts of chapters 2 and 3 in this book also appear in "Prosecutorial Gatekeeping and Its Effects on Criminal Accountability: The Roman Prosecutor's Office and Corruption Investigations in Italy, 1975–1994," by Lucia Manzi, published in the *Justice System Journal*, Volume 43, Issue 3, 2022, copyright ©Owned by the National Center for State Courts, www.ncsc.org, reprinted by permission of Taylor & Francis Ltd, http://www.tandfonline.com on behalf of Owned by the National Center for State Courts, www.ncsc.org.

I also owe an immense debt of gratitude to my family: my mom, for teaching me that a woman's greatest treasure is her education, my dad, for instilling in me the greatest reverence for justice and the rule of law, my brother, for being an incredible adventure companion and one of the kindest people I know, and my grandparents, who are always with me.

Too many friends have helped me grow and thrive and have made this work possible by believing in me and lifting me up when I couldn't do it by myself.

Among them, special thanks go to Domenico Mongiello, who believed in me from the very beginning. I also need to thank Rachele Mocchetti, Antonella Piccinin, Silvia Camilleri, Giulia Borsotti, Danuta Conti, Veronica Ceruti, Ilaria Schnyder, Chiara Bernardini, Justin McDevitt, Fernando Bizzarro, and Thais de Palma for their continued and extraordinary support over the years. I could not have survived my grad school years without a score of incredible people supporting me: Soledad Bertelsen, Theresa MacArt, Jasmin Avila-Sacco, Paul Higson, Emily Ransom, Kate Bermingham, Catherine Sims Kuiper, Maggie Shum, Aaron Pidel S. J., Joseph Riordan S. J., Anna Vincenzi, Brandon Cook, Pietro Bocchia, Martino Rabaioli, Aldo Tagliabue, Michelle Kundmueller, and Elisabeth Kincaid. Moreover, I could not have finished this book without the support and loving company of my dear Vermont-based friends, Gianpiero and Victoria Anelli. Special thanks also go to Marinella Lentis and Doug Davis, without whose support my academic journey would never have started.

Finally, this book would not exist without the enduring support, encouragement, and advice of my husband, best friend, and love of my life, Ben Denison. Every day I am grateful beyond words for the possibility of living this life with Ben. Ben, this book is for you.

Introduction

The Long Failure of Corruption Prosecutions and the Mani Pulite *Operation's Breakthrough*

On February 17, 1992, civil servant and head of the retirement home Pio Albergo Trivulzio, Mario Chiesa, was getting ready to collect another bribe from Luca Magni, one of the many company managers seeking to work with the city-run retirement service (Barbacetto, Gomez and Travaglio 2012, 5–6). The exchange was not unusual: Chiesa had been collecting bribes for decades from several companies and was privy to similar exchanges in other public administration branches (Barbacetto, Gomez and Travaglio 2012, 11–14). These illicit exchanges normally followed a well-established pattern of informal rules and procedures that made them predictable and consistent over time. More importantly, it made them highly profitable: the civil servant, who had received his appointment from the Milan city council as a representative of the Italian Socialist Party, would then proceed to redistribute some of the illegal contributions among members of his political party (Barbacetto, Gomez and Travaglio 2012, 11).

Therefore, Mario Chiesa's intermediary role between corrupt company managers and political parties represented "business as usual," one part of a larger corrupt scheme that allowed Italian political forces to exploit public resources to their own benefit. However, as opposed to previous instances in which similar corrupt exchanges had gone smoothly, this time a local law-enforcement unit led by prosecutor Antonio Di Pietro abruptly interrupted the transaction, catching Mario Chiesa in the act of receiving a bribe and soon after trying to flush further evidence away (Barbacetto, Gomez and Travaglio 2012, 5–6).

Mario Chiesa's arrest gave rise to a chain of events that would turn a routine bribe exchange into the biggest corruption investigation in Italian history, the so-called *Mani Pulite* (Clean Hands) operation. Prosecutor Antonio Di Pietro could have narrowed the inquiry to the illegal exchanges taking place between Chiesa and the local businessman who cooperated with the sting operation. Instead, the investigation gradually expanded beyond the local public administration to include illicit transactions involving state-owned companies and businesses operating across different regions. Consequently, the investigation, which turned into a prosecutorial effort embracing hundreds of cases and requiring a team of prosecutors, slowly moved its target from local politicians to members of Parliament and eventually to national party leaders as suspects at the center of a massive corruption scheme.

By the end of 1996, the year in which the Clean Hands operation formally concluded, the overall number of first-instance convictions had risen to 1,254 (Di Nicola 2003, 121).[1] However, this number only applies to convictions within the Milan jurisdiction. The Clean Hands operation also unleashed a wave of similar local investigations in other Italian jurisdictions. Some of these investigations followed the referral of cases from Milan (Di Nicola 2003, 120–21) and therefore directly derived from the Clean Hands prosecutorial team's efforts. Other investigations represented local autonomous attempts to mimic the Clean Hands prosecutorial team's work. Thus, the Clean Hands operation gave rise to an unprecedented wave of corruption investigations and convictions that propagated, although unevenly, across Italian jurisdictions.

This operation's unprecedented scope and success stand in stark contrast with past legal inquiries into the same type of crime. Certainly, Mario Chiesa was not the first civil servant to undergo investigation for corruption-related crimes. In the past, a few investigations had uncovered illicit transactions between local bureaucrats, businessmen, and elected officials. In 1974, for instance, investigations taking place within the Genoa jurisdiction uncovered a bribery scheme involving the *Unione Petrolifera*, Italy's oil trade association, and elected officials, which was geared toward producing "artificially high oil prices" (Guarnieri 2003, 145). Similarly, toward the end of the 1980s, Milanese prosecutors obtained a glimpse of the corruption system via the so-called Golden Prisons (*Carceri d'Oro*) scandal, which revolved around corrupt exchanges between local officials and businessmen for construction bids in Milan (*Un Pool di Giudici a Consulto sulle Maxitangente a Milano* 1988). Furthermore, at the turn of the 1990s, Palermo prosecutors were pursuing inquiries into bribery schemes involving local politicians and state-owned companies operating in Sicily's regional capital (Mulé 1990).

Nevertheless, none of these prosecutorial efforts managed to fully expose the pervasive corruption scheme that ran through Italian politics with similar informal rules across regions and levels of government. Therefore, these efforts did not jeopardize the corruption system's survival. Moreover, political efforts to enhance accountability, such as the 1974 reform of public funds for political campaigns, may have strengthened corruption, rather than weakened it (Golden 2003, 209–210). Thus, it is safe to conclude that until the Clean Hands operation's breakthrough, the Italian corruption system could adequately be described in Socialist party leader Bettino Craxi's famous words at trial:

> In Italy, funding for political parties and political activities in general has involved irregularities and illegalities at least since the birth of the republic [. . .] only those who did not want to see it could not see it, and only those who intentionally turned their heads the other way were not aware of its existence.[2]

The visible contrast between decade-long prosecutorial ineffectiveness and the Clean Hands operation's momentous breakthrough highlights the salience of this empirical puzzle: Why was the Clean Hands operation so successful in exposing the corruption system in its entirety and holding its participants accountable? What conditions emerged in 1992 to facilitate the start and development of this massive anti-corruption operation? Furthermore, the salience of this empirical puzzle is not confined to Italian politics. Given the enduring presence of corruption across democracies, even consolidated ones, the Clean Hands operation's success provides a powerful precedent for the pursuit of accountability via prosecutorial and judicial means. Therefore, the Clean Hands operation raises important questions about prosecutorial behavior, especially the latter's independence and effectiveness. If prosecutors can be effective enforcers of political accountability against corrupt politicians, then it is fundamental to ask what conditions will allow these legal actors to pursue corruption prosecutions without undue interference and what conditions will enhance prosecutorial work's effectiveness.

Despite the importance of this empirical puzzle, previous scholarly analyses of the Clean Hands operation do not seem to have generated a broader debate about prosecutorial behavior in relation to corruption. Only recently have political scientists turned their attention to prosecutors as key actors in the fight against this criminal issue. Specifically, recent works have focused on the root causes of prosecutorial independence as a key determinant of effective corruption control (Voigt and Wulf 2019; Michel 2017; Van Aaken, Feld and Voigt 2010). Much of this recent literature, however, does not build on the Clean Hands operation, which represents an astonishing demonstration of prosecutorial independence against systemic corruption. Therefore, a deeper analysis of the causes of prosecutorial independence in the Clean Hands operation could fuel and enrich the ensuing scholarly debate on this topic.

More importantly, the Clean Hands operation offers an interesting opportunity to move beyond prosecutorial independence to prosecutorial effectiveness. The Clean Hands operation's success was not limited to bringing hundreds of powerful defendants to trial. Rather, these hundreds of cases resulted in hundreds of convictions, several of which withstood the appeal test. Scholarly analyses of prosecutorial behavior, however, rarely focus on effectiveness, and when they do, they mostly focus on different issues than corruption (Brinks 2007; González-Ocantos 2016). Thus, an examination of the root causes of prosecutorial independence and effectiveness in the Clean Hands operation has the potential to contribute to this scholarly debate, which holds great importance for practitioners as well.

Recent attempts to replicate the Clean Hands operation in Brazil, with the *Lava Jato* (Car Wash) operation, speak to the former's enduring ability to generate demonstration effects. Brazilian prosecutors and judges in the Car Wash operation quite explicitly acknowledged Clean Hands prosecutors' work as the source of their inspiration (Moro 2004). For all these reasons, a scientific study of the causes of prosecutorial independence and effectiveness in the Clean Hands operation still holds great salience for ongoing scholarly debates and for understanding current anti-corruption efforts.

At the same time, previous scientific analyses of the Clean Hands operation offer precious insights into several dimensions of corruption as a criminal phenomenon. For instance, scholarship on the Clean Hands operation has provided important insights on the nature of corruption exchanges (Della Porta and Vannucci 2012; Della Porta, Sberna and Vannucci 2015; Della Porta and Vannucci 2016) and corruption's evolution following the Clean Hands operation (Vannucci and Della Porta 2007; Davigo and Mannozzi 2007). Nevertheless, while using documents and evidence acquired in the Clean Hands operation, none of these works examine the reasons why the latter was so successful.

On the other hand, extant analyses of prosecutorial effectiveness in the Clean Hands Operation tend to focus on some of the Italian prosecutorial system's peculiar institutional features, particularly its inclusion in the judicial branch and its remarkable degree of formal independence from other government branches (Nelken 1996*a*, 1996*b*, 1997, 2002; Guarnieri 2003). In addition, Nelken (1996*a*) points at the "decentralized and unpredictable nature of prosecution decision making" (Nelken 1996*a*, 101) as one of the reasons behind the Clean Hands operation's unprecedented success. However, these analyses also leave ample room for further empirical and theoretical elaboration, especially with regard to the local conditions that made the Clean Hands Operation possible.

My argument in this book contributes to these extant accounts by deepening and expanding this scientific analysis to include local prosecutorial institutions and their internal organizations. Recent works on the Italian criminal justice system have shown that different organizational structures may have momentous effects on justice administration at the local and, on aggregate, at the national level as well (Nelken and Zanier 2006; Montana and Nelken

2011). My analysis builds on these accounts and shows that the Clean Hands operation's success was a product of both the Italian criminal justice system's "decentralization" at the national level as well as key changes in local prosecutors' offices' organizational structure unfolding over time.

Another stream of recent scholarly contributions on the topic has left aside institutional analyses to focus more prominently on prosecutorial behavior, mostly to highlight the latter's attitudinal bias in corruption prosecutions. Ceron and Mainenti (2015) applied the attitudinal model (Segal and Spaeth 2002) to corruption prosecutions and explained the latter as a function of Italian prosecutors' political preferences and strategic targeting of rival political parties. While not focusing specifically on the Clean Hands operation, Ceron and Mainenti (2015) extended the application of the attitudinal model to this instance as well. In this book, I argue that the attitudinal model does not adequately explain the Clean Hands operation's causes and success. While the Clean Hands operation clearly had broad and long-lasting political effects that still reverberate through the Italian political system today, the attitudinal model hardly explains prosecutorial behavior in the Clean Hands operation or its long-lasting effects on politics and the judiciary. Furthermore, the attitudinal model tends to disregard the institutional context in which prosecutorial behavior occurs. Rather than placing judicial and prosecutorial behavior within a broader institutional framework, attitudinal explanations tend to focus on single individuals' choices at a specific moment in time. Thus, this approach tends to ignore the complex evolution of judicial and prosecutorial institutions that preceded and helped produce the Clean Hands operation.

On the other hand, Della Porta's analysis (2001) of the Clean Hands operation's "judicial revolution" took into account the long historical processes that helped produce a broad cohort of prosecutors with more assertive and activist attitudes than their past colleagues. Della Porta's (2001) analysis rightly pointed at the long historical processes that revolutionized the Italian judiciary's understanding of its professional mission, therefore affecting prosecutors as well, who are members of the judicial branch. The deep and gradual transformations that Della Porta mentioned produced a significant reconfiguration of the judicial and prosecutorial roles over time, giving rise to a new professional awareness of the prosecutorial role as the main enforcer of political accountability—what Della Porta, borrowing from Pizzorno (1992), calls "role substitution" mentality (Della Porta 2001, 4). Similarly, Vauchez (2004) also highlighted the gradual re-conceptualization of the judicial role over the years, with the emergence of a new model of judicial professionalism within the Italian context.

My analysis in this book builds on Della Porta's (2001) and Vauchez's (2004) accounts. I expand on their historical analysis to identify the institutional processes that produced highly independent prosecutorial institutions and a significant reservoir of prosecutorial expertise over time, particularly at the local level. In this book, I offer an in-depth analysis of the organizational structures that shaped professional relations within local prosecutors' offices determining either the development of prosecutorial independence and effectiveness or the lack thereof. Moreover, my work illustrates how the emergence of a new model of judicial professionalism resulted from a contested process, especially at the local level, where different judicial factions fought each other for control of local organizational structures within prosecutors' offices. Thus, my analysis fills a gap in Della Porta's (2001) and Vauchez's (2004) works by considering the "politics" of judicial associations and judicial factions, which saw one side sponsoring a democratic and egalitarian understanding of the judicial profession eventually prevailing against a reactionary and hierarchical conception.

OVERVIEW OF THE ARGUMENT

In this book, I show that the Clean Hands operation's unprecedented success was the product of long-developing historical trends that promoted the emergence of strong egalitarian attitudes and egalitarian practices among the Italian judiciary (of which prosecutors are members), transforming this institution in radical ways as opposed to its hierarchical past. The decentralization of national judicial institutions and the introduction of egalitarian decision-making at the local level produced significant increases in prosecutorial independence, by allowing prosecutors to pursue new and innovative approaches to criminal investigations. This, in turn, helped build a reservoir of expertise in the prosecution of complex criminal issues, such as terrorism and organized crime. Therefore, the Clean Hands operation represents the culmination of this long process of expertise accumulation, which was only possible thanks to the restructuring of national and local prosecutorial institutions along egalitarian lines.

Furthermore, increased prosecutorial independence allowed lower-ranked prosecutors to pursue activist attitudes toward rampant social issues, such as systemic corruption. This new judicial activism brought about the creation of more effective legal interpretation and investigative approaches against corruption. In this book, I explore the development and features of these activist attitudes among Clean Hands prosecutors, which shaped the operation's legal strategy and investigative practices contributing to its unprecedented success.

The institutional transformation from a highly hierarchical to an egalitarian judiciary was not devoid of conflict. In fact, this transformation was the product of a long fight between different factions within the Italian judiciary, each with its own views on the nature of the law and the judicial mission. In the first part of this book, I examine these historical developments starting from the Italian judiciary's traditionally hierarchical setting in pre-democratic times and the emergence of Italian legal conservatism during the Fascist regime, with its emphasis on a literal interpretation of the law and deference to political authorities. I then examine the emergence of more democracy-oriented judicial associations and the fight for an egalitarian judiciary before and after the enactment of the 1947 Constitution. I argue that the years from 1945 to 1975 represent judicial associations' fight to bring the Italian judiciary's internal structure in line with the new constitutional principles. This process, which I define as "decentralization," opened up new opportunities for prosecutorial actors.

However, national judicial institutions' transformation along egalitarian lines did not immediately produce the same outcome at the local level. In this book, I argue that institutional diversity among prosecutors' offices in terms of their organizational structure explains much of the variation in the outcome of corruption prosecutions during the Clean Hands operation. For this reason, in this book, I examine four prosecutors' offices from 1975 to 1996: Rome, Milan, Palermo, and Reggio Calabria. My analysis aims to show that the early adoption of egalitarian organizational structures set some of these prosecutors' offices on a trajectory toward enhanced prosecutorial independence and increasing prosecutorial effectiveness against complex criminal issues, including corruption. On the other hand, the persistence of hierarchical organizational structures hindered the development of both.

Furthermore, as I show in my empirical analysis, both changes toward egalitarianism and the resilience of hierarchical structures in some prosecutors' offices were the product of the continued fight between democratic and reactionary legal factions at the local level. While most judicial associations embraced the values of the new democratic Constitution, judges and prosecutors who maintained a traditionally conservative understanding of their profession fought against changes toward egalitarianism. Therefore, the early establishment of egalitarian structures in prosecutors' offices like Milan and Palermo derived from the hard-fought efforts of either enlightened conservative or progressive chief prosecutors, who tried to implement an organization compatible with the new constitutional values. On the other hand, the persistence of hierarchical structures within the Rome and Reggio Calabria prosecutors' offices resulted from the choices of local prosecutors with more traditionalist preferences.

Through the case studies in this book, I show how reshaping professional relationships along egalitarian lines was the foundation of impressive prosecutorial achievements, from the successful prosecution of left-wing terrorist organizations like the Red Brigades and First Line to the successful prosecution of hundreds of Cosa Nostra affiliates in the 1984 Palermo maxi trial. Furthermore, my analysis shows that these were not isolated events. In fact, each prosecutorial achievement built on previous ones, thanks to the formation of an informal judicial network tying together prosecutors and instructing judges in different jurisdictions. The development of this impressive reservoir of prosecutorial expertise is directly connected to the implementation of egalitarian decision-making within these prosecutors' offices. Milan and Palermo's chief prosecutors, who decided to introduce egalitarian structures, afforded their subordinates the necessary independence to pursue new and more effective investigative approaches against complex criminal issues.

On the other hand, Rome and Reggio Calabria's chief prosecutors' insistence on hierarchical structures significantly compressed prosecutorial independence and stifled prosecutorial achievements, creating a long-lasting dearth of expertise among local prosecutors. Once again, this was the product of a reactionary legal mentality. By implementing hierarchical structures, chief prosecutors in Rome and Palermo were showing enduring loyalty to a pre-democratic understanding of the prosecutorial function and the purposes it serves. A deep ideological divide ran between prosecutors with a renewed understanding of their professional role at the service of democratic accountability and prosecutors who insisted that their institutional mission was to act in an illiberal fashion as an arm of the state.

Nevertheless, the conflagration between democratic and reactionary forces within the Italian judiciary soon gave way to the emergence of a new form of judicial activism, rooted in the failure of the Italian political system to uphold accountability. As I explain in this book, political parties' enduring failure if not outright refusal to tackle corruption, along with prosecutors' direct involvement with civil society in the fight against pervasive criminal phenomena, over time led to the emergence of a new activist judicial ethos. Faced with political inaction against corruption, this new activism endowed prosecutors with a compelling duty to use new prosecutorial tools to achieve a specific goal, namely the exposure of the corruption system that had been pervading Italian politics for decades.

This activist mentality, which Della Porta (2001) called "role substitution" (4), animated the development and use of new prosecutorial approaches in the Clean Hands operation, while at the same time building on the pre-existing reservoir of prosecutorial expertise and independence that local egalitarian structures had created. For this reason, the Clean Hands operation's unprecedented success represents the culmination of a long institutional and ideational transformation, which gave rise to enhanced prosecutorial independence and effectiveness and a new activist understanding of the prosecutorial role.

Therefore, in this book, I provide a comprehensive framework for understanding the root causes of prosecutorial independence and effectiveness within democracies, which takes into account both the macro- and micro-foundations of these phenomena. In my theory, I provide a classification of prosecutorial institutions that take into account both the degree to which they are internally or externally directed and their degree of internal hierarchy or decentralization. In addition, I complement this national-level analysis with an in-depth exploration of organizational structures within local prosecutorial offices and how these two levels interact with each other. Thus, my work offers a framework for understanding prosecutorial behavior that considers the interaction between national and local institutions. Given the ongoing salience of corruption prosecutions today, with recent anti-corruption campaigns in Brazil (Winter 2017), South Korea (Gi-Wook and Moon 2017), and France (Corbet 2021), among other democracies, my theoretical framework and empirical analysis provide a few lessons from the Clean Hands operation that may apply well beyond the Italian context.

OVERVIEW OF THE BOOK

In order to provide a thorough examination of prosecutorial independence and effectiveness' root causes in the Clean Hands operation, this book includes both an outline of the general theoretical argument and an empirical test of its implications. In chapter 1, I provide a theory of the macro- and micro-foundations of prosecutorial independence and effectiveness. I offer a general classification of both national and local prosecutorial institutions, along with a discussion of their interactions. I also discuss the causes of prosecutorial behavior. From this general framework, I draw a few hypotheses which I test in the remainder of this book. I conclude chapter 1 with a discussion of the research design in the book, and I address a few alternative hypotheses to my argument.

For my empirical analysis, in chapter 2, I provide a historical longitudinal analysis of Italian judicial and prosecutorial institutions, with a special focus on their post–World War II development up until the mid-1970s. I examine the establishment and evolution of Italian judicial and prosecutorial institutions and the role of new legal factions in bringing about the prosecutorial system's decentralization in the 1970s. This chapter provides the necessary historical background to the case studies in the remainder of my book. In chapters 3–5, I apply process tracing to the case studies of the prosecutors' offices in Rome, Milan, Palermo, and Reggio Calabria, respectively. In each case study, I show how the persistence of hierarchical structures, or the introduction of egalitarian organizational structures, explains the emergence of prosecutorial effectiveness against systemic corruption over time or its lack thereof.

In particular, the case study of the Roman prosecutor's office in chapter 3 and the Reggio Calabria prosecutor's office in chapter 5 illustrates the detrimental effect of hierarchical organizational structures on prosecutorial effectiveness. On the other hand, the case study of the Milan prosecutor's office in chapter 4 and the Palermo prosecutor's office in chapter 5 shows how egalitarian organizational structures may foster the effective prosecution of systemic corruption in the long run. As I explain in my discussion of the research design in chapter 1, I selected these as comparable case studies (Lijphart 1975; Collier 1993; Munck 2004) due to the variation on both the independent and dependent variables, because they allow me to control for key alternative hypotheses. Thus, by applying process tracing to these case studies, I illustrate the conditions for the emergence of effective corruption prosecutions in the 1992 Clean Hands' investigation. Finally, in the conclusion, I draw a few lessons and discuss possible applications of my argument beyond the Italian context.

NOTES

1. These numbers are the author's elaboration on the data offered by Di Nicola (2003, 121).

2. Bettino Craxi, national secretary of the Italian Socialist Party, testimony during trial, December 17, 1993, author's translation from Italian. The testimony's recording is accessible at this website: Radio Radicale. 2010. "Processo Cusani: Il Pubblico Ministero Di Pietro Interroga Bettino Craxi." Last modified January 8, 2010, http://www.radioradicale.it/scheda/294694/processo-cusani-il-pubblico-ministero-di-pietro-interroga-bettino-craxi

Chapter 1

From Hierarchical to Egalitarian

The Root Causes of Prosecutorial Independence and Effectiveness against Systemic Corruption

The Clean Hands operation's unprecedented success offers important insights into the effective prosecution of systemic corruption, which exceed the Italian context. The roots of this effective prosecutorial effort lie in the interaction between extensive structural reforms to the Italian prosecutorial system, both at the national and local levels, and the emergence of new legal ideologies among its members. In this chapter, I develop a theory of the causes underlying the effective prosecution of systemic corruption. Such a theoretical framework is generally applicable to all democracies where judicial and prosecutorial actors enjoy some degree of formal independence from other government branches. The application of this theoretical framework to the Italian case, in turn, can offer important lessons about the effective prosecution of corruption for other democracies where this criminal phenomenon is endemic.

The Clean Hands operation is not the only recent example of a successful prosecutorial response to complex criminal issues. During almost the same years, the rising number of trials and convictions for human rights abuses across Latin American countries, the so-called justice cascade, offered hope for accountability against former authoritarian agents (Lutz and Sikkink 2000; González-Ocantos 2014, 2016). However, transitional justice is qualitatively different from corruption prosecutions. The former implies a change in political regime and therefore often targets state agents who have lost their position of power. On the other hand, the prosecution of systemic corruption seems to present more similarities with the prosecution of police killings. This is because both types of inquiry tend to target state agents currently in office. Furthermore, both types of prosecutorial action tackle a crime, threatening the basic features of the democratic rule of law (Brinks 2007).

In this sense, corruption prosecution presents high stakes because it requires prosecutorial authorities to use their powers not just against civilians involved in illicit activities but also against public officials abusing their current position for economic gains. Within democratic settings, social mobilization may put significant pressure on prosecutorial and judicial authorities to carry out investigations into corrupt politicians (Smulovitz and Perruzzotti 2000; Perruzzotti and Smulovitz 2003). However, social pressure and even political support for corruption prosecutions, while providing strong incentives for legal action (Brinks 2007), may fail to produce the desired outcome without the accumulation of specific legal knowledge and investigative expertise by legal authorities.

For corruption prosecutions to be not only possible but also effective, legal authorities must enjoy enough independence not only to bring legal action against these crimes but also to pursue a diversity of legal approaches while doing so. In other words, prosecutors' *de jure* independence from external interference and backlash is not enough to guarantee effective corruption prosecution. Rather, I argue that the effective prosecution of systemic corruption necessitates both the prosecutorial system's decentralization and the establishment of egalitarian modes of decision-making at the level of local prosecutorial offices. This is because only such an institutional framework can guarantee prosecutors' ability to pursue new legal philosophies and develop innovative approaches to complex criminal phenomena. This institutional setting, in other words, promotes the endogenous emergence of legal innovations, which is crucial to the development of prosecutorial effectiveness, especially in the absence of external pedagogical interventions from advocacy networks or other organizations committed to legal reform, like in the justice cascade (González-Ocantos 2014, 2016).

In what follows, I develop a theory of the causes of prosecutorial independence and effectiveness against systemic corruption within democratic systems. My theory takes into account both the microfoundations of prosecutorial behavior and the overarching institutional context in which it occurs. Therefore, this theoretical framework aims to improve current understandings of prosecutorial independence and effectiveness by offering a systematic and comprehensive understanding of the micro- and macro-causes of prosecutorial behavior. Furthermore, this comprehensive framework may help shine light on the causes of endogenous legal innovation.

First, I provide a conceptual and operational definition of the dependent variables in this study, prosecutorial independence and effectiveness against systemic corruption. I then discuss the dichotomy between hierarchical and decentralized justice systems, and the differences between hierarchical and egalitarian organizational structures within local prosecutorial institutions. My analysis yields a few hypotheses concerning the effects of decentralization and local egalitarian structures on prosecutorial independence and effectiveness. I also offer a brief analysis of the research design underlying the application of this theory to the Italian case. Therefore, in the final sections of this chapter, I briefly discuss the Italian judicial and prosecutorial systems' institutional design and the reasons for my selection of four Italian prosecutors' offices as case studies. Finally, I address a few alternative hypotheses to my theory.

PROSECUTORIAL INDEPENDENCE AND PROSECUTORIAL EFFECTIVENESS

Definitions of prosecutorial independence tend to echo definitions of judicial independence centering either around the existence of formal institutions protecting prosecutors from retaliation or undue influence (Rios-Figueroa 2012; Michel 2017; Carvalho and Leitão 2019), or around legal professionals' assertiveness in pursuing risky legal action despite potential retaliation from political or societal actors (Van Aaken, Feld and Voigt 2010; Voigt and Wulf 2019). While assertiveness is certainly an aspect of *de facto* prosecutorial independence, I utilize a conceptually broader definition. *De facto* prosecutorial independence does not solely express itself in the ability to act despite potential backlash. Prosecutorial independence also consists in prosecutors' freedom to explore different legal and investigative approaches, to subscribe to a variety of legal philosophies, and to pursue different understandings of criminal justice in their investigative and legal practice. In other words, I identify an "intellectual" dimension to prosecutorial independence that is equally essential to its behavioral manifestations. This dimension is essentially informal in nature, as it does not refer to the existence of formal guarantees allowing for legal diversity among prosecutors. Rather, it targets prosecutors' informal ability to pursue the latter without constraints or fear of retaliation.

For this reason, this intellectual dimension is also harder to operationalize than assertiveness as it requires moving beyond the simple number of investigations initiated. While the latter may speak to prosecutors' willingness to pursue risky legal action, it does not capture their freedom to adopt varied legal approaches, including innovative ones. Rather, the operationalization of this new concept entails a deeper examination of the investigative and legal tools prosecutors deploy against specific criminal phenomena. In my analysis, I gather and examine qualitative evidence of prosecutorial independence, or the lack thereof, by detailing Italian prosecutors' freedom to pursue different legal philosophies and legal strategies and to develop new investigative approaches.

I define prosecutorial effectiveness as prosecutorial authorities' ability to uncover the full extent of criminal activities under investigation, leading to a successful case for the prosecution. Therefore, prosecutorial effectiveness implies prosecutorial authorities' ability to apply appropriate legal standards and investigative approaches to the facts of the case and to uncover criminal evidence to the greatest extent possible. While it would be wrong to assume that a successful outcome always follows from effective prosecution, the latter implies the prosecution's ability to hold responsible parties accountable for their crimes in most cases where legal standards and investigative techniques are applied proportionally to the legal issue. For this reason, I operationalize prosecutorial effectiveness in terms of the number of convictions achieved against a specific criminal phenomenon.

The definitions of prosecutorial independence and effectiveness I provided also serve to illustrate the intrinsic relationship between the two. Effective prosecutorial action requires the use of legal and investigative tools apt to the criminal phenomenon under investigation. As a result, effective prosecution stems from legal actors' freedom to pursue new investigative approaches and to develop new legal interpretations of extant norms and procedures. In my analysis of the causes underlying effective corruption prosecution, I show how increases in *de facto* prosecutorial independence necessarily precede the effective deployment of legal action against this criminal phenomenon.

Since this book focuses on the prosecution of systemic corruption, it is also necessary to provide a brief definition of this criminal issue. Systemic corruption entails the evolution of occasional and contingent bribe exchanges into an informal structure of rules and institutions that regulate interactions between bribe-givers and bribe-receivers. This set of informal rules develops to regulate a criminal phenomenon that expands and ramifies, therefore gaining complexity as it grows. For this reason, systemic corruption oftentimes develops into a network, branching together participants from different sectors of politics and society. Thus, effective prosecutorial action against systemic corruption consists in prosecutors' ability to apply legal standards and investigative techniques in a way that uncovers the full extent of this corruption network, leading to the convictions of its participants in accordance with their criminal responsibilities.

The theory I develop in this book may apply to the effective prosecution of other complex criminal issues beyond systemic corruption. Complex criminal issues usually entail the development of informal criminal institutions, such as structured criminal organizations or ramified criminal networks, in order to support the involvement of several individuals in interrelated illegal activities. In the case of systemic corruption, pervasive bribe exchanges combine with other interrelated crimes, such as false accounting (Di Pietro 2017), illegal campaign funding, and other financial crimes. However, this is also the case with other criminal phenomena, such as mafia activities or terrorist acts, to mention a few I discuss in this book. Both aforementioned criminal issues require a well-structured network or criminal organization capable of conducting several interrelated criminal activities. Terrorist groups, for instance, may conduct robberies to support themselves financially and may engage in the trade of illicit goods for the same reason, in addition to conducting terrorist attacks. Mafia organizations may pair extortion with international drug trafficking, in addition to using violence against their rivals (Falcone and Turone 2015). Thus, my research may offer insights into the roots of effective prosecutorial action against several other complex criminal issues beyond systemic corruption.

HIERARCHICAL VERSUS DECENTRALIZED SYSTEMS

My theory is grounded in a new institutionalist perspective on the law and legal behavior (Smith 1988). In other words, I contend that prosecutorial behavior cannot be considered in isolation from the institutional framework in which legal actors operate. Rather, incentives and constraints, formal and informal, on prosecutorial behavior shape and interact with prosecutors' deeply held beliefs. For this reason, the starting point of my theoretical framework is the analysis of institutional structures, both national and local, that condition prosecutorial behavior and contribute to shaping these actors' goals.

Similar to previous scholarship on the subject, my theoretical framework asserts that hierarchical institutions, whether formal or informal, can force legal actors into conformity with specific legal philosophies and therefore contribute to perpetuating the latter's dominance within the legal profession (Hilbink 2007; Couso and Hilbink 2011). On the other hand, the combination of decentralized institutions at the national level with egalitarian decision-making within local institutions may greatly facilitate the emergence and diffusion of new legal ideas. Thus, my theory builds on and clarifies previous institutionalist insights (Couso and Hilbink 2011) to shed light on the emergence of prosecutorial independence and effectiveness.

I argue that it is possible to classify prosecutorial systems as either hierarchical or decentralized depending on who holds the power to promote and appoint legal professionals to prosecutorial offices and the nature of the relationship between the official holding this power and the population of possible candidates. By prosecutorial systems, I mean the complex of institutions and legal actors working for the side of the prosecution in a legal case and/or overseeing prosecutorial work at any level. Scholars have repeatedly shown that the power to select and remove has momentous consequences on judicial and prosecutorial behavior (Hilbink 2007; Couso and Hilbink 2011; Melton and Ginsburg 2014). While most constitutional provisions shielding the judiciary from other branches' interference do not seem to have any effect on *de facto* judicial independence, those concerning the selection and removal of judges do (Melton and Ginsburg 2014). For this reason, the relationship between the institution in charge of prosecutorial promotions and appointments and its lower ranks is the cornerstone of the classification I provide in this theoretical framework.

Within hierarchical prosecutorial systems, the decision to appoint and/or promote resides with an agent or institutional body that is insulated from lower-ranked prosecutors. In other words, within hierarchical prosecutorial systems, lower-ranked professionals have no way to consistently reach out, influence, or select the small elite or public official in charge of appointments and promotions. Hierarchical systems, therefore, leave lower-ranked prosecutors formally powerless over their careers. On the contrary, decentralized prosecutorial institutions diffuse power over promotions and appointments, by creating formal channels through which lower-ranked actors can exert influence over the institutions or officials in charge of these decisions.

This distinction between hierarchical and decentralized systems must take into consideration the multitude of institutional arrangements regulating selection and appointments. Hierarchical or decentralized systems may take different forms, depending on which actors or institutions participate in this process. Therefore, I also distinguish between externally directed and internally directed prosecutorial systems. The former delegates the selection and appointment of prosecutors to actors or institutions outside the prosecutorial or judicial system (including, potentially, a democratic constituency). On the contrary, internally directed prosecutorial systems tend to rely on members of the institution to select and appoint candidates to prosecutorial offices. Previous analyses have relied on a similar distinction between internally and externally directed prosecutorial institutions to draw conclusions about prosecutorial independence (Michel 2017; Rios-Figueroa 2012; Aaken, Feld and Voigt 2010). However, I argue that the distinction between hierarchical and decentralized prosecutorial systems holds more relevance for prosecutorial independence than the system's location vis-à-vis other government branches.

Both of these institutional configurations—hierarchical and decentralized, internally versus externally directed—may harbor "exceptions to the rule," namely pathways to professional advancements onto specific prosecutorial bodies that do not follow the general institutional configuration. This does not invalidate my classification, as each prosecutorial system may intentionally curtail specific exceptions to the rule in order to implement a different set of principles within specific institutional bodies. For instance, the process for appointment of the Spanish Attorney General, the head of the *Fiscalia General*, involves multiple institutions across the three branches of government. On the other hand, the Fiscal Counsel (*Consejo Fiscal*) is the only prosecutorial institution in charge of all other prosecutorial appointments, making the Spanish prosecutorial system internally directed (Ministerio Fiscal n.d.).

Overall, externally directed systems seem to offer greater institutional variety than internally directed ones. Table 1.1 outlines at least three types of institutional designs that represent externally directed prosecutorial systems: political appointment, indirect control, and election. Table 1.2, on the other hand, outlines three types of internally directed prosecutorial systems: elitist, democratic elitist, and democratic. These classifications are by no means exhaustive. The variety of existing prosecutorial systems can hardly fit into a general classification. However, tables 1.1 and 1.2 present ideal types of some of the most frequently observed institutional configurations. Therefore, each country's prosecutorial system may fit within a specific category with some degree of deviation from the ideal type. At the same time, the ideal types in tables 1.1 and 1.2 provide a useful analytical framework to explore the effects on prosecutorial independence and effectiveness of different externally and internally directed prosecutorial systems.

It is also possible for a country to possess multiple institutional configurations at different levels of government, like in the case of the U.S. federal and state prosecutorial systems. American federalism provides an opportunity for the coexistence of two externally directed institutional designs regulating

Table 1.1 Three Types of Externally Directed Prosecutorial Systems

Externally Directed Prosecutorial Systems		
Public officials outside the justice systems hold control over appointments and promotions (Political Appointment)	Public officials outside the justice system control the institution responsible for appointments and promotions (Indirect Control)	Voters elect justice system officials (Election)

Source: Author's elaboration.

Table 1.2 Three Types of Internally Directed Prosecutorial Systems

Internally Directed Prosecutorial Systems		
Higher-ranked members appointed/elected by other higher-ranked peers control promotions and appointments (Elitist)	Higher-ranked members elected by whole system's population control promotions and appointments (Democratic Elitist)	Members elected by whole system's population control promotions and appointments (Democratic)

Source: Author's elaboration.

selection and promotions to prosecutorial offices. As a result, American district attorneys, the legal actors in charge of the prosecution at the state and county level, usually acquire office via election. Therefore, the U.S. states present one type of externally directed system. At the same time, U.S. attorneys receive their appointment directly from the executive branch with the participation of the legislative branch. This procedure clearly embodies the "political appointment" configuration.

On the other hand, the French system between 1958 and 1993 embodies another type of externally directed institutional design that endows one government branch (in this case, the executive branch) with control over the institution responsible for the selection and appointment process. During that time, the French High Council's evaluation could either block or move forward a candidate for prosecutorial office (Guarnieri 2004, 180). While the Council was considered a judicial institution, its composition significantly empowered the executive branch. The French president was both a member of the Council and could also select its nine judicial members (Guarnieri 2004, 180). Therefore, the French system relegated control over council membership and, consequently, control over appointments and promotions, to the executive branch. For this reason, the French system embodied a type of externally directed prosecutorial system based on another branch's indirect control of prosecutorial appointments.

While externally directed systems present a great variety of institutional arrangements, internally directed prosecutorial systems show a significant degree of similarity among them. This is because all internally directed prosecutorial systems relegate promotions and appointments in the hands of institutional members, although they may do so in different ways. The main differences between internally directed systems reside in the degree to which higher-ranked professionals control the appointment and promotion process in isolation from the lower ranks. Based on this principle, internally directed systems include at least the following institutional configurations: elitist, democratic elitist, and democratic. These configurations go from higher-ranked members' complete control over the appointment process in isolation from lower ranks to the "democratization" of the appointment process, with officials in charge of career advancements being democratically selected by the population of potential candidates.

The distinction between externally directed and internally directed prosecutorial systems bears some resemblance to the distinction between career and recognition judiciaries (Georgakopoulos 2000). However, the latter neglects to consider the differences between judicial structures based on their internal degree of hierarchy and decentralization. For instance, the description of career judiciaries' internal functioning seems to assume that these systems will always entail senior judges' hierarchical control of lower ranks' career (Georgakopoulos 2000, 212). Garoupa and Ginsburg (2009), on the other hand, seem to offer an analysis of judicial structures that takes into consideration the presence of hierarchical or non-hierarchical features (122). However, Garoupa and Ginsburg's analysis is limited to judicial councils rather than the judicial system's overarching structure and does not discuss prosecutorial institutions.

As previously mentioned, the difference between hierarchical and decentralized prosecutorial systems resides in lower ranks' ability to influence promotions and selections. Therefore, hierarchy and decentralization are inherently connected to the institutional mechanisms regulating promotions and appointments. Figure 1.1 classifies different types of internally and externally directed systems by their degree of hierarchy and decentralization.

Given the similarities across internally directed systems, it is easier to articulate the reasons behind the different degrees of decentralization associated with the institutional designs in the table. In highly hierarchical, internally directed prosecutorial systems, a small legal elite controls the lower ranks' institutional fate. At the opposite pole, highly decentralized internally directed systems allow lower ranks to influence promotions and appointments by selecting the officials in charge of this process among their own ranks. Intermediate institutional arrangements differ in the degree to which they broaden either the population that can attain the power to select and promote or the population that can elect the officials in charge of this function. As I explain in chapter 2, the Italian prosecutorial system presented different types of internally directed institutional arrangements at different points in time, moving gradually from a highly hierarchical to a very decentralized system.

On the other side of the graph, externally directed systems also line up according to their growing degree of decentralization. Given the variety of institutional arrangements on this side of the graph, discussion of their

Externally Directed Prosecutorial Systems			**Internally Directed Prosecutorial Systems**		
Voters elect justice system officials (election)	Public officials outside the justice system control the institution responsible for appointments and promotions (indirect control)	Public officials outside the justice systems hold control over appointments and promotions (political appointment)	Higher ranked members appointed/elected by other higher ranked peers control promotions and appointments (Elitist)	Higher ranked members elected by whole system's population control promotions and appointments (Democratic Elitist)	Members elected by whole system's population control promotions and appointments (Democratic)

More Decentralized ⟵ More Hierarchical ⟶ More Decentralized

Figure 1.1 Prosecutorial Systems and Degrees of Decentralization. *Source*: Author's elaboration.

different levels of decentralization deserves more elaboration. The most hierarchical institutional setting entails the legislative and/or executive branch's direct role on appointments and promotions to prosecutorial office. Within a democratic context, legal professionals do have a way to influence both government branches, via elections. However, this is qualitatively different from a prosecutorial or judicial institution, such as a judicial council, overseeing promotions and appointments. In the former scenario, legal professionals are further removed from the selection and promotion process due to its occurrence within another government branch's purview. On the other hand, the existence of a judicial or prosecutorial council, though entirely appointed by legislative or executive branch officials, increases legal professionals' proximity to the "selectors." Especially if legal professionals can influence the selection process via the drafting of a candidates' list, the existence of a judicial or prosecutorial council increases decentralization as opposed to the direct and exclusive role of the legislative and/or executive branch in the selection and promotion processes.

Among externally directed systems, decentralization is at its peak when selections and promotions occur via democratic elections. This is because, although legal officials have little way to influence the electorate besides campaigning in the run to elections, democratic constituents' control over selections and promotions to judicial and prosecutorial offices is limited to the electoral moment. Therefore, elections create "diffuse control" over selections and promotions by the general electorate. In other words, elections' inherent dynamics limit the electorate's control over selections and promotions to the moment of the vote and increase this institutional setting's decentralization in comparison to other externally directed justice systems.

The prosecutorial system's institutional design has huge implications for prosecutorial independence. I argue that increasing decentralization will lead to greater *de facto* prosecutorial independence, while a hierarchical structure will significantly reduce it. Several authors make similar claims about hierarchical control over prosecutorial careers (Michel 2017; Rios-Figueroa 2012; Aaken Feld and Voigt 2010), whether the officials in charge of career decisions reside within the prosecutorial systems (Aaken, Feld and Voigt 2010; Rios-Figueroa 2012) or in other government branches (Michel 2017). However, my theory improves on previous analyses by focusing only on the impact of institutional structures on prosecutorial behavior, rather than external conditions (Aaken, Feld and Voigt 2010), and systematizing this intuition about hierarchical power within a coherent theoretical framework.

Hierarchy tends to create a strong principal–agent relationship, which will affect prosecutorial behavior regardless of *de jure* guarantees of independence. This is visible, for instance, in the relationship between U.S. attorneys and the executive branch within the U.S. federal prosecutorial system. Although strong formal guarantees are in place to protect U.S. attorneys' independence, their tight relationship to the executive branch may easily jeopardize their *de facto* independence. Anecdotal evidence of this can be found in the investigation into vice president Spiro Agnew's embezzlement activities (Maddow and Yarvitz 2020). Then, attorney general Kleindienst did not hesitate to reach out to Baltimore's prosecutors involved in a corruption investigation to ask about the nature of their inquiry, even though the latter still had a quite remote connection to vice president Spiro Agnew (52–53). Even more importantly, Baltimore prosecutors were able to document vice president Agnew's ongoing involvement in corruption while in office only thanks to newly appointed attorney general Elliott Richardson's sense of civic duty (82–83). Had Richardson's political loyalty prevailed over his ethical obligation to the rule of law, U.S. attorneys working on Agnew's involvement in criminal activities could well have reached an insurmountable obstacle.

The principal–agent relationship is even clearer within internally directed systems. Lower ranks' dependence on a small and insulated elite for their professional fate will severely limit the former's ability to pursue legal ideas that differ from the elite's legal philosophy (Hilbink 2007). Indeed, the prosecutorial system's hierarchical structure facilitates the perpetuation of the legal elite's ideology throughout this institution's tiers (Hilbink 2007). While focusing on the judiciary, rather than the prosecutorial system, Hilbink (2007) shows these dynamics at work in Chile before and during Pinochet's authoritarian rule. The Chilean judiciary's evaluation-based promotion system, which allowed higher-ranked judicial professionals to control their subordinates' professional fate, forced lower-ranked judges to comply with the institution's legally conservative ideology (Hilbink 2007). Nevertheless, this dynamic does not exclude the possibility that a few courageous prosecutors may decide to stand up to the legal elite's interpretation of the law, like *Justicia Democratica* prosecutors did in Spain during Franco's regime (Hilbink 2012, 598). However, hierarchy creates powerful systemic incentives against this type of behavior, which tends to remain limited to a few highly motivated individuals.

On the contrary, decentralization frees lower-ranked prosecutors from their dependence on a principal's approval. By providing lower ranks with a way to influence the officials in charge of appointments and promotions, this structure significantly diminishes legal elites' control over lower ranks. Consequently, decentralization also paves the way for increased representation of diverse legal approaches, both within internally and externally directed systems. For instance, democratic constituencies that tend to endorse novel and more progressive understandings of criminal justice may decide to elect district attorneys that espouse similar innovative approaches. This has been visible in recent district attorneys' elections in very progressive counties across the United States.[1] Within internally directed systems, the existence of a legal council representative of the broader justice system population may create a significant opportunity for the rise to prominence of new legal philosophies, previously relegated to the margins. Thus, decentralization significantly increases *de facto* judicial and prosecutorial independence, by allowing lower-ranked legal professionals to pursue a variety of legal and investigative approaches without fear for their professional fate.

While the prosecutorial system's overarching structure at the national level clearly has important implications for prosecutorial behavior, it is not possible to fully comprehend its effects without considering the intervening role of local institutions. The effects of both hierarchical and decentralized structures will reverberate across the prosecutorial system via local prosecutors' offices. For this reason, in the next section, I explore local prosecutorial offices' internal dynamics, specifically their organizational structure and how the latter mediates hierarchy and decentralization's effects on prosecutorial behavior.

LOCAL ORGANIZATIONAL STRUCTURES AND THEIR IMPLICATIONS

It is plausible to assume that every local prosecutorial institution will be under the control of a local authority, such as a district attorney or a chief prosecutor. In most cases, local prosecutorial authorities are responsible for setting up their office's internal organization, including key functions such as case distribution. Local prosecutorial authorities, however, will enjoy different degrees of discretion over their offices' internal organization within a hierarchical rather than a decentralized system.

Regardless of formal guarantees of autonomy, hierarchical control over legal professionals' careers, including local prosecutorial authorities, may severely limit the latter's freedom to organize their office as they see fit. Hierarchical structures facilitate oversight and therefore restrict local prosecutorial authorities' *de facto* independence. As a result, within a hierarchical system, most prosecutors' offices will present similar organizational structures. On the other hand, decentralization will significantly increase local prosecutorial authorities' control over their offices' internal organization. By reducing central oversight, decentralization will provide local prosecutorial authorities with increased discretion over how to organize the relationships with their subordinates. Consequently, within decentralized systems, we can expect local prosecutorial authorities to pursue a variety of approaches to their offices' internal organization.

Although local prosecutorial authorities may choose a variety of organizational approaches, I argue that the latter will tend toward either one pole or another of a continuum between hierarchical and egalitarian organizational structures. These are designed to regulate key functions, such as case distribution, case handling (how prosecutors organize investigative work), and choice of prosecutorial strategy (the investigative and legal approach to a specific case). Local prosecutorial authorities who enforce a hierarchical structure within their office will ultimately control all decisions pertaining to each one of these functions without consultation with their subordinates. On the other hand, organizational structures that entail either a partial or comprehensive consultation with lower-ranked prosecutors will tend toward collegiality. Therefore, this set of organizational structures assumes the equality of prosecutorial authorities with their subordinates, whose contributions will equally inform one or more of the office's key functions. Figure 1.2 outlines this continuum and its two poles.

The reason for the conceptualization of hierarchy and egalitarian organizational structures as a continuum, rather than a rigid classification, is due to the variety of practical forms these local institutions may take. Prosecutorial offices' internal organization may find expression in a granular set of formal rules and procedures regulating the most intricate, though important, minutia pertaining to the administration of justice. A rigid classification would inevitably neglect to consider some of the complexity inherent in these local institutions. Therefore, for the purposes of the analytical effort in this book, I believe that conceptualizing hierarchical and egalitarian structures as a continuum is more beneficial and carries as much, if not more, explanatory power than adopting a rigid classification. In conclusion, any organizational structure that relegates decisional power almost exclusively in the chief prosecutor's hands tends to be hierarchical, while organizational structures that rely at least on some consultation with lower-ranked prosecutors tend toward egalitarianism.

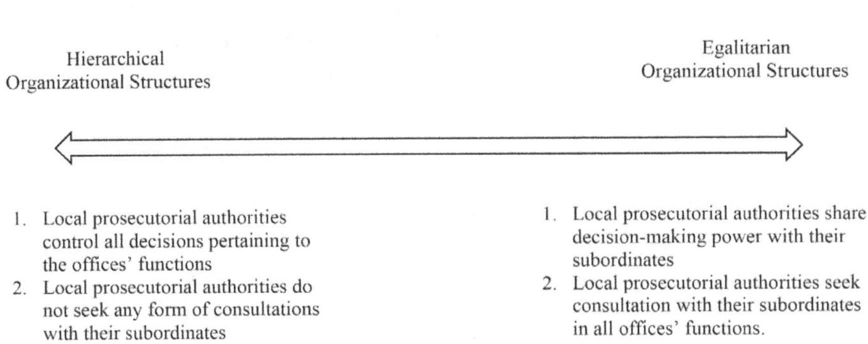

Figure 1.2 Hierarchical and Egalitarian Structures. *Source*: Author's elaboration.

As with hierarchy and decentralization, local organizational structures carry momentous implications for prosecutorial behavior. Hierarchical approaches to an office's internal organization will inevitably limit lower-ranked prosecutors' *de facto* independence. Their superior's constant oversight and control of key functions, such as the distribution and handling of investigations, will limit lower-ranked prosecutors' freedom to pursue new investigative and legal strategies without the local authority's approval. Therefore, within this type of structure, legal innovation can only move from the top down. Chief prosecutors' strict oversight of their offices' main functions implies that the adoption of legal or investigative innovations may only occur as a result of these authorities' interest in adopting them. As a result, hierarchical structures not only hinder prosecutorial independence but also severely diminish prosecutorial effectiveness, by limiting prosecutors' freedom to explore novel and more effective legal and investigative approaches.

On the other hand, organizational structures that tend toward egalitarianism will increase lower-ranked prosecutors' independence. The existence of collegial decision-making and peer relationships between local authorities and their subordinates will empower lower-ranked prosecutors, giving them the opportunity to significantly impact the local administration of justice. Within this framework, lower-ranked prosecutors will enjoy more freedom in choosing investigations they wish to handle and the legal and investigative strategy that seems most appropriate to the case. This will result in a bottom-up approach to the emergence as well as the diffusion of legal innovations. Within an egalitarian framework, lower-ranked prosecutors will enjoy greater freedom in choosing or proposing the adoption of new investigative and legal tools. The latter may well have originated outside the local prosecutor's office and have come to the attention of local actors thanks to their visible results in another jurisdiction.[2] Egalitarian structures facilitate the emergence of a variety of legal and investigative approaches within the same unit and therefore lead to increasing prosecutorial effectiveness.

As I previously mentioned, the effects of hierarchy and decentralization on prosecutorial behavior will be felt through the mediating role of local institutions. Therefore, the combination of hierarchical and decentralized structures with local organizational approaches will yield different observable implications about prosecutorial behavior. Figure 1.3 provides a graphic representation of the implications we can draw from this overarching theoretical framework.

The combination of national and local hierarchy will yield the most significant decreases in prosecutorial independence and effectiveness. On the other hand, decentralization with local egalitarian structures will yield the most significant increases in prosecutorial effectiveness. This is due to the isomorphism between national and local institutions in both scenarios.

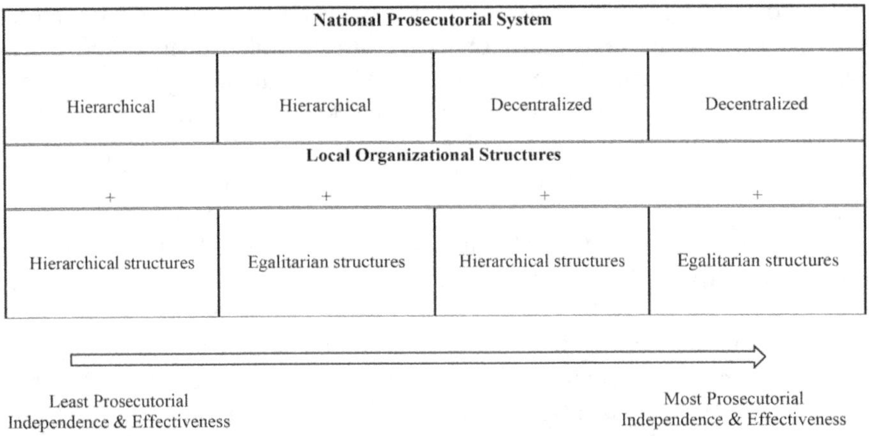

Figure 1.3 The Effects of National and Local Prosecutorial Institutions on Prosecutorial Independence and Effectiveness. *Source*: Author's elaboration.

However, significant differences remain in how this isomorphism may unfold within each combination. Within a hierarchical prosecutorial system, the elite can easily impose similar hierarchical structures at the local level, thanks to its control over professional careers. In the same way, the elite may, theoretically, impose pluri-morphism, if it so desires, by introducing strong career incentives and constraints on local authorities to adopt egalitarian organizational structures. On the other hand, legal officials or legal bodies in a decentralized system do not hold the same degree of power over local authorities. Therefore, local authorities within decentralized systems enjoy more freedom to uphold a hierarchical organization within their office without fear of backlash from the top. Similarly, local authorities' decision to implement an egalitarian structure is less the product of constraints and incentives coming from the top, like in a hierarchical system, and more the result of these authorities' preferences.

In other words, officials in charge of promotions and appointments in a decentralized system may find themselves "disarmed" against local prosecutorial authorities' resistance to specific organizational structures. Thus, within decentralized systems, the top-down push toward isomorphism is inevitably diminished. As a result, decentralization may, unintentionally, facilitate pluri-morphism or the existence of different organizational models across jurisdictions, at least for some time. At the same time, however, decentralization also tends to empower lower ranks vis-à-vis national and local elites, specifically by providing local prosecutors with a set of tools they can use to challenge their local superior to embrace different organizational structures. Thus, while decentralization is less likely to impose specific organizational structures from the top down, it paves the way for the possibility of their adoption as a result of lower-ranked prosecutors' mobilization.

As shown in figure 1.3, pluri-morphism between national and local structures imposes some constraints on prosecutorial independence and effectiveness. This is because the persistence of a hierarchical principal–agent relationship, either at the local or national level, will significantly limit prosecutors' ability to pursue a variety of legal and investigative approaches to achieve criminal accountability. In the presence of a national hierarchy, lower-ranked prosecutors will be under pressure to conform to the national elite's legal preferences to secure their career ambitions. In the presence of a local authority with hierarchical attitudes, lower-ranked prosecutors' freedom to pursue effective investigative and legal approaches will find severe limitations in their immediate superior's strict oversight. Thus, both scenarios undermine prosecutorial independence and effectiveness, to a degree. However, pluri-morphism within a decentralized system may yield different implications than pluri-morphism within a hierarchical system.

Specifically, decentralized systems where different organizational approaches coexist across jurisdictions may promote a higher degree of prosecutorial independence and effectiveness overall than hierarchical systems implementing pluri-morphism at the local level. This is because, even though not all prosecutorial units may choose to adopt an egalitarian approach, decentralization may still provide lower-ranked prosecutors with the tools to pressure their superiors into adopting this organizational form. On the other hand, hierarchical systems, even when they require the presence of different organizational structures across local prosecutorial units, leave lower-ranked prosecutors powerless vis-à-vis national and local prosecutorial authorities, whose preferences still exerts powerful influence over local actors.

THE IMPORTANCE OF LEGAL IDEOLOGY

As I have argued so far, different institutional structures at the national and local levels will have varying effects on *de facto* prosecutorial independence. I defined the latter as prosecutors' ability to pursue a variety of legal and investigative approaches without fear or concern for their careers, and I argued that *de facto* prosecutorial independence is a key precondition to prosecutorial effectiveness. My theoretical framework, therefore, implies the centrality of legal philosophy as a determinant of prosecutorial behavior over another much-debated cause, political ideology. However, legal actors espousing different legal philosophies do not operate in an institutional vacuum. Within decentralized and egalitarian structures, prosecutorial actors will be free to pursue their preferred legal philosophy without fear of retaliation; on the other hand, hierarchical structures tend to force lower-ranked prosecutors into conformity with their superiors' legal ideology

The scholarly dispute about the validity of the attitudinal model (Segal and Spaeth 1996, 2002) versus the legal model does not seem any closer to a definitive answer. In recent years, studies in comparative judicial politics have revived the importance of the legal model. For instance, the emphasis on the role of legal ideas in shaping behavior has emerged clearly among scholars trying to make sense of constitutional courts' rulings in Latin American countries (Couso, Huneeus and Sieder 2010; Ingram 2016). However, the exploration of legal ideas' influence on judicial behavior is not confined to a single region of the world. Woods (2008) examines high court judges' dynamic relationships with "judicial communities" (xii) to understand changes in legal interpretation and the Israeli supreme court's increasing activist role. Furthermore, several of these studies trace the root cause of changes in legal ideas to the interactions between judicial actors and legal organizations mobilizing in support of human rights (González-Ocantos 2014, 2016; Rodríguez-Garavito 2011). Despite this bourgeoning academic literature, the debate about the role of legal ideas versus political ideology has only marginally affected scholarly analyses of prosecutorial behavior so far (Ceron and Mainenti 2015).

I argue that legal philosophy is hugely influential on prosecutorial behavior, much more than political ideology. The choices that prosecutors face are rarely "neutral," meaning that these choices rarely follow from a mechanical application of the law. In their everyday work, prosecutors must decide what legal tools they will deploy to build a compelling case against defendants allegedly involved in a criminal violation. Moreover, prosecutors may enjoy particularly broad latitude in their choice of legal strategy when they operate within egalitarian or decentralized institutional structures, while they may have to strictly follow their superiors' preferences within a hierarchical structure. I argue that, within the constraints and incentives provided by the existing institutional structure, legal philosophy plays a prominent role in orienting prosecutors toward a specific investigative and legal approach. This is because prosecutors, like all legal professionals, are trained to conceive of themselves as the implementers of a fundamental institution of the modern state, the rule of law. The impact of legal socialization, both at the training stage and during an individual's professional career, cannot be overstated.

In this book, I will test the importance of legal philosophy for prosecutorial behavior against the implications of the attitudinal model, which expects prosecutors to be lenient toward public officials they sympathize with and assertive against those they disagree with politically (Ceron and Mainenti 2015). However, it would also be wrong to conceptualize legal philosophy as an entirely apolitical legal construct. Legal philosophies are complex constructions that offer a specific understanding of the legal profession's mission and relationship vis-à-vis other government branches. Consequently, legal philosophies may be more or less inherently supportive of a democratic framework, depending on whether they understand the rule of law to be an instrument of accountability or a tool to consolidate state power. In this book, I will show how Italian legal positivism, a country-specific variation of a much broader conservative legal philosophy, oriented Italian prosecutors against the pursuit of assertive accountability for public officials involved in corruption. The long-lasting influence of this legal philosophy among Italian prosecutors hindered the effective prosecution of systemic corruption more than prosecutors' political preferences.

Despite the prominence of legal philosophies, it would also be unrealistic to presume the absolute dominance of one model of prosecutorial behavior over another (Kapiszewski 2012). Some prosecutors may appeal to specific legal philosophies to disguise much more politically oriented decisions. Furthermore, legal philosophies' inherent understanding of the legal profession may offer cover for the use of prosecutorial powers in politically biased ways. In other words, legal philosophy may provide cover for a few individuals with ulterior motives. However, political ideology does not explain the visible patterns in prosecutorial behavior I explore in my analysis, which instead seem to lend support to legal philosophy's relevance.

More importantly, all legal philosophies may offer philosophical grounding to judicial activism. Scholars usually identify the latter as judges' attitude to move beyond their role's appropriate confines and take up "legislative" powers via a creative interpretation of the legal texts they are applying to a case (Kmiec 2004). Because the discourse around judicial activism developed mostly within the American legal context, in which judges hold the power of judicial review, judicial activism also often presents itself as reading specific values into the Constitution's ambiguous places (Kmiec 2004, 1447). This definition illustrates fairly well that judicial activism is not bound to a specific legal ideology but can attach itself to any of them. Judicial professionals will simply read different values into a legal text depending on their conservative or progressive legal preferences. This is also the reason why, while often used in a derogatory way, within the American context, judicial activism may also possess a positive connotation when applied to civil rights litigation (Kmiec 2004, 1451).

In other words, judicial activism may have different normative implications depending on the type of values that judicial professionals promote via an activist approach to legal texts. As a result, judicial activism also raises important philosophical questions about the nature of judicial decision-making and its normative implications (La Torre 2015; Alexander 2015). Regardless, it is important to point out that judicial activism may apply to judicial professionals within any legal tradition or legal system (Holland 1991) whenever their actions move beyond the simple application of extant laws to the creation of new legal rules via a creative interpretive effort. As a result, judicial activism is also inherently "result-oriented" (Kmiec 2004, 1447), because judicial professionals will pursue a creative interpretation of the law in light of goals they consider valuable. This also means that judicial activism is, and most likely will remain, an inherently contested concept, and one that is empirically hard to measure (Lindquist and Cross 2009). As Hirschl (2008) points out, understanding what constitutes judicial activism – or, as he calls it, the "judicialization of politics" (Hirschl 2009) and of "mega-politics" (Hirschl 2008)—depends very much on a subjective evaluation of what falls within the judiciary's exclusive purview and what falls within other branches' (Hirschl 2008, 99).

In chapter 4, I show that judicial activism provided Clean Hands prosecutors with new legal and investigative approaches to corruption prosecutions geared toward breaking the bonds of loyalty among participants in the corruption system. This new activist approach to corruption prosecutions relied on a creative interpretation of extant legal rules, which allowed for the introduction of informal plea bargains. Furthermore, this activist approach signaled a new understanding of the judicial role, according to which judicial professionals had an obligation to fill the vacuum left by other government branches in tackling systemic issues, like corruption (Della Porta 2001, 4). Thus, my empirical analysis shows how ideas about the judicial role and an activist approach to its duties, more than political preferences, fueled the Clean Hand operation.

As I mentioned before, the role of legal ideology is mediated through the institutional structure in which prosecutorial actors find themselves operating. Decentralized and egalitarian structures enhance prosecutorial actors' freedom to pursue their favorite philosophical approach to the law, while hierarchical structures induce ideological conformity with higher ranks' preferences. At the same time, however, these institutional structures are the result of actors' choices, including legal actors at times. While political actors may hold ultimate control over the design of the prosecutorial system at the national level, legal actors may play a decisive role in influencing the choice of this design. Thus, the main determinant of prosecutorial behavior, legal philosophy, will also play a role in determining the existence of decentralized and egalitarian institutions rather than hierarchical ones. One example of this can be found in Ingram's work (2012, 2015). Ingram (2012) showed that the establishment of judicial councils in Mexico resulted from political actors' "principled ideological commitments" (441) rather than from political incentives inherent in electoral competition. As I discuss in chapter 2, the preeminence of ideas in leading the process of institutional design for judicial and prosecutorial institutions is also visible in the Italian case, where different legal factions lobbied political forces to bring about the prosecutorial system's decentralization in the 1970s.

Furthermore, legal ideology will also play a crucial role in determining the organizational approach within local prosecutors' offices. When given the freedom to organize their office as they please, chief prosecutors will choose to adopt either hierarchical or egalitarian structures depending on the legal philosophy they subscribe to. Nevertheless, legal philosophies' inherent understanding of the legal profession may at times offer cover for the use of prosecutorial powers in politically biased ways. As previously mentioned, while legal ideology is the preeminent driver of legal behavior, it is also possible that political bias will determine a few individuals' choices, including their choice of organizational structure for their offices. In chapter 2, I discuss Italian legal positivism's predilection for hierarchical relationships within the judicial system. This legal philosophy's support for hierarchical structures may also lend itself to abuses of power on the part of prosecutorial authorities who wish to target or protect public officials out of their own political bias.

More importantly, this process of institutional formation, both at the national and local levels, will not be devoid of competition between groups with different legal philosophies. In his discussion of Mexican judicial councils, Ingram (2012) outlines the existence of competing political visions of the judiciary's mission: a more conservative vision that expected the judiciary to work toward ensuring economic rights and another is more progressive vision in which the judiciary would be an engine of democratic progress (442). Similarly, legal factions holding on to different visions of their professional mission may compete for control over the design of prosecutorial institutions. The eventual prevalence of a hierarchical or egalitarian model will depend on which legal faction will prevail at key junctures in this process.

This is particularly visible in the Italian case, both at the national and local levels. In chapter 2, I discuss the emergence of new legal factions within the Italian judiciary with more democracy-oriented legal philosophies rooted in the values of the new Constitution. I also explore these legal factions' continued efforts to bring about decentralization and reshape prosecutorial institutions along egalitarian lines. Furthermore, the case studies in my book highlight the competition between conservative and progressive legal factions among Italian prosecutors for control over the organization of local prosecutors' offices and specifically for control over the appointment of local chief prosecutors, the individuals in charge of these organizational choices. The appointment of chief prosecutors with either a more conservative or more progressive legal philosophy was extremely consequential for the institutional structure of local offices. At times, these appointments reflected the emerging prevalence of a specific legal faction within a prosecutor's office. Other times, they represented a break in the emerging legal culture of the local prosecutor's office and, consequently, often sparked contention and revolt among lower-ranked prosecutors.

Figure 1.4 illustrates the role of legal ideology in bringing about institutional change and connects it to my previous discussion about the effects of decentralized, egalitarian, and hierarchical institutions on *de facto* prosecutorial independence and prosecutorial effectiveness.

In line with what I discussed in the previous sections of this chapter, hierarchical prosecutorial systems will tend to dictate local offices' organizational structure, whether the latter is hierarchical or egalitarian in nature. For this reason, the competition between different legal factions for the appointment of chief prosecutors is less consequential in hierarchical prosecutorial systems. On the other hand, chief prosecutors will enjoy more freedom over their offices' organizational structure within decentralized prosecutorial systems. For this reason, the competition between legal factions over the appointment

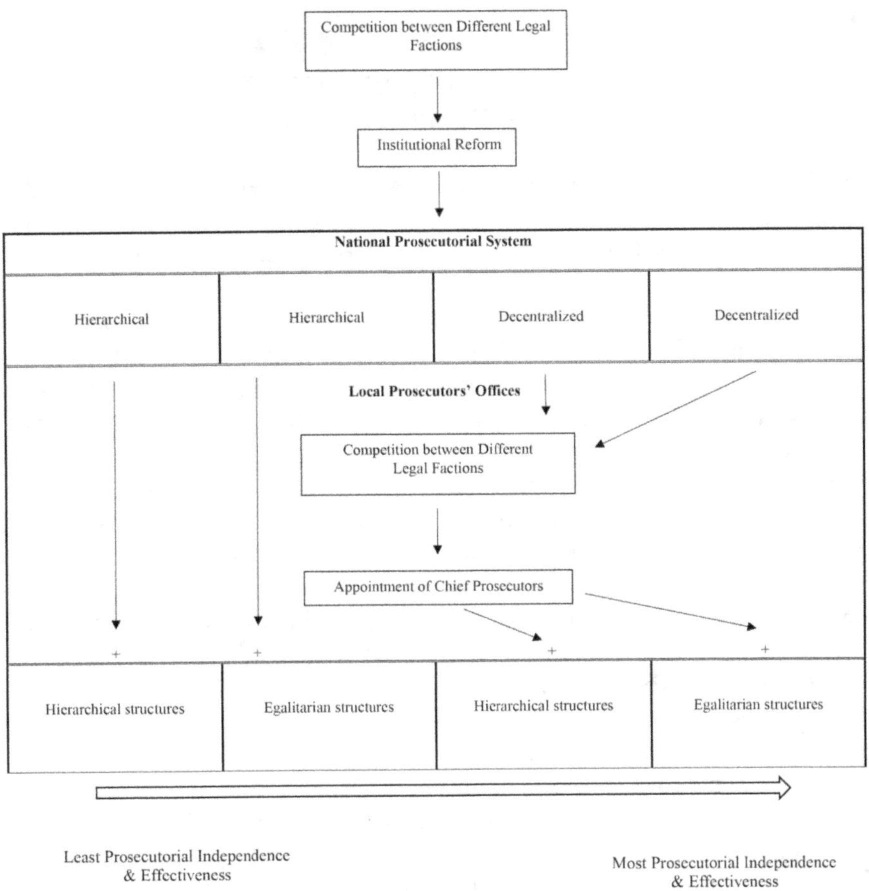

Figure 1.4 The Interactions between Legal Ideology and Prosecutorial Institutions. *Source*: Author's elaboration.

of local chief prosecutors will have significant repercussions on the resulting structure of the local prosecutor's office.

Thus, legal ideology is a crucial factor whose importance cannot be ignored and whose influence pervades the prosecutorial system. Legal ideology motivates actors as they pursue institutional reform and determines their choice of either egalitarian or hierarchical structures. Furthermore, legal ideology shapes prosecutorial actors' behavior within the resulting institutional environment, although the latter will necessarily affect the degree to which lower-ranked prosecutors can freely pursue their favorite legal approach or instead have to comply with their superior's. My theoretical framework therefore is essentially new institutionalist in nature, as it relies on Smith's (1988) intuition that institutions may arise out of actors' ideological visions and at the same time deeply affect the latter.

THE CAUSES OF EFFECTIVE CORRUPTION PROSECUTION

The theoretical framework I outlined so far does not refer specifically to corruption prosecutions. This is because its application may extend well beyond this criminal issue. However, it is worth clarifying how national and local prosecutorial structures affect corruption prosecutions. As mentioned earlier, corruption grows in complexity as it becomes systemic. From occasional illicit exchanges, corruption may evolve into a ramified network of actors from different sectors of society and politics, regulating their interactions via an elaborate set of informal rules. Uncovering such a complex criminal issue requires an enhanced degree of *de facto* independence on the part of prosecutorial authorities, which may grant them the ability to explore a variety of investigative and legal approaches. Furthermore, the ramified nature of systemic corruption, which may extend across institutional bodies, levels of government, and jurisdictions, may require prosecutors' ability to work cooperatively across units, with an enhanced degree of autonomy and freedom in forming collaborations and exchanging information.

Decentralized prosecutorial systems with egalitarian organizational structures at the local level are the most efficient at providing the conditions for the effective prosecution of systemic corruption. Decentralized systems empower prosecutorial authorities and their subordinates, providing them with significant freedom to explore diverse investigative methods and legal approaches to this criminal issue. Furthermore, within these systems, the development of effective corruption prosecution will particularly unfold in those prosecutorial units that opted for an egalitarian structure of professional relationships. This is because the collegial relationship between lower-ranked prosecutors and their superiors will allow the former to propose new legal and investigative approaches to systemic corruption.

On the other hand, local prosecutorial units that choose to implement a hierarchical organization, even within a decentralized system, will tend to lag behind in the effective prosecution of corruption as a result of the obstacles to prosecutorial independence imposed by this structure of professional relationships. Moreover, a hierarchical organization within a prosecutorial unit will provide the local chief prosecutor with significant control over subordinates. While ethical chief prosecutors may simply use this hierarchical control to run their office, chief prosecutors with strategic or unethical goals may use the same oversight powers to discourage or hinder specific investigations. Hierarchy, in other words, provides several opportunities for chief prosecutors to unduly influence or direct their subordinates' investigations toward a pre-decided conclusion.

Similar observations apply to hierarchical structures at the national level. Hierarchical systems will impose severe constraints on effective corruption prosecutions because central oversight creates significant pressure to conform to the legal philosophy or preferences of the principal in the principal–agent relationship. Within hierarchical prosecutorial systems, innovation can only move from the top down, and lower-ranked prosecutors are under momentous pressure to conform to the elite's preferred legal philosophy. If the latter is antithetical to the effective prosecution of systemic corruption, there is little room for local prosecutors to pursue alternative, more effective legal and investigative approaches. Furthermore, hierarchical structures facilitate the obstruction of potentially important corruption investigations on the part of the legal elite or officials at the top of the prosecutorial system. Strategic or unethical officials may use their position of power to discourage or prevent prosecutorial authorities from investigating corrupt activities. For this reason, hierarchical systems tend to negatively affect the likelihood of effective corruption prosecution.

Based on this general theoretical framework, the effective prosecution of systemic corruption will more likely emerge out of decentralized systems, specifically from prosecutorial units that have adopted an egalitarian approach to their internal organization. On the other hand, the persistence of hierarchical approaches, either at the national or at the local level, will consistently hinder the emergence of effective corruption prosecutions. To complete this theoretical framework, it is necessary to consider another potential obstacle to successful prosecutorial action, namely the existence of prosecutorial gatekeepers.

PROSECUTORIAL GATEKEEPING

As I argued so far, decentralization empowers lower-ranked prosecutorial actors vis-à-vis the institutional body or officials in charge of the former's professional fate. This results in a weakening of central oversight over local prosecutorial units. One unexpected implication is the possible emergence of strong prosecutorial gatekeepers at the local level, or among local prosecutorial units. "Prosecutorial gatekeeping" has been previously used to refer to prosecutors' discretion in bringing charges (Benson 1988; Olson 1984). However, I offer a new meaning of this concept. I define prosecutorial gatekeeping as the strategic use of jurisdictional issues for the appropriation of investigations in order to influence the latter's outcome.

Jurisdiction is the legal concept that determines which prosecutorial or judicial body will have a legitimate claim over an investigation or a case. In most cases, jurisdiction consists of the geographical boundaries limiting a prosecutorial office or a court's territory, over which the latter can raise a legitimate claim to a case. However, sometimes formal rules will establish a legal body's special jurisdiction over a specific set of cases, depending on the charges or the individuals involved. One example is the Brazilian code of criminal procedure's rules about lawsuits against members of Congress. Brazilian criminal procedure establishes that only the Brazilian Supreme Court can adjudicate this type of cases (Moro 2018, 158–159). Therefore, Brazilian criminal procedure formally establishes a prosecutorial gatekeeper in the Brazilian Supreme Court. Under these rules, the Brazilian Supreme Court may raise legitimate jurisdictional claims against any other judicial body intending to adjudicate charges against members of Congress.

However, prosecutorial gatekeepers can also emerge from an informal set of conditions, above all their geographical proximity to centers of power, either political or criminal power. When jurisdiction depends on a legal body's geographical boundaries, courts and prosecutorial units operating in proximity to centers of criminal power, such as drug cartels or mafia territory, will hold a jurisdictional advantage over cases related to these issues, compared to other judicial bodies. Jurisdictional conflict between prosecutorial units may arise due to these criminal activities' complex structure: mafia activities, for instance, will encompass a host of different criminal enterprises. This complexity will manifest itself in huge geographical reach, which might raise jurisdictional issues. However, courts and prosecutorial offices located next to centers of criminal power will enjoy an informal jurisdictional advantage over others. In other words, their ability to raise and win jurisdictional claims over specific criminal issues will make these institutions informal prosecutorial gatekeepers.

Prosecutorial gatekeepers may also arise as a result of their proximity to the center of political power. Political capitals will inevitably facilitate the concentration of political activities within a specific territory, thanks to the presence of legislative and executive institutions, political parties' branches, and even lobbying activities. As a result, courts and prosecutorial units in proximity of these political centers may enjoy a disproportionate jurisdictional advantage over cases involving elected officials and other political actors. Systemic corruption will tend to form a well-ramified criminal network with nodes overlapping with centers of political power, which may give rise to jurisdictional conflict. Nevertheless, prosecutorial units located in a country's political capital may enjoy the ability to raise and win jurisdictional issues and appropriate corruption investigations from other prosecutorial offices.

It is important to note that legal actors at these gatekeeping institutions will use this jurisdictional advantage for different reasons. Appropriating an investigation from another jurisdiction may be a strategic move to ensure accountability or to undermine it. For instance, chief prosecutors may use their office's gatekeeping powers to appropriate a case if they fear that another jurisdiction will not pursue criminal accountability to its full extent. Under this scenario, gatekeeping may promote more effective prosecution. On the contrary, chief prosecutors who wish to undermine criminal accountability may use their gatekeeping powers to appropriate and neutralize a sensitive investigation. Prosecutorial gatekeeping may serve either strategy, depending on prosecutorial authorities' intentions. However, given its inherent gatekeeping function, I argue that legal actors may more easily deploy this power to undermine accountability, rather than to strengthen it.

To fully understand a prosecutorial system's dynamics, it is necessary to consider the presence of prosecutorial gatekeepers. Hierarchy and decentralization will also create different expectations concerning these institutions' behavior. Within hierarchical systems, it is plausible to expect that prosecutorial gatekeepers will simply fall in line with the elite's legal preferences. If the officials at the top of the hierarchy controlling prosecutors are hostile to effective corruption prosecution, they will easily direct prosecutorial gatekeepers to use their power to appropriate and undermine corruption investigations. Therefore, the existence of prosecutorial gatekeepers is less relevant within hierarchical systems, where the former will act in accordance with the elite's preferences. On the other hand, decentralization will empower prosecutorial gatekeepers. The weakening of central oversight may increase gatekeepers' influence over specific sets of cases.

It is possible to derive some important implications for the prosecution of systemic corruption from the existence of prosecutorial gatekeepers within decentralized systems. Specifically, the presence of a prosecutorial gatekeeper that opposes criminal accountability may undermine the successful prosecution of corruption. If the prosecutorial gatekeeper wishes to undermine prosecutorial efforts to uncover systemic corruption, it can do so by appropriating investigations regardless of where they originated and neutralizing the "threat." More importantly, the inherent weakness of central oversight in decentralized systems may facilitate the use of gatekeeping powers against corruption investigations, even despite a growing consensus in favor of criminal accountability. Within decentralized systems, prosecutorial gatekeepers enjoy significant prosecutorial independence, like any other prosecutorial unit. This will allow them to use their gatekeeping powers more easily against the pursuit of accountability if they wish so.

However, as opposed to hierarchical systems, decentralized systems also offer important pathways to change, even with regard to prosecutorial gatekeepers. Decentralization may provide lower-ranked prosecutors, even those operating within a gatekeeping institution, with tools to pressure their immediate superior. This might result in significant conflict between a chief prosecutor who wishes to undermine corruption investigations via gatekeeping and their dissenting subordinates. Moreover, the existence of institutional channels through which lower ranks may influence promotions and appointments within decentralized systems may also lead to significant changes. Specifically, it may facilitate a gatekeeping institution's takeover by a different legal faction, which may in turn refrain from using gatekeeping power to neutralize corruption prosecutions. Thus, decentralization simultaneously empowers prosecutorial gatekeepers, while also providing pathways to significant changes in the use of their powers.

THE ITALIAN COURT SYSTEM AND PROSECUTORIAL INSTITUTIONS

The purpose of my analysis in this book is to apply the theoretical framework outlined so far to the Italian prosecutorial system in order to explain the Clean Hands operation's unprecedented success against systemic corruption after decades of failed attempts. For this reason, it is first necessary to provide a brief outline of judicial and prosecutorial institutions responsible for litigation at different levels in Italy. Figure 1.5 provides a simplified outline of the Italian court system and prosecutorial offices. As I explain in detail in chapter 2,

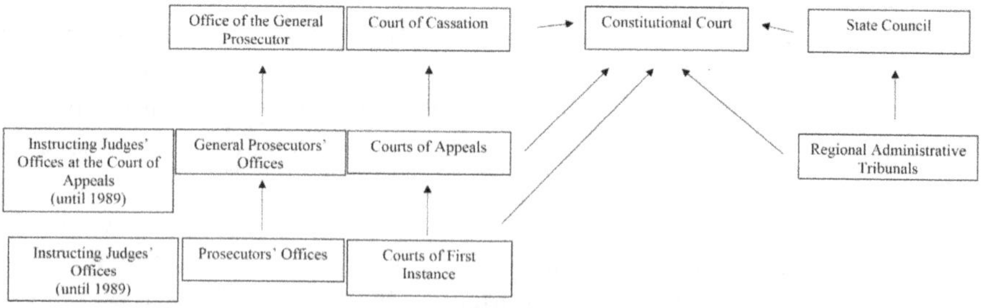

Figure 1.5 The Italian Court System and Prosecutors' Offices. *Source*: Author's elaboration.

Italian prosecutorial institutions and actors are considered part of the judicial branch. Like any other court system, the Italian judicial system includes several levels of review, with the Court of Cassation, the State Council, and the Constitutional Court representing three distinctive apical points. As it is often the case in civil law systems, in the Italian judicial system, the Court of Cassation represents the last level of review for criminal and civil disputes. The State Council, on the other hand, is the court of last resort for administrative matters. Finally, the Constitutional Court is the only judicial body in charge of deciding the constitutionality of laws.

Civil and criminal disputes normally move upward through three levels of review: courts of first instance (lower courts), courts of appeal, and the Court of Cassation. On the other hand, administrative and constitutional reviews follow distinct pathways. The former will move from regional lower courts with jurisdiction over administrative matters (so-called *tribunale regionale amministrativo*) to the State Council, the final level of review for administrative issues. Constitutional review directly connects lower courts to the Constitutional Court. If lower court judges identify a constitutional issue during litigation, they have an obligation to suspend legal proceedings and defer the issue to the Constitutional Court for resolution. Therefore, the latter is the only judicial body with the power to decide constitutional issues. At the same time, this method of review connects any lower court of any type (including regional administrative tribunals) directly to the Constitutional Court. As I explain more in detail in chapter 2, the latter dynamic holds massive implications for legal reform via constitutional review.

Every level of criminal and civil litigation includes a prosecutorial institution. As a result, figure 1.5 shows the first level of prosecution, with lower prosecutors' offices operating in conjunction with first instance courts. General prosecutors' offices operate at the appellate level, while the office of the General Prosecutor at the Court of Cassation argues for the prosecution before the court of last resort for criminal and civil matters. While this system creates multiple prosecutors' offices at different levels, lower prosecutors' offices represent the most salient center of investigative activity. Prosecutors at the appellate and final level of review will mostly rely on the evidence collected by lower prosecutors for the first instance trials. Consequently, lower prosecutors' offices will disproportionately affect the overall degree of prosecutorial effectiveness within this system. For this reason, my research design predominantly focuses on lower prosecutors' offices.

As is also shown in figure 1.5, prosecutors' offices were not the only institutions with investigative powers. Until 1989, prosecutors' offices were paired with so-called "*uffici instruzione*" or instructing judges' offices. The latter closely mirrored prosecutors' offices' investigative powers and supported their prosecutorial counterpart's investigative efforts (Reale 2018,

3–4). The 1989 criminal procedure reform brought instructing judges' offices to an end (Reale 2018). In most cases, this produced an influx of qualified personnel into local prosecutors' offices. While the focus of my analysis is on prosecutors' offices, I also examine organizational structures and investigative practices within their respective instructing judges' offices when necessary. This allows me to explore whether the later personnel migration from these institutions into prosecutors' offices had any effect on prosecutorial independence and effectiveness.

RESEARCH DESIGN

In this book, I pursue two research strategies: first, I use historical longitudinal analysis to explore the Italian prosecutorial system's institutional transformation over time, especially from re-democratization in 1945 to the 1970s, and this transformation's repercussions on prosecutorial behavior. As I explain in chapter 2, during those years, the Italian prosecutorial system went from a hierarchical to a decentralized system. This longitudinal analysis, therefore, shows how the Italian system's hierarchical structure prevented the pursuit of aggressive criminal accountability against corruption, among other issues, until decentralization occurred.

After the Italian prosecutorial system's decentralization came to completion in the mid-1970s, incentives and constraints on corruption prosecutions moved from the national to the local level. As explained in my theory, within a decentralized system, local prosecutorial units and their internal organization become salient factors for the emergence of prosecutorial independence and effectiveness. For this reason, in chapters 3–5, I apply process tracing to the case studies of four prosecutors' offices from 1975 to 1996 to explain the delay and final emergence of effective corruption prosecutions. This period of time covers the years from the completion of the decentralization process to the conclusion of the Clean Hands operation.[3] The data for process tracing comes from a multitude of sources: national and local newspapers, civil society organizations' journals, memoirs, and interviews I personally conducted with journalists, lawyers, prosecutors, judges, and civil society activists. Given the ongoing political divisions around the meaning and effects of the Clean Hands investigation, I decided to keep the identity of most of my interviewees confidential, to the greatest extent possible, to protect the free expression of their ideas on the topic. This was done as a precaution but does not in any way imply the existence of dangers, reputational or of another nature, for the individuals involved in this study. The exceptions to this rule concern a few individuals for which identification would have been inevitable, given the content of their interviews and their centrality to the events under examination. All interviewees were asked to sign a consent form, and evidence was handled in accordance with IRB-approved guidelines.

The case studies in my analysis include the prosecutors' offices in Rome, Milan, Palermo, and Reggio Calabria. Therefore, these case studies include prosecutorial units in different regions, from the North of Italy, to its political capital, to two Southern jurisdictions. I selected these case studies as comparable pairs of cases (Lijphart 1975; Collier 1993; Munck 2004) with significant similarities between them. The Milan and Rome prosecutors' offices are comparable in size (Cazzola and Morrisi 1996, 37–38), and they have been historically at the center of the two essential nodes of the corruption network: Milan, the country's "business capital," as its economic and financial node, and Rome, the nation's capital, as its political node. In addition, the Roman prosecutor's office has long enjoyed the status of informal prosecutorial gatekeeper, as I explain in chapter 3. For this reason, its inclusion in this research design is necessary to understand potential obstacles to effective corruption prosecutions. The prosecutors' offices in Palermo and Reggio Calabria are also comparable cases on many important dimensions, first of all their size (Cazzola and Morrisi 1996, 37–38). More importantly, both offices sit at the center of local organized crime networks that shaped corruption exchanges within these jurisdictions. For this reason, these cases highlight the evolution of corruption prosecutions within similar criminal contexts.

Furthermore, these case studies offer interesting variation on the dependent variables, prosecutorial independence and effectiveness. While I discuss qualitative evidence for the degree of prosecutorial independence in each prosecutor's office in my empirical analysis, figure 1.6 offers an operationalization of prosecutorial effectiveness by presenting the number of appellate corruption convictions in Rome, Milan, Palermo, and Reggio Calabria from 1992 to 1997, one year after the formal conclusion of the Clean Hands operation at the lower court level. The reason I included one more year was to capture corruption convictions that might plausibly result from the Clean Hands' wave of corruption investigations. Moreover, focusing on the appellate level is an inherently "conservative" way of measuring prosecutorial effectiveness, since appellate review will inevitably throw out some first-level convictions.

As it is clearly visible from figure 1.6, Milan recorded a higher number of appellate corruption convictions than Rome, and Palermo recorded a higher number of appellate corruption convictions than Reggio Calabria. At the same time, the variation between Palermo and Reggio Calabria does not immediately stand out, given the lower number of convictions for this pair of cases compared to Rome and Milan. This is partially a result of the criminal context within these Southern jurisdictions. As I explain in chapter 5, in both Palermo and Reggio Calabria, corruption was deeply integrated into the local network of mafia activities. For this reason, prosecutorial effectiveness

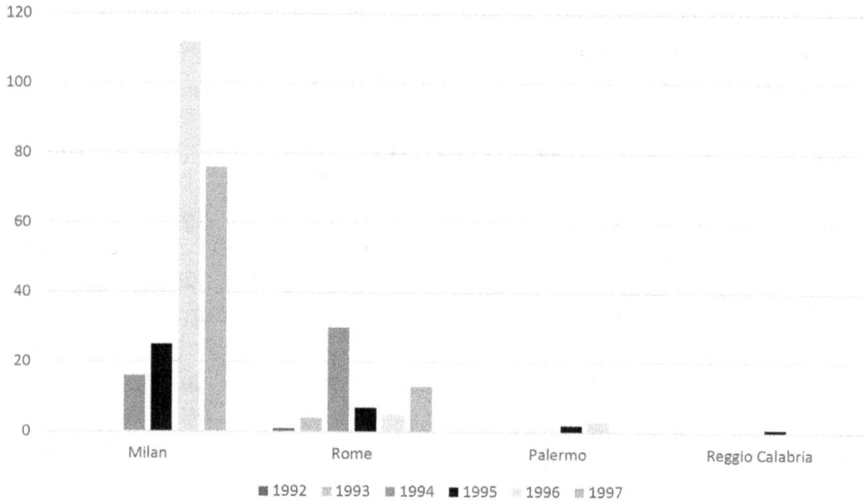

Figure 1.6 Appellate Corruption Convictions in Milan, Rome, Palermo, and Reggio Calabria, 1992–1997 Data in Davigo and Mannozzi (2007). *Source*: Author's elaboration.

against the former might find expression in legal action against mafia crimes, rather than corruption-specific activities, such as embezzlement and bribery. Qualitative evidence, which I present in chapter 5, clearly confirms Palermo's higher levels of prosecutorial effectiveness in prosecuting mafia and corruption crimes than Reggio Calabria's.

In addition, these case studies present significant variation on the independent variable, namely the organizational structure of professional relationships within a prosecutor's office. Table 1.3 illustrates the diversity of organizational approaches implemented in each prosecutor's office at different points in time. While chief prosecutors in Milan and Palermo pushed early on for the adoption of egalitarian approaches, the prosecutors' offices in Rome and Reggio Calabria remained impervious to these approaches for

Table 1.3 Organizational Structures in Milan, Rome, Palermo, and Reggio Calabria Prosecutors' Offices, 1975–1996

	Hierarchical	*Egalitarian*
Rome, 1975–1992	✓	
Rome, 1992–1996		✓
Palermo, 1979–1986		✓
Palermo, 1986–1993	✓	
Palermo, 1993–1996		✓
Milan, 1975–1978	✓	
Milan, 1978–1996		✓
Reggio Calabria, 1978–1996	✓	

Source: Author's elaboration.

most, if not the whole time period considered. In the case studies, I explore the effects of these different choices on prosecutorial independence and effectiveness.

ORGANIZATIONAL STRUCTURES IN MILAN, ROME, PALERMO, AND REGGIO CALABRIA PROSECUTORS' OFFICES, 1975–1996

As I explained in my theory, within decentralized systems, local chief prosecutors hold significant discretion over their offices' internal organization. In the case studies, I explore chief prosecutors' legal philosophy and how it affected their approach to their office's internal structure. I also examine the interactions among different legal factions within each prosecutor's office. As I explain in chapter 2, Italian legal positivism, a conservative legal ideology, entailed a strong preference for hierarchical approaches. On the other hand, Italian legal progressivism, based on the values of the new democratic Constitution, supported the development of egalitarian structures. In chapter 2, I show that decentralization afforded both conservative and progressive chief prosecutors the freedom to pursue organizational approaches in line with their preferences. At the same time, decentralization offered lower-ranked prosecutors, often younger and more progressive than their superiors, new means to push for the adoption of egalitarian approaches. In the case studies, I explore the interactions between chief prosecutors and lower ranks and how they affected the choice of local organizational structures.

I apply process tracing to the case studies in this research to show how the adoption of egalitarian structures or the persistence of hierarchy within a prosecutor's office affected the development of effective corruption prosecutions over time. Via process tracing, I show that the early adoption of egalitarian structures was the leading reason behind the effective prosecution of systemic corruption in the Clean Hands operation. In the Milan prosecutor's office, the early adoption of an egalitarian structure laid the foundation for the development of prosecutorial effectiveness against systemic corruption. In particular, an egalitarian setting allowed local Milanese prosecutors to experiment with new activist approaches to corruption prosecutions, which turned out to be extremely effective in breaking through the corruption system. This set of conditions explains the Milan prosecutor's office's central role in the Clean Hands operation.

At the same time, process tracing also illustrates the different effects stemming from the intermittent introduction of egalitarian structures in Palermo, their late adoption in Rome, and persistent hierarchical structures in Reggio Calabria. Furthermore, process tracing allows me to outline the informal networks forming across several of these jurisdictions and their role in the diffusion of new investigative techniques and new legal ideas about the prosecutorial mission. Finally, process tracing also sheds light on prosecutorial gatekeeping. In chapter 3, I explore the dynamics underlying the Roman prosecutor's office's use of gatekeeping powers along with gatekeeping's effect on corruption prosecutions, both within and outside the Roman jurisdiction.

ALTERNATIVE HYPOTHESES

Before delving into my empirical analysis, it is worth outlining the main alternative theories to the argument in this book and addressing a few. Specifically, it is worth discussing both theories that revolve around corruption prosecutions and theories that discuss judicial and prosecutorial independence more broadly. Most alternative hypotheses argue that the political context is essential to explaining judicial and prosecutorial behavior. For instance, Political Fragmentation Theories (PFTs) argue that increases in judicial independence follow from the presence of divided government in a presidential system (Rios-Figueroa 2007; Iaryczower, Spiller and Tommasi 2002), or the occurrence of minimal coalitions or minority governments in parliamentary systems (Carrubba et al. 2015). Therefore, PFTs would explain the Clean Hands operation as the result of the "thinning" or weakening of government coalitions, which hindered elected officials' ability to retaliate against prosecutors and judges investigating corruption. In chapter 2, I show how empirical evidence does not support PFTs as a possible explanation for successful systemic corruption prosecution in the Clean Hands operation.

Other theories rely on judicial professionals' political ideology to explain their behavior (Segal and Spaeth 1996, 2002), including their willingness to prosecute corruption within the Italian context (Ceron and Mainenti 2015). Ceron and Mainenti (2015) argue that Italian prosecutors tend to direct their investigative efforts against politicians with opposite ideological convictions than their own. In my case studies, I present evidence against this attitudinal argument. While Italian political parties' repeated attempts to influence and co-opt judicial elements are undeniable (Nelken 1996*a*, 103), prosecutors' political ideology does not explain systemic patterns in prosecutorial independence and effectiveness, especially in the Clean Hands operation. In general, there is a little evidence that the Clean Hands operation may have been a "judicial coup" orchestrated against the political class (Nelken 1996*a*). As Nelken (1996*a*) points out, there was a little coordination between the several investigative units scattered around the country that decided to imitate Milanese prosecutors in tackling systemic corruption immediately after the start of the Clean Hands investigation (Nelken 1996*a*, 105–106). Where cooperation happened, as in some of the case studies I discuss in this book, it required significant effort and it was not a foregone conclusion.

Furthermore, the Clean Hands operation's overwhelming focus on political parties necessarily followed from the latter's central role in the corruption system. As Nelken (1996*a*) explains, because political parties were the chief "controllers of public resources" (Nelken 1996*a*, 105), for whose distribution they had engineered complex informal rules like *lottizzazione*, they were also the "prime movers of corruption" (Nelken 1996*a*, 105). In other words, there is a little evidence that the Clean Hands operation represented a well-designed plan to retaliate against the First Republic's main political forces (Nelken 1996*a*, 105–106; Nelken 2002b, 57).

On the other hand, it would be inappropriate to disregard the Clean Hands Operation's momentous effects on the Italian political system (Nelken 1996*a*, 106). Public opinion's backlash against political parties' involvement in corruption brought about the possibility of alternation in power for the first time since re-democratization (Nelken 1996*a*, 107). While this resulted in an increased chance of electoral victory for left-wing political parties like the PDS (the former Italian Communist Party) in the long run (Nelken 1996*a*, 106), it also paved the way for the rise of new political forces, such as Silvio Berlusconi's *Forza Italia* (Go Italy). The latter won the 1994 election—with the Clean Hands operation still moving ahead in the background—after having been created in a matter of months. I briefly explore the Clean Hands operation's political consequences in the conclusion.

Another argument relies on structural changes in the economic sphere and points at declining GDP growth and public spending as conditions facilitating corruption investigations (Davigo and Mannozzi 2007, 58–61). According to this argument, economic downturns and decreases in state investments withdraw significant resources from corruption exchanges, pushing the actors involved to reconsider the pros and cons of these illicit bargains. This often results in the spontaneous emergence of confidential informants (Davigo and Mannozzi 2007, 59). However, this argument hardly explains the timing and success of the Clean Hands operation. While GDP growth and public spending were both declining in the years leading to 1992, this was by no means the first such economic slowdown. On the other hand, corruption had been widespread in Italian politics since the return to democracy. Therefore, it is not clear why the early 1990s' economic outlook should lead to the successful prosecution of systemic corruption, as opposed to previous similar circumstances.

Furthermore, even when economic conditions might seem to facilitate the surfacing of corrupt exchanges, this does not necessarily entail a successful outcome to their prosecution. The 1970s oil crisis, for instance, significantly depressed Italy's GDP growth. In 1974, Genoese prosecutors uncovered a bribery scheme organized by the Italian oil trade association, *Unione Petrolifera Italiana*, to increase its own profits (Guarnieri 2003, 145). Nevertheless, the "oil scandal," as it was labeled by the press at the time, did not lead to a single indictment against the politicians involved (Almerighi 1993). As this demonstrates, while economic conditions may facilitate the surfacing of corruption, they do not necessarily lead to its successful prosecution. Furthermore, reliance on external conditions to prompt spontaneous collaboration from corruption network participants entails a very narrow understanding of prosecutorial action. In the case studies, I detail prosecutors' extensive efforts in spurring collaboration from actors in the corruption network and other criminal organizations, such as the mafia. Over time, Milanese and Sicilian prosecutors developed investigative techniques that would facilitate the emergence of confidential informants.

Finally, an alternative explanation for the successful prosecution of systemic corruption in the Clean Hands operation focuses on the radical changes to the Italian code of criminal procedure that took place in 1989. The purpose of this reform was to introduce adversarial elements into Italy's traditionally inquisitorial criminal justice system (Pizzi and Marafioti 1992). One could argue, then, that this new adversarial framework may have improved prosecutorial effectiveness against corruption and could therefore explain the Clean Hands operation's success. Nevertheless, the 1989 reform also introduced stronger guarantees for defendants' rights, without necessarily chipping away at existing ones (Nelken and Zanier 2006, 144). Moreover, there is little evidence that Italian prosecutors modeled their behavior and legal practice after this new adversarial framework. Rather, the Italian judiciary continued following an inquisitorial understanding of criminal procedure (Nelken 2002*a*, 126–127). Even decades after the 1989 reform, Italian prosecutors seemed to have persisted in an inquisitorial mentality that emphasizes concerns for criminal procedure over "crime fighting" (Montana and Nelken 2011, 846). Thus, it is unlikely that the 1989 reform may explain enhanced prosecutorial effectiveness in the Clean Hands operation.

The 1989 reform introduced a procedure superficially resembling plea bargaining (Pizzi and Marafioti 1992). As I explain in my empirical analysis, the Clean Hands operation would come to rely greatly on plea bargaining for its success. However, the type of plea bargaining formally introduced by the new criminal procedure code did not allow Italian prosecutors to "bargain over the nature of the crime to which the defendant will plead guilty" (Pizzi and Marafioti 1992, 22). As I explain in chapter 4, the prosecutorial strategy driving the Clean Hands operation was based on an informal bargaining of charges, which required some degree of discretion in choosing whether to pursue *concussione* or *corruzione* charges. Therefore, this bargaining procedure represented a significant departure from extant legal rules. In chapter 4, I trace the development of this informal plea bargaining, which prosecutor Di Pietro created by introducing another legal novelty, namely the concept of *dazione ambientale*. Furthermore, in chapter 5, I examine the development of a similar informal plea bargaining process in the prosecution of mafia organizations in Palermo, which occurred before the 1989 reform. Thus, formal legal reform only goes so far in explaining prosecutorial effectiveness in the Clean Hands operation and other prosecutorial achievements against complex criminal issues.

On the other hand, the reorganization of investigative offices introduced by the 1989 reform did, in some cases, contribute to increased prosecutorial effectiveness. This is because the elimination of instructing judges' offices brought an influx of new personnel into local prosecutor's offices. This resulted, at times, in significant increases in local expertise among prosecutors. I explore this dynamic in my case studies.

CONCLUSION

In this chapter, I offered a theoretical framework for the development of *de facto* prosecutorial independence and prosecutorial effectiveness in relation to systemic corruption prosecutions. Previous scholarly analyses have focused on national judicial and prosecutorial systems' design and its relationship vis-à-vis other government branches (Skaar 2011; Michel 2017). The theoretical framework I offer provides a granular systematic analysis of prosecutors' offices' internal organization, within the broader institutional context of hierarchical and decentralized prosecutorial systems. Therefore, this theoretical framework connects the microfoundations of prosecutorial independence and effectiveness to the overarching institutional context in which they develop. By doing so, this theory also allows me to explore the causes behind the endogenous emergence of legal innovations among prosecutors.

While this theoretical framework may extend to prosecutorial systems in all democracies, in this book, I apply this theory to the Italian system. In accordance with the research design outlined above, in chapter 2, I develop a longitudinal study of the Italian prosecutorial system's transformations, from its establishment to its full decentralization in the 1970s. In chapters 3–5, I conduct case studies of the prosecutors' offices in Rome, Milan, Palermo, and Reggio Calabria.

NOTES

1. In 2019, San Francisco elected Chesa Boudin as the local district attorney. Boudin's progressive legal views are visible in his commitment to a comprehensive

restructuring of the criminal justice system to address the persistence of racist practices (Hawkins 2019). While Boudin was eventually ousted from office, other progressive prosecutors recently won elections in other jurisdictions across the country, including Larry Krasner in Philadelphia (PA) (Smith 2021) and Sarah George in Burlington (VT).

2. Scholars have stressed a policy's visibility as one of the potential reasons for its diffusion (Weyland 2005*a*, 2005*b*).

3. This refers to the conclusion of the investigation at the level of first instance trials, not the appellate level.

Chapter 2

A More Democratic Judiciary

The Transformation of Italian Judicial and Prosecutorial Institutions

In the previous chapter, I offered a theoretical framework aimed at explaining *de facto* prosecutorial independence and effectiveness. One of the key aspects of my theory is the distinction between hierarchical and decentralized prosecutorial systems in relation to the appointment and promotion power. As I explained in chapter 1, the implications of each institutional setting for prosecutorial independence and effectiveness are momentous. Hierarchical systems tend to entrench and perpetuate the legal philosophy that is most prevalent among the elite in charge of promotions and appointments. As a result, hierarchical systems tend to compress prosecutorial independence among lower ranks. On the other hand, decentralized systems promote a higher degree of independence among lower-ranked prosecutors. Thus, decentralization facilitates the emergence of a variety of legal approaches to the same issue across local prosecutorial institutions.

Transformations from one type of prosecutorial system to another rarely occur due to the radical institutional restructuring they entail. Democratic transitions may offer an opportunity for such institutional overhaul. This is because these events often entail the drafting or amending of constitutional texts. Nevertheless, constitutional drafters may at times overlook changes to the prosecutorial system's internal structure, especially the appointment and promotion processes, in favor of a focus on formal autonomy guarantees, what scholars usually call *de jure* independence. This is because the former's political implications are less clear than the prosecutorial system's overall formal autonomy from other government branches. Therefore, even constitutional drafters risk neglecting a key aspect affecting the prosecutorial system's performance, namely the extent to which it is either hierarchical or decentralized.

The transition to democracy in Italy well embodies this paradox. The new democratic framework enhanced judicial and prosecutorial actors' formal autonomy from other government branches. The inclusion of prosecutorial actors in the judicial branch further increased this formal autonomy. At the same time, the new constitutional text did not entail a significant restructuring of the judiciary's internal organization, which remained very hierarchical. For instance, while strengthening the High Council of the Judiciary's insulation from other government branches, the new democratic constitution did not lay out clear rules for its members' selection. This intentional omission resulted in the entrenchment of a conservative judicial elite's dominance over the judicial branch, which now included prosecutors as well. This, in turn, had a profound impact on prosecutorial independence and effectiveness.

When constitutional drafters miss an opportunity to decentralize the prosecutorial system after democratization, institutional restructuring may come to depend on the protracted interactions between legal and political actors within the newly democratic framework. The Italian case also embodies this dynamic: it took almost thirty years for judicial associations and political parties to agree on a set of institutional reforms that would bring about decentralization. When the latter occurred in 1975, it led to the corresponding empowerment of local prosecutorial actors. Without the High Council of the Judiciary's hierarchical oversight over the prosecutorial system, local chief prosecutors became the leading actors in shaping their offices' internal organization and prosecutorial work. Thus, starting in 1975, the roots of prosecutorial independence and effectiveness lie in local chief prosecutors' decisions about their office's internal organization.

In this chapter, I explore the Italian prosecutorial system's gradual institutional transformation from the country's founding to the mid-1970s. My analysis briefly outlines the historical roots of the Italian prosecutorial system's hierarchical structure, which came to full fruition under the Fascist regime. This structure entrenched the power of a conservative legal elite and resulted in a significant compression of prosecutorial independence among the lower ranks. This analysis also allows me to trace the historical development of Italian legal positivism, a conservative legal philosophy. I also explore the struggle between different legal and political factions around the prosecutorial system's restructuring after the transition to democracy in 1945. I show that progressive legal forces championed decentralization in order to bring the system in line with the new democratic principles in the constitutional text. Thus, I also conduct a thorough examination of the institutional changes that gradually decentralized the Italian prosecutorial system, completing this transformation in 1975.

This historical analysis is the background to the cases in the following chapters of this book. As I theorized in chapter 1, decentralization empowers local prosecutorial actors. As a result, paradoxically, the Italian prosecutorial system's decentralization strengthened conservative chief prosecutors' control over their offices at the local level. On the other hand, decentralization also afforded Italian prosecutors with new tools they could use to hold their local superiors accountable. Therefore, understanding decentralization and its implications is necessary to explain the differences in prosecutorial independence and effectiveness among the prosecutors' offices in Milan, Rome, Palermo, and Reggio Calabria.

In what follows, I start by briefly summarizing the Italian prosecutorial and judicial system's development from its foundation to the end of the Fascist period. This brief analysis allows me to discuss the formation of Italian legal conservatism as a result of the alliance between the Italian legal elite and the Fascist regime. I then discuss the prosecutorial system's restructuring after democratization, the emergence of new legal philosophies, and judicial associations. I also outline decentralization's implications for local prosecutors' offices to set the background for the case studies in the following chapters. Finally, I conclude the chapter by addressing a few alternative hypotheses to my argument, especially political fragmentation theories (PFTs) (Rios-Figueroa 2007 and Iaryczower, Spiller and Tommasi 2002).

THE HISTORICAL ROOTS OF ITALIAN JUDICIAL AND PROSECUTORIAL INSTITUTIONS

In chapter 1, I offered a typology of hierarchical and decentralized systems, along with a typology of externally and internally directed prosecutorial systems. For the greater part of its existence, the Italian prosecutorial system has been hierarchical in nature, as I explain in this chapter. However, a brief historical background shows that at its foundation, the Italian prosecutorial system was established as an externally directed system. Nevertheless, its hierarchical nature has been its defining feature until the 1970s. Far from being an exhaustive account, this section provides the historical background necessary to understand the Italian system's traditionally hierarchical institutional design.

While the focus of my analysis in this book is on prosecutorial institutions, in what follows, I also briefly discuss the development of judicial institutions. This is necessary as Italian prosecutors would later become part of the judiciary after re-democratization. For this reason, when discussing prosecutorial institutions after re-democratization, I refer to the judicial and the prosecutorial system interchangeably. This is because the two systems "merged" together, to the point that judicial professionals could switch from prosecutorial to judicial roles and vice versa over the course of their careers without too much difficulty. For the same reason, in the sections of this chapter discussing developments after re-democratization, I often refer to both prosecutors and judges as "judicial professionals."

At its establishment in 1864, the Italian prosecutorial system did not enjoy a significant degree of formal autonomy from other government branches—as is to be expected for prosecutorial systems in nineteenth-century Europe. Western European prosecutorial systems generally emerged as one more ramification within a large state bureaucracy serving, above all, the interests of the monarch. For this reason, government officials controlled selection and promotions within the Italian judicial and prosecutorial system (Guarnieri 2003, 88–90). The typologies I elaborated in chapter 1 apply to consolidated democracies where the prosecutorial system enjoys some degree of formal independence from other government branches. Although late 1800s' Italy may not neatly fit this category, it is fair to say that at this time, its prosecutorial system approximated an externally directed system based on political appointment. Moreover, the uniform social and ideological outlook between legal professionals and the political elites lessened the need for external control over the prosecutorial systems. As Guarnieri (2003) explains, politicians and legal professionals came from the same elites that had spearheaded the movement for Italian unification under the Kingdom of Piedmont (89).

More importantly, members of the Italian legal profession overwhelmingly adhered to a positivist understanding of their role. Legal positivism provided Italian legal professionals with the philosophical underpinnings that supported their textualist approach to norms and legal texts. This legal philosophy, widespread among civil law countries, shaped judicial professionals' understanding of their own professional mission for at least a century. According to legal positivism, judicial professionals are simply the "mouth of the law," bound to apply and not interpret legal provisions. Therefore, legal positivism encourages judicial professionals to think of themselves as removed from politics (Hilbink 2012, 605–606). This, in turn, contributes to limiting the judiciary's role as a possible check on legislative and executive power. Because of its highly bureaucratic understanding of the judicial mission and its hostility toward interpreting legal norms in light of current circumstances, legal positivism, therefore, represents a "conservative" legal philosophy. The Italian legal profession's adherence to legal positivism reinforced its submission to other government branches. In the name of legal positivism, legal professionals understood their chief mission to be solving legal disputes in a highly "mechanical" manner on behalf of the monarch.

While later institutional changes would increase the Italian judicial system's formal autonomy over the years, these developments did not apply to prosecutors. For instance, in 1890, political appointment to the judiciary was abolished and replaced by a national examination, which would work as a gateway to this institution for law graduates (Guarnieri 2003, 90). In addition, in 1907 and 1908, the mechanism for judicial promotions and appointments changed. Starting in 1908, the newly established *Consiglio Superiore della Magistratura* (High Council of the Judiciary) would hold significant influence over promotions and appointments (Guarnieri 2003, 91). The most important exception to this procedure concerned prosecutorial appointments. The latter remained firmly under the executive branch's control (Guarnieri 2003, 92).

Even though Italian judges improved their autonomy from other branches, higher-ranked judges still maintained strong oversight powers over the lower ranks. This is because Court of Cassation judges would appoint High Council members from among higher-court judges (Guarnieri 2003, 91). Government officials could only appoint a minority of Council members (91). In 1921, another reform further insulated the High Council from political influences by establishing that the whole judicial population would elect Council members, but only among Cassation judges (Guarnieri 2003, 92). Thus, until the 1970s, most High Council members would belong to an extremely selective judicial elite sitting on the courts of appeals and the Court of Cassation. As a result, Italian higher-court judges established their long-lasting control over judicial appointments and promotions.

As the High Council's control over appointments and promotions solidified, so did higher-court judges' influence over the judiciary's lower ranks. Through their control over the High Council, higher-court judges with conservative views held ultimate control over the rest of the judiciary, which they could force into compliance with their legal preferences. Furthermore, the enduring control of higher-court judges over lower-ranked ones explains why the rise to power of the Fascist party "did not represent a disruption in our judiciary's institutional development" (Guarnieri 2003, 92). Rather, the Fascist regime "brought to fulfillment" some of this institution's bureaucratic features (92).

While Fascist authorities drastically changed representative institutions, such as the legislature, to assert their power, they did not modify the Italian judiciary's institutional structure in equally drastic ways. Rather, Fascist authorities made sure to have control over "politically salient" cases by establishing a few special courts (Guarnieri 2003, 93). Clearly, Fascist officials did have an interest in affirming their control over the prosecutorial and judicial systems. Nevertheless, the latter did not require significant institutional changes other than transferring control of judicial promotions and appointments back into the hands of the executive branch. For this reason, in 1926, Fascist authorities indirectly extended their control over the judicial branch by allowing the executive to appoint all High Council members (Del Mastro 2014, 34–35). In addition, new legislation stripped the Council of its consultative powers in relation to promotions and appointments, leaving the Minister of Justice in complete control of this fundamental task (Del Mastro 2014, 37). As a result, Fascist officials indirectly controlled the judiciary while they continued to appoint prosecutors directly. This institutional configuration was enough to guarantee the authoritarian regime's subjugation of the Italian judicial and prosecutorial systems.

Interestingly, even during the Fascist era, the High Council's composition continued to consist, for the most part, of higher-court judges (Del Mastro 2014, 37–38). This might have represented the beginning of a bond of loyalty between the Italian judicial elite and Fascist authorities. Far from vocally opposing the rise to power of Mussolini and his party, judicial professionals sitting on appellate courts and on the Court of Cassation proved to be, if not loyal, at least passive recipients of autocratization. At the same time, Fascist authorities may have specifically looked for sympathizers or loyalists to appoint to the High Council. It is, therefore, a stretch to assume that all members of the judiciary espoused the regime's ideology.

At the same time, the absence of significant efforts on the part of Fascist authorities to indoctrinate judicial personnel (Guarnieri 2003, 93) is stark and telling. The only visible attempts to indoctrinate judicial professionals started toward the end of the regime (Guarnieri 2003, 94). Only then did Fascist authorities decide to request party membership of all judicial professionals and to hold mandatory workshops for new judicial trainees (94). However, for the greater part of the Fascist regime, there was no prolonged and concerted effort at judicial indoctrination. Indeed, there was no need for it, as the prevalence of legal positivism across all levels of the Italian judicial system guaranteed that its members would think of themselves as mere implementers of the law rather than its interpreters (Guarnieri 2003, 93). Therefore, the Italian judicial system's institutional structure and its elite's prevalent legal philosophy made it easy for this institution to comply with Minister of Justice Rocco's infamous invitation to "apoliticism":

> We do not require that the judiciary pursue pro-regime, Fascist politics [. . .] However, we do firmly require the judiciary not pursue anti-regime, anti-Fascist politics. And judges comply with this request in most cases.[1]

At the same time, some judges believed that adherence to legal positivism would constrain the excesses of the Fascist regime (Borgna 2017). Even though the Fascist regime had already altered the pre-existing legal framework by introducing abhorrent anti-Semitic laws, for instance, some members of the legal elite still believed that strict adherence to the pre-Fascist body of laws would limit the regime's atrocities and abuses of power (Borgna 2017). In their opinion, adherence to the letter of the law was preferable to judicial interpretation that would adapt existing laws to present circumstances. According to some members of the judicial elite, this type of interpretation would have opened the door to more legal abuses, therefore benefiting the current authoritarian regime (Borgna 2017).

Italian judicial professionals' adherence to positivist legal ideas and their tacit acceptance of the Fascist regime shaped the nature of Italian legal positivism for years to come. Moreover, Italian judicial professionals' understanding of their role as mere executors of the letter of the law, even under authoritarianism, created a deep aversion on their part to the use of judicial powers to hold public officials accountable. For instance, in the years immediately following the fall of the regime, Italian judges opposed the establishment of *ad hoc* military tribunals to try Fascist officials (Borgna 2017), because this would have clearly contradicted established criminal procedure (Borgna 2017). Furthermore, as I will discuss later, the Court of Cassation would play a crucial role in putting an end to any attempt at transitional justice. Thus, the Italian judiciary's posture toward the Fascist regime would shape Italian legal conservatism's hostility toward accountability way past the return to democracy.

THE FAILURE TO DECENTRALIZE THE PROSECUTORIAL SYSTEM AFTER DEMOCRATIZATION

Italy's transition to democracy in 1945 embodies the dilemmas that constitutional drafters face and the traps they might fall into when reforming prosecutorial institutions. As I previously mentioned, constitutional drafters will rarely consider changing the prosecutorial system's internal structure and organization. This is because the latter's political implications are often less clear than prosecutorial institutions' placement vis-à-vis other government branches. This omission often combines with democratic officials' unwillingness or difficulty in pursuing judicial purges. Replacing authoritarian judicial elements is not as easy as replacing government officials with authoritarian loyalties. Because the judiciary requires a specific type of professional knowledge, judicial purges, if they occur, are likely to be narrow and circumscribed events. The constitutional discussion about changes to the Italian prosecutorial system after World War II highlights all of these trends.

Italian constitutional drafters were eager to enshrine fundamental principles of autonomy and independence for the Italian judiciary into the new text. However, the constitutional drafters barely contended with several key issues about the judiciary's internal organization. Therefore, these questions were left to the *Associazione Nazionale Magistrati* (National Judicial Association), or ANM, the official association representing all judicial professionals, and its internal factions to decide. This was, however, not an even playfield: thanks to their long-lasting privileged status, even under the Fascist regime, higher-court judges clearly enjoyed an overwhelming advantage over other ANM factions. In a thorough study of the Italian judiciary's institutional ideology, Moriondo (1967, 94) finds that the principle of hierarchical control as a corollary to formal independence was overwhelmingly present in ANM publications, where high-court judges' contributions prevailed. Therefore, political forces' unwillingness to address changes to the judiciary's internal structure allowed higher-court judges to preserve their position of privilege.

This resulted in the survival of a very hierarchical institutional structure, which would soon extend to prosecutors as well, with momentous implications for prosecutorial independence and effectiveness. While constitutional drafters were negotiating a new fundamental text, the temporary government moved to establish a functioning judicial and prosecutorial system that would improve on previous weaknesses. Specifically, the 1946 Togliatti decree withdrew the executive branch's direct control over prosecutors by including the latter in the judicial branch (Del Mastro 2014, 45–46). In addition, the decree assigned consultative powers in relation to appointments and promotions to the High Council of the Judiciary (Del Mastro 2014, 45).[2] Finally, the decree established that all local *consigli giudiziari* (judicial councils), along with a group of Court of Cassation judges and court of appeals judges, would select Council members via a vote (Del Mastro 2014, 47).[3] Consequently, all High Council members would belong to the higher ranks of the judicial branch, either as judges or appellate-level prosecutors (47–49). As a result of these changes, in the aftermath of World War II (and before the enactment of a new, more democratic Constitution), the Italian prosecutorial system embodied an internally directed elitist type of system, because, ultimately, higher-court judges were the only ones choosing High Council members in charge of promotions and appointments.

While prosecutors' inclusion in the judicial branch clearly enhanced the prosecutorial system's formal autonomy from other branches, the latter's hierarchical structure was not in question. Therefore, the new hierarchical structure strengthened higher-court judges' control over the prosecutorial system, handing over to an elite group with lasting authoritarian tendencies control over appointments and promotions to judicial as well as prosecutorial posts, thanks to the absence of extensive judicial purges. New political forces had made some attempts to replace judicial professionals with authoritarian tendencies, but most purges had narrowly targeted a few individuals at the top of the judicial hierarchy (Guarnieri 2003, 95). The survival of authoritarian-leaning elements at the top of the judicial elite would last well after re-democratization. As Meniconi notes:

> in 1968 all Court of Cassation judges (and about seventy percent of those sitting on courts of appeal) had been serving on this Court since before 1944, while

almost ninety percent of judges on lower courts had entered the profession after that critical juncture. (Meniconi 2015, 225)

Despite widespread agreement among ANM representatives on hierarchical control, the emergence of discordant voices among the judiciary's lower ranks soon became increasingly noticeable. For instance, in 1946, a regional journal published an article from a local judge arguing that the judicial branch's hierarchical structure was essentially "anti-democratic" and, therefore, contrary to the profession's institutional mission (Moriondo 1967, 94). In the same year, an article in *La Magistratura*, the official ANM publication, argued, on the contrary, that hierarchical control over the lower ranks should increase rather than decrease (94–95).

These contrasting publications illustrate fairly well the nature of the conflict that would develop among judicial professionals in the following years, and that would also reflect a "geographical" divide. While high-court judges leading the ANM, particularly those residing in Rome, shared profound agreement on hierarchical control, strong opposition to this principle was developing in peripheral jurisdictions, such as Milan and Naples (Moriondo 1967, 266–267). This opposition would particularly manifest itself in the fight against the evaluation system regulating promotions. When deciding on career advancements, the High Council relied on a series of evaluations administered by higher-court judges. As I will explain later in this chapter, these evaluations assessed a candidate's knowledge of the law, but, more importantly, they determined a candidate's compliance with a conservative understanding and approach to jurisprudence (Di Federico 1978, 808–809). Thus, the evaluation system was a powerful tool to induce compliance with the legal elite's preferences among lower-ranked judicial professionals.

In 1946, Milanese judges signed a declaration asking the ANM to abolish the evaluation system that regulated promotions (Moriondo 1967, 266). At the same time, the proclamation asked that representation to the High Council include a higher quota of judicial professionals residing outside Rome (267). Similar complaints about the prevalence of Roman judges among the ones promoted to the Court of Cassation came from the local ANM branch in Turin after the first round of evaluations in 1949 (267). Several other peripheral jurisdictions raised their voices against a promotion system that overwhelmingly favored judicial professionals residing in the capital (269).

The dominance of Roman judicial professionals over promotions to higher posts was also a legacy of the authoritarian past. Fascist authorities, obsessed with centralization, had previously re-structured the High Council appointment procedures to make sure that it would include solely higher-ranked judicial officials. This meant that the only judicial and prosecutorial authorities[4] included in the High Council would be picked among those residing in Rome (Del Mastro 2014, 37–38). This produced a deep bond between high-ranking judicial and prosecutorial professionals residing in Rome and Fascist authorities. Furthermore, the executive branch's exclusive control over judicial and prosecutorial appointments during the Fascist era had long-lasting effects on high courts' composition long after democratization (Meniconi 2015, 225).

During the drafting of the constitutional text, the higher-ranked judicial professionals controlling the ANM convinced political forces to maintain a hierarchical judicial and prosecutorial system. The ANM pressured members of the Constituent Assembly to enhance the judiciary's formal autonomy without fundamentally questioning its internal organization (Moriondo 1967, 93). As a result, the Constituent Assembly formalized the judicial branch's insulation from political influences in the new text, creating an internally directed system. However, it was left up to regular legislation to establish what type of internally directed system this would turn out to be.

For instance, the new Constitution formalized the existence of the High Council of the Judiciary as the sole institution in charge of "transfers, promotions, and disciplinary proceedings for both judges and prosecutors" (Guarnieri 2003, 100). It also established that two-thirds of the Council members would be elected by all judicial professionals every four years (Italian Constitution, art. 104). Parliament obtained the power to appoint the remaining one-third of Council members among candidates with specific legal qualifications.[5] These council members came to be called "lay members" and their appointment would closely reflect the balance of power among parties in Parliament.[6] Therefore, Italian political parties obtained limited formal influence over prosecutorial appointments: the number of lay members in the Council represented a minority in relation to the number of judicial members. Overall, the new constitutional text limited political influence on the Italian judiciary and granted the latter a high degree of formal independence from other government branches (Nelken 2013, 250).

However, the Constitution did not clarify how judicial professionals would be called to choose their Council representatives, and political forces waited until 1958 to pass legislation clarifying this electoral process. The 1958 law, while guaranteeing access to Council members' selection to all judicial professionals, created a structural electoral advantage for higher-court judges, especially Court of Cassation judges (Del Mastro 2014, 85–86). As a result, the law adhered to the new constitutional principles but severely limited their implications by entrenching higher-court judges' dominance over Council membership. Thus, the 1958 law created an internally directed democratic elitist prosecutorial system.

REBELS IN THE PERIPHERY: THE FIGHT FOR EQUALITY AMONG JUDICIAL PROFESSIONALS

In the years following the return to democracy, lines of conflict started forming between central and peripheral members of the judicial branch over its institutional structure, as well as between younger lower-ranked professionals and senior judges on appellate courts (Moriondo 1967, 277). Freddi (1978) argues that this type of conflict is cyclical and inevitable: the inequalities created by the evaluation system had already produced similar conflicts in the past. In 1909, similar divisions between lower- and higher-ranked judges had led to the formation of the *Associazione Generale fra i Magistrati Italiani*, or AGMI (Guarnieri 2003, 91–92). This professional organization advocated for better salary conditions and the introduction of elections to the High Council (Guarnieri 2003, 92). Therefore, the AGMI's requests were similar to the ones raised by younger and peripheral judicial professionals to the ANM after 1946. In addition to questioning the evaluation system and the centrality of Roman judges, judicial professionals in Turin, Milan, and Naples, particularly newly appointed ones, took issue with their job's economic conditions (Moriondo 1963, 277–282).

However, this new series of protests were qualitatively different from previous ones. This time, complaints against the evaluation system relied on the principles in the new constitutional text. This is visible in the proclamation that the Naples ANM branch issued in 1957 (Moriondo 1967, 288). The latter stated that all members of the judicial branch were equal in relation to each other, given art. 107 in the new democratic Constitution. The latter declared that the only relevant distinctions among judicial professionals consisted in the diversity of their functions (Moriondo 1967, 288–289). Taking this principle to its extreme consequences, Neapolitan judges argued that moving from one judicial post to another, particularly those on higher courts, should not reflect a difference in rank. Furthermore, the proclamation declared that the main reason for advancement to a higher post should be an individual's aspirations rather than the judicial elite's control over lower ranks (288).

As opposed to previous mobilizations, Neapolitan judicial professionals, along with several of their colleagues scattered across the country, were appealing to the new constitutional principles as the foundation for a radical restructuring of judicial and prosecutorial institutions. Mobilization spread rapidly. After the Neapolitan judges' statement, the Bologna ANM branch put forth a similar document, requesting to postpone the upcoming evaluations for selection to the courts of appeals and the Court of Cassation (Moriondo 1967, 304). This request received support from more than twenty local judicial associations all over the country, forcing the ANM's national committee to request a suspension of the scheduled evaluations to the Ministry of Justice (305). Despite the national government's refusal to abide by this request (305), the consensus around a substantial restructuring of the judicial branch's internal organization continued growing. As Moriondo (1967) points out, during the 1959 ANM national assembly, "the votes in favor of suspending evaluations were an overwhelming majority of 2298 against 351" (305).

Adherence to the principles enshrined in the new democratic Constitution drove the growing mobilization over institutional reform among lower-ranked judicial professionals. As Moriondo (1967) reports, most, if not all, declarations released by local ANM branches relied on constitutional provisions to call for institutional change. These constitutional principles, in turn, offered a highly egalitarian understanding of the judicial profession, as evidenced by Neapolitan judges' interpretation of article 107. Therefore, judicial professionals understood the Constitution to uphold radical egalitarianism, namely the absence of hierarchical distinctions among judicial professionals if not for "administrative" reasons, such as the distinction between different judicial functions (Moriondo 1967, 288–289). Therefore, according to this reading of the foundational text, the latter enshrined the radical equality of judicial professionals against power relationships based on hierarchical oversight. Thus, young and democracy-oriented judicial professionals adopted egalitarianism as the animating principle behind their professional mission and started lobbying for judicial institutions to reflect this constitutional principle in their structure.

Egalitarianism, therefore, motivated judicial professionals and shaped their request for institutional change. At the same time, egalitarianism also became a contested principle. While younger, more democracy-oriented judicial professionals started mobilizing in favor restructuring of the Italian judiciary along egalitarian lines, senior elements, especially those on higher courts, deeply opposed this transformation. As I have showed so far, reactionary elements with a preference for Italian legal positivism and a hierarchical understanding of the judicial profession dominated the ANM even after re-democratization. The growing mobilization among junior judicial professionals in favor of egalitarian changes convinced several appellate judges with traditionalist views to split from the ANM and form a new organization, called *Unione Magistrati Italiani* (Italian Judicial Union), or UMI, in 1961 (Guarnieri 2003, 103). Therefore, while not strictly a political position, egalitarianism did become a contested idea among judicial professionals. The latter's attitude toward egalitarianism, namely their support or opposition to this constitutional principle, created a deep divide between judicial groups and prompted the emergence of a "political" fight among these for control of the Italian judiciary. I explore these dynamics later in my analysis, when discussing the emergence of new judicial associations.

Despite the ongoing fight between conservative higher ranks and more democratic lower ranks, the Italian prosecutorial system remained firmly under the former's control until the 1970s. Higher-court judges' dominance in the High Council entailed their continued control of promotions and appointments well into the 1960s. Only with final reforms to the High Council's electoral law in 1975 did higher-court judges' dominance eventually end. Thus, until the mid-1970s, the Italian prosecutorial system remained an internally directed democratic elitist system where conservative judicial professionals could force lower ranks into conformity with their legal views. To show how this institutional setting significantly compressed prosecutorial independence and, therefore, also prosecutorial effectiveness, in the following section, I examine the evaluation system. I also explore the Court of Cassation's application of Italian legal positivism to transitional justice to outline the obstacles this conservative legal philosophy poses to criminal accountability.

THE DOMINANCE OF ITALIAN LEGAL POSITIVISM VIA THE EVALUATION SYSTEM

As I explained so far, in the aftermath of democratization, the Italian judicial profession showed a clear generational divide: senior high-court judges demonstrated continued loyalty to Italian legal positivism's main tenets, such as hierarchy, while lower-ranked judicial professionals demonstrated a commitment to the new democratic principles. Furthermore, conservative judicial professionals' dominance at the top of the judicial system entailed their ability to force their legal views onto the lower ranks via the evaluation system. Court of Cassation judges on the High Council relied on the evaluation system to select worthy candidates for judicial and prosecutorial posts. As a result, the conservative judicial elite could impose conformity with its legal views by forcing candidates to demonstrate mastery of Italian legal positivism in their day-to-day rulings, one of the elements in the evaluation system. The latter left no room for legal innovation.

Di Federico (1978) provides an extensive analysis of High Council members' evaluations of lower ranks. In particular, Di Federico (1978) found that negative evaluations relied on three types of considerations: disagreement between a candidate's interpretation of the law and the Court of Cassation's understanding of the same legal provision (808), "the use of extra-judicial considerations" in court rulings (808), and lack of engagement with hard cases (808). What higher ranks meant by "extra-judicial considerations" was any kind of language that may show a candidate's own ideological beliefs or political inclinations (Di Federico 1978, 808).

This set of criteria ensured that lower-ranked judges would pursue the application of abstract legal provisions without consideration for the current socio-political context (808). In other words, by using these guiding principles in its evaluations, the High Council aimed to enforce a strict textualist approach to legal interpretation. It also aimed at preventing lower ranks from adopting the equivalent interpretive approach of what American legal scholars call "living Constitutionalism." In addition, cases involving civil law rather than criminal law presented a better opportunity for professional advancement because they provided a chance to engage in legal reasoning of the most abstract and rigorous kind. Thus, this created a strong incentive for ambitious judges to engage with civil cases (Di Federico 1978, 808–809).

The implications of these evaluation criteria were momentous. Above all, the enforcement of Italian legal positivism through the evaluation system severely hindered the emergence of legal innovations. Lower-ranked judges and prosecutors who wished to follow a different legal approach had to accept that this would doom their prospects of professional advancements. Therefore, judicial professionals had to choose between adopting "extra-judicial" considerations (Di Federico 1978, 808) in their rulings and losing any hope of a successful career or conforming to the Court of Cassation's conservative understanding of the law in exchange for a better post. In addition, the dominance of conservative elements on appellate courts also increased the risk of overruling on appeal for the use of innovative legal approaches. Thus, overall, the Italian prosecutorial system's hierarchical structure severely discouraged the bottom-up emergence of legal innovations.

As a result, the High Council ensured the preservation of a legal framework that still included significant authoritarian elements. The last comprehensive revision of the Italian penal code had been completed in 1930. Democratic legislators did not consider any comprehensive reform of the "*Rocco* code," as it came to be called after then Minister of Justice for the Fascist government Alfredo Rocco. The *Rocco* code, therefore, remained valid law despite its clearly authoritarian framework. Thus, by rejecting any interpretive approach that might take into consideration new social and political conditions, the High Council all but ensured the survival of this code in its entirety.

This structure of incentives had significant effects on prosecutorial and judicial behavior, which are immediately visible in relation to transitional justice. On the one hand, the legal framework litigants would have to rely on to sue former Fascist officials had remained unchanged after the fall of the regime. The legal framework, therefore, was the same that had allowed these atrocities to go unpunished. On the other hand, the Italian prosecutorial system's hierarchical structure prevented any judicial professional from considering a new interpretation of the criminal code that would open the door to transitional justice demands under the new Constitution. Thus, Italian judicial professionals found themselves in the paradoxical situation of living under a democratic framework that held no legal power over a persistently authoritarian legal structure. Via the evaluation system, higher-court judges sitting on the High Council could "hollow out" new constitutional principles' application to the legal system.

The only potential challenge to the former Fascist legal framework could have come from the legislative branch. New legislation could have created a serious legal dilemma for the High Council and the Court of Cassation, whose members overwhelmingly believed in the primacy of legislation over judicial interpretation. In fact, the latter principle was the foundation for higher-court judges' strict loyalty to the words of the text: no other interpretive approach would have fully preserved the dominance of the legislative branch over the judicial function. However, the legislative effort that could have opened the door to transitional justice left just enough room for the Court of Cassation to undermine this attempt at its foundation.

In 1946, the so-called Togliatti amnesty promised to address the atrocities of Italy's authoritarian past while paving the way to peaceful reconciliation (Borgna 2017). The law pardoned some of the violent acts performed by Fascist regime supporters but also excluded others from amnesty (Borgna 2017). This exemption represented an invitation to the Court of Cassation to fill a legislative vacuum. Despite being usually averse to "creative" judicial interpretation, the Court of Cassation managed to extend the confines of the amnesty to their greatest length possible without openly challenging or adapting the letter of the law. As Caroli (2015) explains, the amnesty law used the words "particularly cruel brutality" (169). However, amnesty decree drafters had shied away from clearly explaining what they meant by these words. Therefore, the Court determined this to be a new category and established that acts of such nature would not be pardonable (169). The Court then proceeded to include all acts of torture, such as "gang rape, and de-nailing practices" (Caroli 2015, 169), into other categories than "particularly cruel brutality," therefore emptying the decree law of any punitive elements (Borgna 2017).

Thus, the Court of Cassation's twisted application of legal positivism brought all hopes for transitional justice to an end. Furthermore, the Court of Cassation's interpretation of the amnesty law clearly highlighted Italian legal positivism's aversion toward accountability. The Court's reasoning made it impossible to hold former Fascist officials accountable for their crimes against humanity. This tendency to shield public officials from accountability would become a lasting feature of Italian legal conservatism, as I outline in the case studies. Moreover, the entrenchment of Italian legal conservatism via the evaluation system ensured the survival of an authoritarian legal framework for criminal law. Higher-court judges' enduring control over promotions and appointments forced judicial and prosecutorial lower ranks into conformity with an authoritarian understanding of criminal law, which shut the door to transitional justice efforts.

Only with the establishment of a new judicial body, the Constitutional Court, would a gradual process of reform start. The new constitutional text established the Constitutional Court as the only institution allowed to consider questions of constitutionality. Furthermore, members of the Constitutional Court would receive their appointment by Parliament rather than the High Council of the Judiciary (Barsotti et al. 2015, 18). This partially fits with the Court's role as a completely distinct avenue of litigation. Like many other civil law countries, in Italy, the power of constitutional review resides solely with the Constitutional Court. No other judicial body at any level can review and decide the issues of constitutionality.

At the same time, the procedure for constitutional review creates a direct channel between any judicial professional and the Constitutional Court. According to the "incidental method of judicial review" (Barsotti et al. 2015, 54), any judge can raise the issue of constitutionality while adjudicating a case. If the judge detects a constitutional issue, without whose resolution the case cannot proceed, then the trial is suspended until the Constitutional Court resolves the issue (54). An expansive understanding of this constitutional review procedure, which prevailed until the 1970s (55–57), created a significant direct connection between lower judges and the Constitutional Court (56).

Consequently, the Constitutional Court's peculiar place within the judicial system and its ability to directly intervene in any type of litigation at any level made it the only available venue of legal change as long as the rest of the system remained hierarchical in nature. The Court did not shy away from this responsibility. In its first ruling, the Constitutional Court explicitly argued that constitutional provisions also applied to legislation issued prior to the enactment of the new Constitution and that it was the Court's duty to perform this constitutionality check (Barsotti et al. 2015, 33–34). This paved the way for constitutional review of all laws issued during the Fascist regime (Barsotti et al. 2015, 33–34).

Over the 1960s, the Constitutional Court would end up playing a key role in reforming extensive parts of the Italian legal corpus, particularly in the field of criminal law and criminal procedure (Guarnieri 2007, 447–448). Bruti Liberati (2017) points out that the Constitutional Court frequently allowed review of "issues that the Court of Cassation had previously deemed uncontroversial" (4). Therefore, the Constitutional Court became a powerful ally to lower-ranked judges in their effort to reform broad areas of the law dating back to the Fascist regime (Guarnieri 2007, 448). The Court's work was most visible in the area of criminal procedure, where the Court helped introduce key civil rights, such as the right to counsel at every stage of adjudication.[7]

In doing so, the Constitutional Court entered a harsh fight with the Court of Cassation over the right to counsel. According to Bruti Liberati (2017), "the Court of Cassation could not tolerate that the Constitutional Court would have the last say" on this issue (4).

The Court also strengthened defendants' rights in relation to warrants, searches, and seizures.[8] Merryman and Vigoriti (1967) argue that "a sort of alliance between low-ranking judges, the Constitutional Court, academic doctrine and a group of civil rights attorneys was able to report a victory in the fight" to reform broad sections of Italian law in light of the new constitutional principles (Guarnieri 2007, 448). Therefore, in the decades following its establishment, the Constitutional Court played an essential role in reforming Italian criminal law in light of the fundamental civil rights in the new Constitution, even against harsh opposition from other higher-court judges.

The role of the Constitutional Court as the only venue of legal change confirms and illuminates the constraints imposed on lower-ranked judicial professionals by the prosecutorial system's still fairly hierarchical structure. Given its composition via political appointment and exemption from the evaluation system, the Constitutional Court was in a unique position to promote a new legal approach rooted in the Constitution's principles, which radically differed from the Italian judicial elite's conservative preferences. On the other hand, lower-ranked judicial professionals could not enjoy the same freedom as long as their professional future depended on the conservative judicial elite sitting on the High Council. Thus, legal innovation remained limited to the intervention of the Constitutional Court until decentralization occurred in the 1970s.

THE PATH TOWARD DECENTRALIZATION: JUDICIAL ASSOCIATIONS AND INSTITUTIONAL REFORMS

As I discussed in the previous sections of this chapter, younger and more democracy-oriented judicial professionals mobilized against the prosecutorial system's hierarchical design after re-democratization. These protests did not result in the formation of one single movement for reform, but in the emergence of several judicial associations with different legal philosophies within the ANM. Each association formed around a specific approach to law and legal interpretation. Some associations embraced a reformed and more democratic approach to legal positivism while others espoused a more progressive understanding of the law and the legal mission. The growing strength of judicial associations and their interactions with political forces paved the way for the institutional restructuring of the Italian prosecutorial system. Judicial associations spearheaded a process of institutional reforms that culminated in 1975, with decentralization. In this section, I explore Italian judicial associations' formation and the Italian prosecutorial system's gradual transformation.

The first judicial association to form focused more on corporatist requests about the profession's socioeconomic status rather than its commitment to the new constitutional values. In 1957, a group of judges decided to create the association *Terzo Potere* (Third Power) or TP (Guarnieri 2003, 111). TP did not hold progressive legal ideas but organized around judicial professionals' requests for better salaries and other socioeconomic guarantees (Guarnieri 2003, 111). In this respect, TP embodied the corporatist dimension of the protests ensuing after democratization. However, the protests' focus on the democratic principles in the new Constitution also prompted the reaction of conservative elements within the ANM. In 1961, a group of mostly higher-court judges formed the *Unione Magistrati Italiani* (Italian Judicial Union) or UMI (Guarnieri 2003, 103). This new association became the strongest bulwark of traditional Italian legal conservatism. UMI defended the hierarchical principle and a strict understanding of the judicial profession as a merely bureaucratic role. In this sense, UMI inherited the legacy of the most conservative, and most authoritarian-leaning, type of Italian legal positivism in response to the growing consensus around new democratic principles among the younger ranks (Guarnieri 2003, 103).

In the following years, several more groups formed, each one with a distinctive understanding of the new democratic Constitution and how its principles applied to the law and the legal profession. *Magistratura Democratica* (Democratic Judiciary), or MD, embodied the most "progressive pole" (Guarnieri 2003, 109) of the ideological spectrum, which subscribed to an understanding of the Constitution as a "living document" (Guarnieri 2003, 109). MD's legal progressivism found expression in the understanding of the judicial role as an integral part of democratic politics (Guarnieri 2003, 110). According to MD, judges and prosecutors had an obligation to advance the social goals in the new constitutional text through their work (Guarnieri 2003, 109–110). Therefore, judicial professionals should seek to take into consideration the social impact of their decisions and to interpret the law in accordance with the societal conditions to which it applied. In other words, MD's goal was to "fulfill constitutional values and reject the conservative mindset inherited by the judiciary from the Fascist regime" (Meniconi 2015, 225). In one of the first issues of MD's journal, MD members explicitly rejected the ideal of "apoliticism" inherent in legal positivism: "We do not believe in the neutrality of the law; instead, we believe that jurisprudence could and should contribute to fulfilling the promise of equity, and not just formal equality, spelled out in the Constitution" (Meniconi 2015, 225–226).

This progressive understanding of the judicial role also implied deep engagement with civil society and politics. From the beginning, MD pursued so-called *collateralismo* (Guarnieri 2003, 110), namely working alongside elected officials and popular movements toward the fulfillment of constitutional rights (Guarnieri 2003, 110). However, the association eventually reconsidered the importance of *collateralismo* during the 1980s and shifted its focus on a stronger understanding of judicial independence from other government branches (Guarnieri 2003, 110).

In many respects, *Magistratura Indipendente* (Independent Judiciary), or MI, represented the specular opposite of MD. MI's legal philosophy built on the main tenets of Italian legal positivism but understood them in light of the new constitutional values (Guarnieri 2003, 111–112). Above all, MI continued upholding a textualist approach to the constitutional text and other legal provisions (112), given that judges were meant to be the mouth of the law. Furthermore, if judges were to only apply, not interpret, the letter of the law, it followed that they also had to remain completely "apolitical" in their work (Guarnieri 2003, 111–112). Over the years, MI firmly defended a strict understanding of the separation between legislative and judicial power (Guarnieri 2003, 111–112). This turned into a strong emphasis on the judicial profession's absolute independence from other government branches (112). Therefore, MI proposed a "reformed" version of legal conservatism, in line with the constitutional values and the democratic framework in the new Constitution. At the same time, the survival of legal conservatism in this new form may have offered shelter to more traditionalist supporters of this legal philosophy (Colombo 2010, 28).

While MI and MD easily represent the conservative and progressive ends of an ideological spectrum, *Unita' per la Costituzione*, or UniCost, hardly falls on either one. UniCost is usually considered a "centrist" association, mostly due to the way it was formed. Between 1971 and 1979, two smaller groups, *Terzo Potere* (Third Power) and *Impegno Costituzionale* (Constitutional Commitment), formed, only to eventually join together in a new association in 1980 (Guarnieri 2003, 109). I previously described *Terzo Potere* as a judicial association mostly concerned with protecting the judicial profession's corporatist guarantees (Guarnieri 2003, 111). For this reason, *Terzo Potere* lacked a strong attachment to a specific legal philosophy (111). *Impegno Costituzionale*, on the other hand, had formed in response to MD's early ideological excesses, which pushed away less ideological elements (Guarnieri 2003, 109–110). As a result, the merging of these two moderate associations produced a centrist, moderately progressive new conglomerate.

In addition to a strong emphasis on a corporatist defense of the judicial profession (Guarnieri 2003, 111), UniCost maintained similar ideas about the judicial role as MD, without the latter's excessive *collateralismo* (Guarnieri

2003, 111). UniCost members essentially agreed that judicial professionals should seek to apply the new constitutional values to their work but strongly dissented with MD on the necessity to establish an alliance with sympathetic political forces (Guarnieri 2003, 111).

Table 2.1 outlines MI, MD, and UniCost's main legal principles and briefly situates each association on a conservative to progressive legal spectrum. I excluded UMI, as well as TP and IC, from the table, given these associations' limited period of activity. It is fair to say that MD, MI, and UniCost deeply shaped the legal discourse in post–World War II Italy, at least until the formation of a new judicial association, *Movimento per la Giustizia*, which I discuss in-depth in chapter 4.

As shown in table 2.1, it is possible to place these three judicial associations on a legal spectrum from most conservative to most progressive. One must ask if this placement, based on each legal association's legal philosophy, necessarily reflects these groups' political attitudes as well. It is tempting to think of these judicial associations as the equivalent of political groupings within the judiciary tasked with pursuing left-wing or right-wing political agendas via judicial work

To an extent, some of these judicial associations did in fact show active engagement with politics. For instance, especially in the years following its founding, MD explicitly pursued open collaboration with political forces and social actors to bring about outcomes it envisioned as part of the Constitution's promise for Italian society. This might seem to bring evidence to the

Table 2.1 Major Judicial Associations and Their Legal Philosophies, 1964–1990

Magistratura Democratica (MD)	*Unita' per la Costituzione (Unicost)*	*Magistratura Indipendente (MI)*
Legal progressivism 1. Judges have a civic duty to implement constitutional values in their rulings 2. Judges should cooperate with civil society and political forces 3. Judicial role is a political role: to help with societal transformation	Moderate progressivism 1. Judges have a civic duty to implement constitutional values in their rulings 2. This does not mean that judges have a political role 3. Mostly concerned about corporatist defense of career and guarantees	Reformed Legal conservatism 1. Judges must be apolitical 2. Judges carry out a technical role in simply implementing the words of the law (judges are the mouth of the law) 3. Judges must avoid any relationship with non-judicial actors (political actors, civil society)
Progressive	Moderately progressive, centrist	Conservative

Source: Author's elaboration.

idea that judicial associations were nothing more than political groups within the Italian judiciary. Nevertheless, MD also suffered a deep backlash from its own members due to its political proximity with left-wing forces. The deepening of *collateralismo* brought to a flight of MD members (Tony 2015, chapter 2) and to harsh internal divisions (Tony 2015, chapter 2). Toward the early 1980s, MD abandoned its most political orientations (Tony 2015, chapter 2) and shifted its focus to judicial independence from politics (Guarnieri 2003, 110) and stronger defendants' rights (Tony 2015, chapter 2).

However, judicial associations' legal ideologies do not often neatly map over any clear political agenda, whether left-leaning or right-leaning. For instance, MI's preference for textualism and apoliticism does not necessarily yield litigation outcomes that are identifiable as "right-wing" in nature. In addition, all judicial associations in table 2.1 share an important similarity, their loyalty to the democratic values in the constitutional text. As I previously mentioned, MD explicitly promoted the pursuit of constitutional values via judicial rulings. On the other hand, even MI, though devoted to a mechanical view of judging, recognized the importance of carrying out judicial functions in light of the democratic principles in the new constitutional text. UniCost also shared a similar emphasis on democratic constitutionalism.

These shared legal values among judicial associations do not square with a purely political understanding of these groups' purposes, which would pit them against each other in terms of opposite political agendas. Instead, judicial associations' convergence around democratic constitutionalism soon became publicly visible. During the keynote address at the ANM's national assembly, in 1965, renown legal scholar Giuseppe Maranini summed up the Italian judiciary's understanding of its mission with the following statement:

> The idea that legal interpretation is a purely formalistic activity, detached from the content and concrete social impact of a law on the life of the country [. . .] on the contrary, every judge should be aware of the political and constitutional implications inherent in the judicial role, so as to ensure, within the strict confines of the law, the latter's interpretation in conformity with the Constitution's ends.[9]

More importantly, judicial associations' shared emphasis on adherence to democratic constitutional values created a deep ideological divide with those elements within the Italian judiciary that held a profoundly reactionary and positivist understanding of the purpose of the law and the judicial mission. Italian legal positivism continued holding a place of prominence with several higher court and senior judicial professionals, most of whom joined UMI and some of whom eventually joined MI after UMI's disbandment.

Thus, if it is possible to identify an ideological divide among Italian judicial professionals, the latter does not lie so much in different political agendas among judicial associations, but in the contrast between a democratic understanding of the judicial mission rooted in the new Constitution, and a reactionary, positivist understanding of judicial professionalism, more compatible with an authoritarian framework. Italian legal positivism's authoritarian instincts were in full display in the Court of Cassation's jurisprudence on the amnesty decree law, for instance, which I previously discussed.

Furthermore, judicial associations' shared emphasis on constitutional values would also be visible in their unanimous support for decentralization. All judicial associations (except for UMI) supported the political efforts to increase the Italian judiciary's independence as a check on political power. Guarnieri (2003) suggests that Italian political parties started actively seeking relationships with judicial associations for strategic reasons (128–131). The Italian Communist Party and the Socialist Party, for instance, supported institutional reforms that would enhance the judiciary's independence in order to counterbalance the Italian Christian Democracy's control over the legislative and executive branch (129–131). At the same time, Christian Democracy's internal fighting pushed different party factions in the same direction, seeking a closer relationship with some judicial associations and endorsing institutional reforms that would increase lower judicial and prosecutorial ranks' independence (131).

Consequently, in the years from 1963 to 1979, a series of bills passed that would bring about the Italian prosecutorial system's decentralization. In 1963, a bill established that all judicial professionals worthy of promotion would obtain it, regardless of the actual number of vacancies available (Guarnieri 2003, 103–104). By eliminating constraints on the number of available promotions, the bill chipped away at the foundations of the hierarchical system. Furthermore, in 1970, another bill got rid of evaluations as the basis for professional advancements from the lowest professional status, namely judicial trainee (De Vito 2017, 59). In 1963 and in 1977, the so-called law "Breganze" and law "Breganzone" continued the dismantling of the Italian judiciary's hierarchical structure, by significantly modifying the procedure for promotion to higher judicial posts (De Vito 2017, 59). With these laws, the system of evaluations ceased to be in effect. While judicial professionals still had to formally undergo regular performance assessments, the latter were set up to produce positive results in the overwhelming majority of cases. As a result, by the end of the 1970s, seniority became the sole principle regulating career advancements among judicial professionals (Guarnieri 2003, 104).

This set of reforms deprived the judicial elite of the main instrument they could use to force lower ranks into conformity with their legal philosophy. Therefore, these bills significantly weakened the prosecutorial system's hierarchical structure. However, Court of Cassation judges still held control over appointments and promotions, thanks to their dominance over the High Council. Between 1967 and 1975, a series of reforms introduced proportional representation for elections to the High Council and opened Council candidacies to all judicial professionals, not only higher-court judges (Guarnieri 2003, 106). The 1967 law allowed all judicial professionals, regardless of rank, to vote for any of the candidates in a pre-selected list including a majority of higher-ranked judges and a few lower-ranked ones (Del Mastro 2014, 91–93). This was a significant improvement on the 1958 law, which forced judicial professionals to vote solely for candidates within their same professional rank (Del Mastro 2014, 85–86). The latter mechanism guaranteed higher-court judges' dominance in Council elections (85–86).

Finally, the 1975 law introduced pure and simple Open List Proportional Representation, giving judicial professionals complete freedom to vote for Council members by choosing candidates from lists drafted by judicial associations (Del Mastro 2014, 100–101). As a result, any semblance of "vote by professional rank" disappeared (101–102). Rather, "associational affiliation" became a candidate's most important characteristic. Judicial associations became the primary vehicles through which judicial professionals would elect their representatives (101–102). The 1975 law, therefore, brought Cassation judges' dominance over the High Council to an end and made the Council truly representative of the judicial profession. Therefore, the 1975 law completed the decentralization process. The result was the "gradual dismantling of the bureaucratic structure typical of the civil-law systems" (Nelken 1996*a*, 99), which freed lower-ranked judicial professionals from their superiors' oversight (Nelken 1996*a*, 99–100; Nelken 1996*b*, 195). Consequently, the 1975 electoral law completed the Italian prosecutorial system's transformation into an internally directed democratic system.

In addition to creating a democratic prosecutorial system, decentralization also shaped the Italian judicial professionals' corporate interest ever since. As I explained, the legislative framework that introduced decentralization created a safe pathway to professional advancement for any member of the Italian judiciary, including prosecutors. Any lower-ranked member of the judicial branch could now expect to finish their career in a better professional position and enjoy automatic salary increases associated with the number of years in office. This institutional structure not only empowered lower-ranked prosecutors significantly increasing their independence, but also came to define the Italian judiciary's interest as a professional group.

After decentralization, Italian judicial professionals from all associations would strongly defend this institutional setting (Nelken 1996*a*, 100) against any government attempt to change its fundamental features (Nelken 2013, 252), especially the centrality of seniority to judicial promotions. Judicial professionals' corporate defense of the seniority principle is visible, for instance, in the controversy surrounding Palermo instructing judge Giovanni Falcone's candidacy to the office of Palermo chief prosecutor. The High Council of the Judiciary rejected Falcone's candidacy despite his remarkable achievements against mafia organizations. As I show in chapter 5, this instance shows how important it became for Italian judicial professionals to maintain seniority as the sole formal justification for promotions over other principles, even professional merit.

The institutional reforms I have described so far effectively brought about the Italian prosecutorial system's decentralization. Starting in 1975, the High Council ceased to be in the hands of a conservative judicial elite holding complete control over lower ranks' professional fate. Thanks to decentralization, lower ranks could now exert some influence over the institutional body in charge of promotions and appointments by electing High Council members among their peers. In addition, these institutional reforms increased lower ranks' *de facto* independence in choosing the legal approach they wished to apply to cases. With the end of the evaluation system, lower-ranked judges and prosecutors could now enjoy more freedom to pursue other legal philosophies than Italian legal positivism. Thus, decentralization produced increases in prosecutorial independence by allowing lower-ranked judges and prosecutors to experiment with legal approaches that might yield more effective results, therefore paving the way for similar increases in prosecutorial effectiveness as well.

THE RISE OF LEGAL FACTIONS: JUDICIAL ASSOCIATIONS AND *LOTTIZZAZIONE*

The Italian prosecutorial system's decentralization significantly empowered lower-ranked prosecutors in the pursuit of legal innovation. Decentralization, however, also had an unexpected consequence: it increased the importance of judicial associations, which became the main vehicles to High Council membership. As a result, judicial associations acquired growing influence over promotions and appointments (Guarnieri 2003; Di Federico 1990).

On the one hand, this is consistent with decentralization. This institutional process redistributed power away from the judicial elite and into the hands of the larger judicial population. Because Italian judicial professionals were organizing in judicial associations, decentralization inevitably shifted power over promotions and appointments into the hands of these newly formed groups. On the other hand, this process also elevated judicial associations to a position of dominance. Judicial associations started competing fiercely during High Council elections, and their influence over appointments and promotions led to the establishment of practices like *lottizzazione correntizia*. Furthermore, judicial associations' role and potential proximity to political parties opened a potential "backdoor" to external political influences over the judicial branch (Di Federico 1990; Guarnieri 2003, 110). In what follows, I discuss each one of these dynamics.

The rising importance of judicial associations within the High Council had significant effects on the promotion system. Formally, evaluations were still in place, although most personal evaluations were unequivocally positive (Di Federico 1990, 289–290). As previously mentioned, seniority became the only formal requisite necessary for eligibility to a higher judicial post (289–290). However, the overwhelming presence of association members sitting on the High Council introduced an informal requirement for promotions: membership in the same group (Di Federico 1990, 289–290). The relationship of trust between a Council member and a candidate through their shared belonging in the same association came to play a crucial role in the distribution of higher posts, especially when the latter represented positions of authority (Di Federico 1990, 289–290; Nelken 1996a, 100). While membership in an association was not necessary to career advancements, judicial associations, via their members on the High Council, made sure that a certain number of posts would be assigned to their affiliates.

As a result, judicial associations soon adopted informal rules to distribute judicial and prosecutorial posts among their members, which reflected each association's bargaining power within the Council and ability to distribute appointments to its own members (Di Federico 1990, 290). This practice closely mimicked *lottizzazione*, a similar informal practice that Italian political parties followed to assign public offices to party-loyal civil servants, in accordance with each political party's seat share in Parliament.[10] For this reason, Italian scholars soon came to label judicial associations' informal rules of judicial posts' distribution as *lottizzazione correntizia* (Di Federico 1990). This label has become common parlance even among members of the judicial profession and often holds a derogatory nuance.

The similarities between *lottizzazione correntizia* and Italian political parties' public posts' redistribution dynamics, which used almost the same label (*lottizzazione*), highlight one important development stemming out of decentralization. As I previously argued, judicial associations' "platforms" do not neatly overlap with political parties' agendas. While judicial associations do hold either a conservative or progressive understanding of jurisprudence and the judicial mission, the latter neither clearly reflects any political manifesto nor does it yield litigation outcomes systematically benefiting either right-wing or left-wing political forces. However, judicial associations' dominance within the Italian judiciary's newly decentralized setting created strong incentives for these groups to act like "judicial parties" representing different legal ideologies. In other words, judicial associations became very much like "quasi-political groupings" (Nelken 1996*a*, 100) capable of creating strong bonds of loyalty among their members (Nelken 2013, 251).

For instance, judicial associations' competition for votes to the High Council closely resembled competition between different political parties during elections. This entailed creating a list of candidates and running an electoral campaign for High Council seats. Similarly, judicial associations' concern in appointing their own members to specific offices (Nelken 1996*a*, 100) via so-called *lottizzazione correntizia* speaks to their commitment to see their legal vision implemented within judicial and prosecutorial institutions. This "political" behavior is similar to political parties' desire to control the levers of power in order to pursue a specific political vision. Therefore, even though judicial associations did not act on behalf of political parties and did not clearly share the latter's political agendas, they did engage in significant "politicking" when competing for representation both on the High Council and in local judicial and prosecutorial institutions, often adopting practices that closely mimicked political parties' behavior. As I explain in chapter 4, politicking among judicial associations, and especially the practice of *lottizzazione correntizia*, would eventually open the judiciary to harsh criticism from some of its own members, who saw in these practices a corruption of the institution's civic duty.

Even though judicial associations' behavior started resembling widespread political practices, the Italian judiciary's institutional insulation from other government branches still guaranteed significant independence from undue political influences. However, Italian political parties had access to important material resources they could use to build a direct relationship with some judicial professionals. One such resource was the allocation of public offices. Political parties started appointing members of the judiciary temporarily to different branches of the public administration (Di Federico 1981, 63–64). Most, if not all, of these appointments to administrative offices remained subject to approval by the High Council (16–17). Di Federico (1981) estimated that in 1974, as many as 571 judges held a public office in addition to their judicial post (21). Therefore, these judicial appointees served on several public administration branches and special commissions while at the same time adjudicating cases. Moreover, political parties recruited a significant number of judicial professionals to work full time for the Ministry of Justice (Di Federico 1981, 37–40). Over the years from 1959 to 1980, the number of judges working for the Ministry of Justice slowly but constantly increased from 94 to 108 (Di Federico 1981, 38).

The number of public offices held by judicial professionals is an indication of the close relationship that formed over time between some members of the judiciary and political forces both in government coalitions and at the opposition.[11] Despite the troubling ethical implications inherent in this collaboration, the High Council never prevented members of the judiciary from accepting these political appointments. The Council also did not forbid judicial professionals from pursuing their political aspirations. Judicial professionals could run for office while still formally on the bench and did not lose their judicial status while in office (Di Federico 1981, 28–29). This was also the case for several Constitutional Court judges, who worked as elected representatives either before or after their judicial tenure.[12] Moreover, the political appointment of judges to the Constitutional Court also followed the logic of *lottizzazione* among political parties (Volcansek 1999, 23). However, the number of judicial professionals who held either an elected or an administrative office represents only a fraction of the overall judicial population. Thus, while these appointments hold troubling ethical implications, it would be wrong to draw broad generalizations that apply to the whole judiciary.

Overall, decentralization brought about both opportunities and challenges for Italian judicial professionals. On the one hand, decentralization put an end to the judicial elite's control over the lower ranks. This increased the latter's *de facto* independence and established the conditions for the emergence of legal innovation via a bottom-up approach. Decentralization's implications were especially clear for prosecutors working within this renewed institutional framework. Even judicial professionals with differing legal ideologies agreed on the enhanced independence that decentralization granted them. For instance, on MI's journal Montoro (1990) argued the following while discussing decentralization:

> This has gradually produced an even more innovative effect, namely an unprecedented capacity for action, for pursuing the full potential inherent in the principle of compulsory prosecution [. . .] to the point of flirting with excessive activism in a way that is the opposite of the previously suffered inertia and conformism. (15–16)

Similarly, when discussing decentralization on MD's journal, De Vito (2017) argued:

> Without this re-definition of the institutional path to professional advancement, we would not have witnessed the later developments in the role of judges working in the field of labor law, or the emergence of the so-called "*pretori d'assalto*[13]" [. . .] their work and cultural interests were outside the scope of the legal issues that would have facilitated career advancements [under the old evaluation system]. (60)

ALTERNATIVE HYPOTHESIS: POLITICAL FRAGMENTATION AND CORRUPTION PROSECUTIONS

Judicial professionals of every association fully understood the significant implications inherent in decentralization. However, as I just discussed in this section, decentralization also paved the way for judicial associations' increasingly dominant role within the prosecutorial system. Given these associations' proximity with political forces in some cases, it is worth asking whether the development of increasingly assertive prosecutorial behavior against corruption among Italian judicial professionals may have been a function of the changing political context. My argument in the rest of this book significantly diverts from this hypothesis. In the following chapters, I will focus on legal ideologies and institutional structures within each prosecutor's office to explain the development of effective corruption prosecution over time. However, the existence of significant relationships between judicial associations and political forces requires at least an empirical evaluation of this alternative hypothesis.

One theoretical approach that attempts to explain judicial behavior based on strategic interactions with political forces is the so-called Political Fragmentation Theories of judicial independence, or PFTs.[14] According to this set of theories, the likelihood of political retaliation against judicial professionals is the main driver of judicial behavior. As a result, divided government in presidential systems (Rios-Figueroa 2007) and narrow legislative majorities in parliamentary systems (Carrubba et al. 2015) will increase *de facto* judicial independence, because both scenarios lower the risk of retaliation. On the contrary, any situation of consolidated power for the ruling coalition or ruling party will present a credible threat to judicial professionals, who will restrain themselves out of fear of retaliation. On top of the theory's main causal mechanism based on fear of retaliation, the Italian scenario offers a possible adaptation of PFTs based on the availability of resources for co-optation. Political forces with consolidated control of the legislative branch will also have more resources available to co-opt judicial professionals via *lottizzazione*, or the distribution of public offices I previously described. On the other hand, narrow legislative minorities will lack access to similar resources.

The application of PFTs' empirical framework to the Italian case produces several observable implications. First of all, PFTs would predict increases in *de facto* judicial and prosecutorial independence concurrent with what Mershon (1996) calls "minimal winning coalition," namely a situation in which the departure of even just one of the government coalition's components is enough for the former to lose its relative advantage over other political forces within the legislative chamber (Mershon 1996, 535).[15] One straightforward way of measuring Italian prosecutors' willingness to uncover corruption is the number of requests to press charges against MPs sent to Parliament. Scholars used to believe that the number of such requests, also called "*richieste di autorizzazione a procedure*," or RAPs, was a proxy for the presence of corruption (Golden and Chang 2001; Chang, Golden and Hill 2010). However, Golden, and Picci (2006) later found that the number of RAPs seems to be more indicative of prosecutorial activism, rather than corruption (474).

Therefore, if PFTs hold any explanatory power over Italian prosecutors' behavior, we should see a rise in RAPs concurrently with the occurrence of minimal winning coalitions. Figure 2.1 outlines the number of RAPs by legislature. Interestingly, the peaks observed in this distribution contradict PFTs' expectations. For instance, the number of RAPs increased unexpectedly during the Sixth Legislature, from 1972 through 1976. However, despite the frequent changes in government coalitions, for most of this Legislature, the ruling coalition was above the minimal threshold of seats in Parliament.[16] Therefore, this trend contradicts PFTs' main expectation. On the other hand, this observation would seem to lend at least initial evidence to the idea that decentralization increased prosecutorial independence. The increase in RAPs at the same time as the completion of this institutional transformation, in 1975, points at increasing freedom among prosecutors to focus their efforts on political corruption.

Furthermore, the observable number of RAPs during the Seventh Legislature also seems to contradict PFTs' expectations. The years from 1976 to 1979 represent a peculiar moment in Italian politics. For the first time,

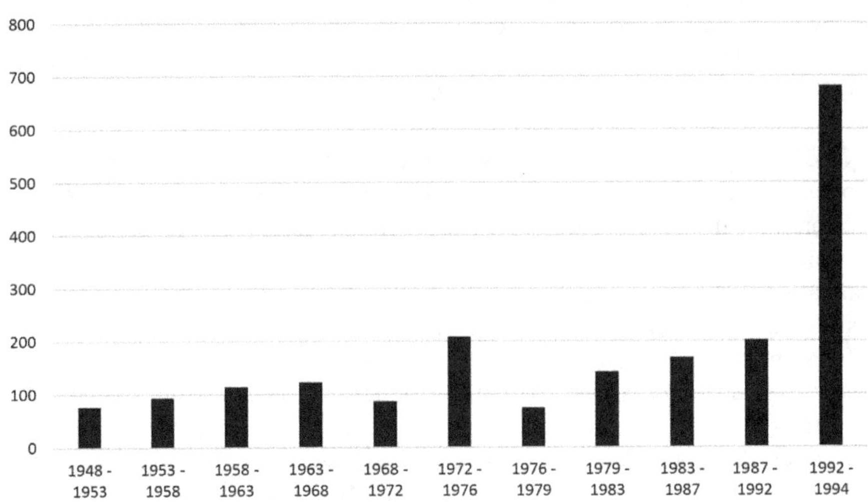

Figure 2.1 *Richieste di Autorizzazione a Procedere* (RAPs) for Corruption, 1948–1994 Data in Cazzola and Morisi 1996, 46. *Source*: Author's elaboration.

the appointment of a Christina Democratic prime minister and his cabinet occurred thanks to the abstention of the Italian Communist Party.[17] As a result of this peculiar collaboration, the ruling coalition was a minority coalition. According to PFTs' expectations, we should expect a rise in the number of RAPs during the Seventh Legislature. On the contrary, the number of RAPs decreased significantly, as opposed to the previous peak during the Sixth Legislature.

Therefore, the observable trends in the number of RAPs over time do not appear to fit PFTs' expectations. This is also visible in the slowly rising number of RAPs from 1979 to 1992, in which the start of the *Mani Pulite* investigation produced a skyrocket-like increase in the number of these requests. The years from 1979 to 1992 witnessed the alternation in government of solid coalitions well above the minimal winning threshold (Mershon 1996, 535). Therefore, the increasing number of RAPs over this period of time also contradicts PFTs' expectations. While PFTs do not explain visible patterns in prosecutorial behavior, this does not conclusively mean that prosecutorial actors' political sympathies may not have any effect on their behavior. I further address this alternative hypothesis, rooted in the attitudinal model (Segal and Spaeth 1996, 2002) via the case studies I conduct in the following chapters.

Decentralization might help explain, at least in part, the trends in the number of RAPs I just described. For instance, the peak in the number of RAPs observed between 1972 and 1976 significantly overlaps with the completion of the decentralization process in 1975. It is plausible that these drastic changes to professional careers and oversight bodies like the High Council might have encouraged prosecutors to pursue more aggressive inquiries into corruption. However, as visible in figure 2.1, steep decline in the number of RAPs followed this sudden peak. RAPs then started growing again gradually until the Clean Hands operation.

The trends in RAPs following decentralization call for an explanation that moves beyond PFTs theories. My argument, which I develop in the following section and in the case studies in this book, is that decentralization did not completely get rid of hierarchical structures at the local level. Rather, decentralization had the paradoxical effect of empowering local chief prosecutors. As a result, hierarchical structures persisted within some local prosecutors' offices and continued undermining prosecutorial independence and effectiveness. After decentralization, the High Council was left with little retaliation measures that would force local chief prosecutors into compliance with its directives. Thus, the weakening of central oversight strengthened local prosecutorial authorities' control over their own offices and personnel.

As a result, conservative chief prosecutors with reactionary tendencies tightened their control over local offices and were able to keep in place highly hierarchical structures with little backlash from central institutions, most of the time. While the High Council provided local prosecutors with new tools they could use to hold their superiors accountable, such as the ability to invite the Council' scrutiny (Di Federico 2012, 20–21), these new tools did not always prove to be effective. Therefore, decentralization allowed some chief prosecutors to maintain an at times almost tyrannical control over their subordinates. On the other hand, the same institutional framework provided local progressive movements and more moderate elements with a tentative pathway for change, which, however, could receive little help from central oversight institutions. In the following section, I explore local prosecutors' offices' typical organizational structures before and immediately after decentralization. I also briefly explore the Council's attempt to encourage a revision of these structures and the new tools it introduced to this end.

DECENTRALIZATION AND LOCAL PROSECUTORS' OFFICES

For a long time, organizational structures regulating the relationships between judicial prosecutorial authorities and their subordinates reflected the overall hierarchical outlook of the Italian judicial branch. Freddi (1978) describes these organizational structures in light of the evaluation system that determined careers before decentralization. As I previously explained, the evaluation system relied heavily on one essential assumption: that civil law was more rigorous than criminal law, and therefore that its mastery was the pathway toward professional advancements (Di Federico 1978, 808–809). The importance of civil law for professional advancements in turn had profound effects on local offices' organizational structures. This is because the evaluation system's emphasis on the scientific perfection of abstract legal reasoning supported a "scholarly" understanding of the judicial role (Freddi 1978, 107). As a result, the culmination of a successful legal career was a judicial post on an appellate court, possibly dealing with civil lawsuits rather than criminal cases.

The evaluation system placed administrative tasks at a much lower level of professional prestige (Freddi 1978, 107). For this reason, judicial professionals tended to consider administrative posts, such as the head of a courthouse or one of its sections, as actual "demotions" (Freddi 1978, 106).[18] For the same reason, judicial professionals in important administrative posts usually attempted to fulfill their duties while maintaining a certain detachment from the most practical aspects of their office (106–107). Therefore, the Italian judicial branch's hierarchical structure, built upon a strict evaluation system, created serious obstacles to the efficient administration of justice at the local level, given its inherent support for "scholars" over "administrators.[19]" In addition to fostering inefficiencies, this hierarchical structure also deeply affected the relationships between local judicial authorities and their subordinates.

Local judicial authorities were both in charge of assigning cases as well as assigning young judicial trainees to their first posts. Given the importance of civil law practice for professional advancements, this gave local judicial authorities' absolute power over their subordinates' future careers (Freddi 1978, 98). Generally, the most prepared judicial trainees were assigned to the civil law section of a court[20] (96), and the most complex civil law cases were assigned to those trainees who showed high intellectual qualities (99). However, these determinations were not always clear-cut and often implied a certain degree of subjectivity (95–96). Consequently, judicial trainees and lower-ranked judicial professionals in general felt significant pressure to conform to their local superiors' preferences (98). Thus, in addition to creating a two-tiered system in which civil law sections held significantly more prestige than criminal law ones, this institutional structure also discouraged collegiality and strengthened local judicial authorities' hierarchical oversight over their subordinates (Freddi 1978, 101).

These incentives applied to prosecutorial offices as well. Indeed, prosecutors' offices' internal organization tended to be even more hierarchical than other offices' (50). The code of criminal procedure stated that local chief prosecutors were effectively responsible for every prosecutorial act, even when one of their subordinates had technically issued the decision. Therefore, the code identified lower-ranked prosecutors as simple "implementers" of the chief's preferences. These procedural norms inevitably subjected lower-ranked prosecutors to strict hierarchical control by their local superiors (50). In general, local prosecutors enjoyed little agency, and, like the rest of the judiciary's lower ranks, their careers depended almost entirely on their superiors' evaluation.

When decentralization finally came to completion in 1975, it significantly impacted local offices' organizations. In particular, the decision to make evaluations irrelevant for judicial careers freed lower-ranked judicial professionals from the pressure to focus on abstract civil cases and allowed them to pursue criminal law without concerns for their career prospects. On the other hand, these effects were mostly indirect. Decentralization concerned national institutions and did not directly impact local organizational structures. Immediately after decentralization, local judicial authorities' almost absolute control over their subordinates remained untarnished.

For this reason, starting in the 1970s, the High Council issued directives that would regulate how local judicial authorities could organize professional relationships within their offices (Di Federico 2012, 21). These directives applied also to local chief prosecutors and therefore were meant to have a significant impact on the rigidly hierarchical structure typical of prosecutors' offices. The Council's directives outlined how local judicial authorities should assign their subordinates to offices and tasks, how they should assign cases, and how they should organize professional relationships within the office (Di Federico 2012, 20). More specifically, the directives required local judicial authorities—including chief prosecutors—to involve their subordinates as much as possible in the office's decision-making process. For instance, chief prosecutors should hold regular assemblies with their subordinates to discuss office organization (20). Moreover, the directives established that any lower-ranked prosecutor had a right to appeal to the Council if they found their superior's handling and organization of the office to be unfair (20–21). Similarly, every prosecutor had the right to gather their peers to jointly assess the chief prosecutor's handling of the office's work and organization (20–21).

The High Council's intention in issuing these directives was to extend the process of decentralization to the local level by empowering lower-ranked judicial professionals vis-à-vis their immediate superiors. The Council believed that this process would improve the administration of justice (Di Federico 2012, 20). At the same time, decentralizing authority at the local level was necessary to implement art. 25 in the Italian Constitution (Di Federico 2012, 21). The latter stated that "no one may be removed from the natural jurisdiction of the court previously established by law."[21] A rigid hierarchical organization might endanger this principle (Di Federico 2012, 21) by compromising a lower-ranked judicial professionals' ability to make decisions without undue influence from their superior. Therefore, with these directives, the High Council and the judicial associations sitting on it were promoting the pursuit of egalitarianism as the main constitutional principle regulating judicial relations not just at the national but also at the local level. Egalitarianism, rooted in the new Constitution's provisions, would increase lower-ranked judicial professionals' independence, especially prosecutorial independence, by promoting their inclusion in key decision-making processes within their office, on an equal footing with their local superiors.

However, in line with the theoretical expectations I outlined in chapter 1, the process of decentralization also partially undermined the effectiveness of the High Council's efforts. First of all, the Council's directives represented very important "suggestions" with no binding legal value. Until 1988, the Council did not formally possess the power to regulate local offices' internal organization. Nevertheless, the Council attempted to do so even before it possessed any legally binding authority over the issue (Di Federico 2012, 20–21). Even so, the High Council could no longer rely on evaluations, which had in the past been the most effective means for forcing judicial professionals into compliance. However, as I previously explained, evaluations did not entirely disappear. The Council did issue a few negative evaluations of local judicial authorities for not complying with its organizational directives (Di Federico 2012, 21).

The Council's directives and the new powers the institution bestowed on lower-ranked prosecutors set the stage for conflict between these individuals and their local superiors. As a result of decentralization, lower-ranked prosecutors could now invite the Council's intervention against their superior's resistance to a more egalitarian organization of the office. While new generation of younger, more progressive judicial professionals were entering the ranks of the institution, local judicial authorities, especially chief prosecutors, often held very conservative preferences, which found expression in a rigid hierarchical organization of their office. On the other hand, lower-ranked prosecutors could now appeal to the High Council and officially file complaints against their superiors. As a result, several prosecutors' offices became the site of a struggle between different legal factions. For the most part, this struggle manifested in the fight between conservative superiors against a growing group of more moderate or progressive lower ranks. Other times, however, moderate or progressive chief prosecutors sought to reform their offices' organizational structures along more egalitarian lines despite their subordinates' resistance.

The argument I develop in this book revolves around local prosecutors' offices' internal organization. I argue that the delayed occurrence of effective corruption prosecution in the Clean Hands operation was a function of local developments, specifically the gradual evolution of organizational structures within local prosecutors' offices. As other authors have highlighted before, different "styles of management" may have a deep impact on the administration of justice within local prosecutors' offices (Nelken and Zanier 2006). The way chief prosecutors decide to organize their office and the informal rules they create to handle caseload may make the difference between the effective prosecution of a criminal issue and the lack thereof (Nelken and Zanier 2006, 153; Montana and Nelken 2011). This, in turn, may be a product of the local office's "legal culture" (Nelken and Zanier 2006, 153). Therefore, in order to explain the Clean Hands operation's unprecedented success, it is necessary to examine prosecutorial offices' internal organizations. I argue that the Clean Hands operation was made possible by the replacement of local hierarchical structures with egalitarian ones, which allowed lower-ranked prosecutors to pursue new and more effective approaches to complex criminal phenomena without obstacles or backlash from their superiors.

In the following chapters, I develop this argument through the examination of organizational structures within four prosecutors' offices: Rome, Milan, Palermo, and Reggio Calabria. As I will show, each office's internal organization had momentous consequences on prosecutorial independence and effectiveness in tackling systemic corruption in the long run. My analysis in the following chapters will focus on both formal and informal institutions. Only by taking into consideration both types of institutions, it is possible to outline each office's actual mode of internal organization.

CONCLUSION

In this chapter, I provided a brief outline of the Italian prosecutorial system's institutional transformations, especially after re-democratization. First of all, the abolition of the evaluation system for promotions and appointments secured safe career paths for judicial professionals. Furthermore, institutional reforms empowered lower judicial ranks, by giving them the means to influence their own promotions and appointments via their participation in elections to the High Council of the Judiciary. This set of reforms brought to completion the Italian prosecutorial system's decentralization. In chapter 1, I argued that decentralization is fundamental to the emergence of legal innovations via a bottom-up approach. The historical background I provided in this chapter shows how the Italian prosecutorial system remained impermeable to legal innovations as long as it maintained its hierarchical outlook. The latter empowered a legally conservative judicial elite, who could force the lower ranks into conformity with its views. On the other hand, decentralization finally freed lower-ranked judges and prosecutors to pursue new legal approaches without fearing for their careers.

Therefore, decentralization was essential to building increasing prosecutorial independence and effectiveness over time. Thanks to decentralization, professional careers in criminal law ceased to appear as less worthy alternatives to careers in civil litigation. Hence, decentralization created the conditions for the emergence of legal innovations among lower-ranked prosecutors, whose careers no longer depended on a legally conservative elite's evaluation of their work. Thus, increasing freedom to experiment with new legal approaches brought along the possibility of increasing prosecutorial effectiveness as well.

Nevertheless, decentralization did not eliminate all obstacles to prosecutorial independence. In chapter 1, I argued that a prosecutorial system's decentralization may empower local authorities, whose freedom from central oversight inevitably increases under this process. As I showed in this chapter, decentralization affected national institutions but left local organizational structures within local prosecutors' offices almost untarnished initially. More importantly, decentralization weakened the Council's power of oversight, which resulted in the latter's weakened ability to force institutional changes at the local level. As a result, decentralization partially empowered local chief prosecutors, who remained the undisputed authorities in charge of their office's internal organization.

Consequently, decentralization sparked a harsh competition among judicial associations for control over local prosecutors' offices. The diffusion of power to lower ranks awakened significant hopes for similar change at the local level. Indeed, as I show in the following chapters, some prosecutors' offices replaced conservative leadership with more moderate chief prosecutors, open to restructuring their offices' organization and to the emergence of progressive voices among their subordinates. The Milan prosecutor's office and to an extent the Palermo office as well illustrate this dynamic. Other prosecutors' offices instead remained firmly in the hands of traditionally conservative elements, who worked to maintain hierarchical control over their subordinates. Both the Roman prosecutor's office and the Reggio Calabria prosecutor's office embody this dynamic. In the remainder of this book, I explore changes in organizational structures, along with their long-term effects on the prosecution of systemic corruption, in each of these four prosecutor's offices.

NOTES

1. The quote can be found in Guarnieri (2003, 93). Author's translation.

2. The decree also assigned some of these consultative powers to the so-called *consigli giudiziari,* local judicial councils (Del Mastro 2014, 45). The latter consisted for the most part of higher-ranking judges (Del Mastro 2014, 48). However, the executive branch maintained the power to appoint judges and prosecutors to the highest offices (Guarnieri 2003, 96), such as the General Prosecutor at the Court of Cassation (Del Mastro 2014, 46–47).

3. Technically, all judicial professionals participated in electing members of their local judicial council. However, the latter consisted solely of higher-court judges (Del Mastro 2014, 47–48).

4. The General Prosecutor at the Court of Cassation was a member of the High Council (Del Mastro 2014, 37).

5. Candidates can either be "university professors of law and lawyers with fifteen years of practice" (Italian Constitution, art. 104, translation found at https://www.constituteproject.org/constitution/Italy_2012.pdf?lang=en).

6. On page 151, Guarnieri (2003) presents an outline of the lay members' party affiliation over the years.

7. See rulings 52/1965, 190/1970, 63/1972 and 64/1972, referenced in Borgna (2017).

8. See rulings n. 86/1968 and n. 148/1969 as discussed in Borgna 2017.

9. Quote in Edmondo Bruti Liberati's (2017) lecture "Magistratura e Società nell'Italia Repubblicana. Esperienza Storica e Problemi Aperti." Author's translation.

10. LaPalombara (1989) describes it as "an endemic, much-maligned patronage system whereby jobs and other valued things are apportioned among the leading political parties roughly in proportion to their electoral strength" (78).

11. LaPalombara (1989) explains that both opposition and ruling parties amicably participated in *lottizzazione* (128–129), which allowed them to assign offices within the public administration to judicial professionals as well.

12. By law, Constitutional judges can only serve for nine years on the Constitutional Court.

13. "Pretori" were lower-ranked judges whose competences included both civil law and criminal law cases. The expression "pretori d'assalto" came to describe an increasingly assertive group of lower-ranked judges, willing to take up controversial cases with significant political and social consequences, De Vito (2017).

14. See Rios-Figueroa (2007) and Iaryczower, Spiller and Tommasi (2002) for an example of PFTs.

15. Mershon relies on Riker's (1962) definition of a minimal winning coalition.

16. I draw this conclusion based on Mershon's (1996) classification of government coalition, in Appendix A (551).

17. Like in all parliamentary systems, in the Italian case the prime minister and his cabinet must be voted into office through a vote of confidence. In the Italian case, the prime minister and cabinet members were usually drawn from the Christian Democracy and allied parties, such as the Liberal Party and the Republican Party, or the Italian Socialist Party as well for a limited period of time. Usually, the Italian Communist Party voted against confidence. However, during the Seventh Legislature, the Communist Party's abstention from its usual opposition was enough to vote into office a Christian Democratic prime minister.

18. In one of his interviews, Freddi (1978) even found that, according to one of his interviewees, promotion to an administrative post meant the end of a judge's career (106).

19. This was particularly visible within civil courts, where judges were competing against each other to adjudicate complex, abstract, and extremely time-consuming legal cases whose long resolution created severe backlogs (Freddi 1978, 105).

20. Italian courthouses normally house both a criminal section and a civil section. There are no distinct "civil courts" and "criminal courts."

21. Translation in Barsotti et al. (2015), Italian Constitutional text in Appendix.

Chapter 3

All Investigations Lead to Rome

The Roman Prosecutor's Office

The Roman prosecutor's office clearly illustrates the theoretical argument I outlined in chapter 1 about the roots of prosecutorial independence and effectiveness. Local hierarchical structures, even within a decentralized system, compress prosecutors' independence to explore new legal and investigative approaches and therefore hinder prosecutorial effectiveness. Furthermore, local actors' choice of organizational structures reflects their deeply held legal beliefs. However, within a decentralized system, local organizational structures are not static, and they can change over time, thanks to the diffusion of power to the lower ranks that decentralization produces. The Roman case study illustrates not only the enduring persistence of hierarchical structures and their effects on prosecutorial independence and effectiveness but also the opportunities for change inherent in a decentralized system.

At the time of re-democratization, in 1945, the Roman judicial community was among the most legally conservative communities in the country. Furthermore, as I showed in chapter 2, Roman judicial professionals had long enjoyed a competitive advantage in terms of professional advancements within the judicial branch, thanks to their proximity to the centers of political power in the nation's capital. This geographical and political proximity to political power reinforced the adherence of the Roman legal community to legal positivism. Given Roman judicial professionals' tight relationship to state officials during the Fascist regime, authoritarian elements remained within this legal community alongside democracy-oriented ones. Until the end of the 1980s, traditionally conservative elements maintained control over the Roman prosecutor's office. Only with the start of the 1990s, a growing legally progressive faction finally reached a critical threshold of consensus to take control of this office.

The enduring control of the legally conservative community over the Roman jurisdiction is visible in the repeated appointment of conservative chief prosecutors. Until 1992, Roman chief prosecutors clearly espoused, or at least supported, Italian legal positivism's central tenets. This adherence translated into a hierarchical mentality, which shaped the Roman prosecutor's office's internal organization. From 1974 to 1992, Roman chief prosecutors implemented a strictly hierarchical organization to regulate the relationships with their subordinates. This organizational structure increased chief prosecutors' control over sensitive investigations and hindered lower-ranked prosecutors' ability to pursue legal innovations. In addition, this hierarchical organization effectively insulated the Roman prosecutor's office from the larger judicial network forming across several Italian jurisdictions at the end of the 1970s. The effects of this organizational structure are visible in the handling of sensitive investigations into terrorist groups like the Red Brigades and First Line. Roman prosecutors fell short of adopting those legal innovations that had led to significant prosecutorial achievements on these same types of cases in other jurisdictions, especially in Milan. Thus, the hierarchical structure implemented by conservative Roman chief prosecutors created a long-lasting dearth of expertise among local prosecutors.

More importantly, until 1992, Roman chief prosecutors' persistent legal conservatism led to the use of prosecutorial gatekeeping in investigations into elected officials. As I outlined in chapter 1, some prosecutorial institutions may become critical nodes in the prosecutorial system. Namely, they may become "gatekeeping institutions." The Roman prosecutor's office represents a clear example of a gatekeeping institution. Given this office's proximity to the central governing institutions, national agencies, and national party branches, Roman chief prosecutors could potentially extend their control over any investigation involving elected officials and state agents, even if they originated in another jurisdiction.

In this chapter, I show that, until 1992, Roman chief prosecutors worked to have investigations involving high-level political personalities or state agents transferred from other jurisdictions into their control. Prosecutorial gatekeeping was especially aggressive when investigations alleged the involvement of center-right and right-wing political actors, including military and intelligence service members, in illicit activities. An examination of these cases shows that these investigations often concluded with lenient sentences or the dismissal of charges. The appointment of the first moderate chief prosecutor, Vittorio Mele, in 1992, led to an important suspension in the use of prosecutorial gatekeeping. This suspension, in turn, allowed for the Clean Hands operation to unfold without Roman prosecutorial authorities' interference.

While the wave of corruption prosecutions unleashed by the Clean Hands operation eventually reached the Roman jurisdiction, Roman prosecutors could not deploy the same legal and investigative means adopted by their peers in Milan and Palermo. The long-standing implementation of a hierarchical structure within the Roman prosecutor's office had undermined learning and insulated Roman prosecutors from the diffusion of legal innovations. This resulted in fewer corruption convictions in Rome than Milan, despite the former jurisdiction's central place in the corruption network. Thus, the suspension of prosecutorial gatekeeping in 1992 explains why effective corruption prosecution only occurred with the Clean Hands operation and not before. However, the suspension of gatekeeping powers might have been the Roman office's most significant contribution to the fight against systemic corruption.

In this chapter, I examine the Roman prosecutor's office from 1975 to 1996. First of all, I show how the conservative legal faction's enduring control of this office led to the appointment of conservative chief prosecutors until 1992. Second, I explore the different ways in which Roman chief prosecutors organized the relationship with their subordinates. I then examine how conservative chief prosecutors used prosecutorial gatekeeping to have investigations into elected officials and state agents transferred under their control, and how this practice ceased in 1992. Finally, I explore the effects of the long-standing hierarchical structure in place within the Roman office on complex criminal prosecutions, such as those into terrorism and corruption. I also assess alternative hypotheses to my argument, particularly those rooted in the attitudinal model of judicial behavior (Segal and Spaeth 2002). I conclude the chapter by showing how the lack of expertise created by this long-standing hierarchical structure undermined Roman prosecutors' efforts to emulate their peers investigating corruption in the Clean Hands operation.

SELECTING ROMAN CHIEF PROSECUTORS

From 1975 to 1992, the Roman prosecutor's office remained a bulwark of legal conservatism. The progressive judicial associations *Magistratura Democratica* (MD) did not significantly increase its membership within the Roman jurisdiction until the 1980s (Ceron and Mainenti 2015, 227). Until then, the office of Roman chief prosecutor remained consistently under the control of conservative elements. Furthermore, appointments to the Roman chief prosecutor's office drew heightened scrutiny on the part of both judicial and political actors. Both elected officials and judicial professionals recognized the nature of this office as a gatekeeping institution. Appointing the Roman chief prosecutor may guarantee control over this office's strategic use of jurisdictional issues, and therefore over the outcome of sensitive investigations beyond the confines of the Roman jurisdiction. For this reason, political parties believed the Roman chief prosecutor's office to be worth three cabinet posts (Bianconi 2015). For the same reason, the appointment process to the Roman prosecutor's office is less opaque than other appointments. The heightened scrutiny coming from the political and judicial community also drew the attention of national and local newspapers, which started closely documenting the appointment process.

While Italian political parties did not shy away from attempts to buy the loyalty of Roman judicial officials, including the Roman chief prosecutor,[1] the appointment process to this office is best explained in light of the competition between judicial associations in the High Council of the Judiciary. As I explained in chapter 2, by the end of the 1970s, judicial associations had become the primary vehicle for promotions and appointments within the judicial hierarchy. Decentralization had significantly reduced the power of the most conservative elements within the system. Nevertheless, conservative control of the Roman prosecutor's office would entrench this faction's influence over the prosecutorial system for decades, thanks to this office's gatekeeping powers. Thus, although decentralization had dealt a fatal blow to the conservative legal movement's prominence, the latter managed to remain a powerful force shaping criminal prosecution long after its loss of status. Table 3.1 outlines Roman chief prosecutors' associational affiliation and professional status before their appointment from 1974 to 1994.

As table 3.1 shows, chief prosecutors Mele and Coiro were the first appointees affiliated with more progressive judicial associations. Until 1992, Roman chief prosecutors were either outspoken legal conservatives, such as De Matteo, a member of the ultra-conservative association UMI, or moderate supporters of legal positivism with some ties to MI, like Boschi. The professional status of Roman chief prosecutors immediately before their appointment also provides helpful information about their legal preferences. For instance, Gallucci had served as the Roman chief instructing judge at a time when MI held significant electoral consensus among judicial professionals, and the more progressive association MD collected only a minority of votes within the Roman jurisdiction (Ceron and Mainenti 2015, 227). Thus, although Gallucci lacked formal affiliation with an association, before his appointment as chief prosecutor, he had already achieved a position of power within a very conservative environment.

On the other hand, Giudiceandrea's appointment would seem to signal a significant change in the profile of Roman chief prosecutors, given his former belonging to the progressive association MD. However, Giudiceandrea's prior conduct as chief prosecutor in Bologna fell perfectly in line with the expectations of the conservative legal community. While in Bologna, Giudiceandrea had behaved like a conservative chief prosecutor in cases implicating political personalities, refusing to aggressively prosecute the

Table 3.1 Roman Chief Prosecutors' Profiles

	Giovanni De Matteo (1975)	*Achille Gallucci (1980)*	*Marco Boschi (1984)*	*Ugo Giudiceandrea (1988)*	*Vittorio Mele (1992)*	*Michele Coiro (1994)*
Associational Affiliation	UMI	None	Proximity with MI (no formal membership)	Former member of MD	UniCost	MD
Previous Appointment	UMI secretary	Chief instructing judge in Rome	Minister of Justice, legal consultant	Chief prosecutor in Bologna	Court of Cassation	Lower-ranked prosecutor in Rome

Source: Information from *Il Corriere della Sera*, *La Repubblica*, Fracanzani (2014). Author's elaboration.

defendants involved (D'Avanzo 1992). This behavior, which had sparked his subordinates' outrage in many cases, stemmed out of Giudiceandrea's overly broad understanding of defendants' rights (D'Avanzo 1992). Thus, Giudiceandrea's extensive interpretation of defendants' rights in the prosecution of political personalities made him a perfect fit for the traditionally conservative community. Furthermore, Giudiceandrea's associational profile highlights the inadequacy of the attitudinal model (Segal and Spaeth 2002) to explain prosecutorial behavior. Giudiceandrea's former adherence to MD does not accurately predict the chief prosecutor's attitudes in the prosecution of right-wing elements, like in the *Gladio* investigation, which I discuss later.

The repeated appointment of conservative chief prosecutors resulted from the conservative legal movement's control over the selection to the Roman office within the High Council of the Judiciary. Conservative dominance over the appointment to the Roman prosecutor's office continued well into the 1980s, until conservative Council members could not hold off the emergence of a progressive legal front any longer. Table 3.2 shows the distribution of votes among Council members on the appointment of Roman chief prosecutors from 1980 to 1994. The table reports the distribution of votes among judicial associations' representatives and lay Council members.[2] Table 3.2 does not include the appointment of chief prosecutor De Matteo. This is because his appointment occurred before the 1975 introduction of proportional representation for High Council elections.

De Matteo was the last Roman chief prosecutor appointed by the Council before new members elected by the whole judicial population could take office in 1976 (Fracanzani 2014, 145). Before his appointment, De Matteo had been one of the leading members of UMI, the judicial association representing higher court judges (145). Therefore, his appointment marked the last affirmation of power by traditionally conservative judicial professionals over the Roman office (145). However, the institutional reforms that changed the High Council composition in 1975 did not immediately alter the conservative legal community's influence over appointments to the Roman prosecutor's office.

Table 3.2 shows that MI, the conservative judicial association, consistently found itself in the majority selecting Roman chief prosecutors. The appointments of chief prosecutors Gallucci and Giudiceandrea created significant divisions in the Council: as many as ten members voted against Gallucci's appointment. Similarly, six Council members (mostly belonging to UniCost) decided to abstain from confirming Giudiceandrea. In both cases, MI found a way to assemble a relative majority over these appointments.

Importantly, however, lay members of the High Council supplied MI representatives with the necessary votes to appoint Gallucci. This was the only instance in which lay members, the sole political appointees to the High

Table 3.2 Vote Distribution on Appointments to the Roman Chief Prosecutor's Office, 1980–1994

	Achille Gallucci (1980)[1]	*Marco Boschi (1984)*	*Ugo Giudiceandrea (1988)*	*Vittorio Mele (1992)*	*Michele Coiro (1994)*
Votes in Favor	Eighteen in favor Judicial associations: MI Lay members: DC, PSI	Unanimity	Twenty in favor Judicial associations: MI, MD UniCost: three votes Lay members: DC, PSI, PCI	Twenty-four in favor Judicial associations: MI, UniCost Movement for Justice Lay members: DC, PSI-PSDI, PDS	Twenty in favor Judicial Associations: MI, MD, UniCost Lay members: DC, PDS, PSI-PSDI
Votes Against	Ten votes against	No votes against	No votes against	Three against: MD	One vote against: PdR, lay member
Abstentions	Two abstentions	No abstentions	Nine abstentions: Unicost: six abstentions	Three abstentions	One abstention: MD: one abstention

Table 3.2 Party Labels:
PSI: *Partito Socialista Italiano* (Italian Socialist Party)
DC: *Democrazia Cristiana* (Christian Democracy)
PCI: *Partito Comunista Italiano* (Italian Communist Party)
PSDI: *Partito Socialista Democratico Italiano* (Italian Democratic Socialist Party)
PDS: *Partito Democratico della Sinistra* (Democratic Party of the Left—former Italian Communist Party)
PdR: *Partito dei Radicali* (Party of the Radicals—liberal party)
Table 3.1 Judicial Associations Labels:
MD: *Magistratura Democratica*
MI: *Magistratura Indipendente*
UniCost: *Unità per la Costituzione*
[1]: It was not possible to trace the exact distribution of votes among judicial associations and lay members. The table reports all available information about this vote.
Source: Information from *Il Corriere della Sera, La Repubblica.* Author's elaboration.

Council, used their votes strategically to sway this institution's selection of a Roman chief prosecutor. Even more noticeably, it was lay members representing the most important parties in the current ruling coalition, Christian Democrats and Socialists, to support Gallucci's appointment. Table 3.2 shows that, otherwise, lay Council members, both from the ruling coalition and the opposition, aligned with the majority of judicial members even when the Council started electing less conservative chief prosecutors to the Roman office in 1992 and 1994.

Giudiceandrea's appointment, on the other hand, promised to reflect the growing influence of the legally progressive community. By selecting one of the former founding members of MD, conservative Council members managed to secure the endorsement of this minoritarian, though growing, judicial association. However, as I previously mentioned, Giudiceandrea's profile fell perfectly in line with the requirements sought out by the conservative legal community.

Therefore, both Gallucci and Giudiceandrea's appointments stemmed from MI's relative control over appointments to the Roman prosecutor's office. On the contrary, chief prosecutor Boschi's appointment would appear to be the fruit of a "bipartisan" agreement, given the unanimity surrounding it. Furthermore, Boschi was the first candidate to have worked for the Minister of Justice before taking office as the Roman chief prosecutor. For this reason, Boschi's profile would seem to identify him as an "outsider." However, Boschi's proximity to MI, in whose events he participated (Scottoni 1985), was naturally appealing to conservative Council members. Being an "outsider," on the other hand, helped garner a broad majority over his appointment without revealing its partisan character. This did not spare Boschi's appointment of partisan fights. During Boschi's confirmation process, MD members tried to vet the candidates (Nese 1984). The Council commission in charge of proposing the initial appointment rejected this attempt (Nese 1984).

Until 1988, MI representatives in the High Council were able to consistently select their preferred candidate for the office of the Roman chief prosecutor. However, different dynamics started emerging in 1992 and 1994. As table 3.2 shows, Mele's appointment created a harsh partisan divide, raising significant opposition, especially from MD representatives. Mele was probably not MI's favorite candidate, given his clear affiliation with UniCost, a less conservative judicial association than MI. In addition, he had no prior experience as a prosecutor (Coppola 1992*b*). In this instance, however, MI was unable to push for a candidate more aligned with its legal views, and Mele seemed to be the only candidate with the potential to ratchet up enough votes against Coiro, who had been ranking first in the race until the final vote (Coppola 1992*b*). As table 3.2 shows, Coiro eventually became the first chief prosecutor to belong to MD, the legally progressive judicial association.

Council members repeatedly rejected his candidacy until his choice became unavoidable in 1994 (Coppola 1992*b*).

Therefore, both Mele and Coiro's appointments signal the end of the conservative legal community's control over the Roman prosecutor's office. Conservative representatives in the High Council were no longer capable of gathering enough votes to secure the election of a Roman chief prosecutor in line with their preferences. Instead, in a final attempt to delay inevitable change, the conservative legal community opted for a less preferable, though more electable candidate in 1992. Coiro's appointment in 1994 marked the progressive legal community's takeover of this key prosecutor's office.

THE ROMAN PROSECUTOR'S OFFICE'S ORGANIZATIONAL STRUCTURE

As I explained in chapter 1, chief prosecutors' legal preferences are of key importance to understanding a prosecutorial institution's organizational structure. Local chief prosecutors may be under an obligation to follow specific guidelines, ethical codes, or regulations in the organization of their office. However, they are also in a position to informally mold this organizational structure as they desire. For instance, local chief prosecutors might establish an "informal hierarchy" to regulate the relationship with their subordinates, despite the existence of formal rules dictating otherwise. Therefore, local chief prosecutors' legal preferences and goals crucially affect how they will organize the relationship with their subordinates.

In this section, I explore how Roman chief prosecutors structured the relationship with their subordinates. I show that, regardless of High Council guidelines, conservative chief prosecutors consistently implemented informal hierarchies within the Roman office. This, in turn, provided them with extensive discretion and control over their subordinates' work. This organizational structure was in line with legal positivism's main tenets, which tended to support a hierarchical understanding of the relationships between judicial professionals. More importantly, conservative chief prosecutors used this hierarchical structure to direct their subordinates' investigations, which often resulted in tenuous accountability or a lack thereof when directed against powerful defendants.

On the other hand, when moderate and progressive chief prosecutors took control of the Roman office, they pursued a more egalitarian organization of professional relationships. This choice was in line with progressive legal philosophies, grounded in the values of the democratic constitution. As a result, moderate and progressive chief prosecutors refrained from interfering with their subordinates' work, paving the way to increased prosecutorial independence and effectiveness.

Conservative Roman chief prosecutors' attempt to implement a hierarchy within their office had to be informal in nature. This is because, as I explained in chapter 2, in previous years, the High Council had issued guidelines aimed at introducing egalitarian elements into prosecutorial offices' organization. For instance, despite the High Council's mandate to hold regular consultations with subordinates, these gatherings did not serve the purpose of encouraging collective decision-making within the Roman office. Instead, conservative Roman chief prosecutors maintained undivided decision-making power over all office functions. Furthermore, most conservative chief prosecutors created informal rankings among their subordinates, establishing a group of "loyalists" and further isolating other lower-ranked prosecutors.

Chief prosecutor De Matteo's tenure, from 1975 to 1980, perfectly embodied these hierarchical tendencies. A member of the ultra-conservative judicial association UMI, De Matteo's preference for hierarchy undermined salient investigations into right-wing elements, including violent neofascist groups. De Matteo's relationship with his subordinate, prosecutor Mario Amato, epitomizes De Matteo's hierarchical tendencies and hostility toward criminal accountability.

Prosecutor Mario Amato had been conducting extensive investigations into the rising number of violent attacks perpetrated by the N.A.R, a neofascist group with openly subversive goals (Balzanelli 1988). Seeking to examine all criminal actions pursued by this group, Amato asked chief prosecutor De Matteo for permission to collaborate with another prosecutor (Balzanelli 1988). Creating a special unit to prosecute all N.A.R.-related activities would have increased the resources invested in this type of investigation. De Matteo discussed his subordinate's request during one of the office's meetings with lower-ranked prosecutors (Balzanelli 1988). However, it soon became evident that De Matteo's goal was not to encourage collective decision-making on this issue. Rather, the chief prosecutor's intention seemed to be to isolate Amato (Balzanelli 1988). Amato's request was ignored, and he was killed by N.A.R. members later in the same year (Balzanelli 1988).

Prosecutor Amato's killing enraged Roman prosecutors, who loudly protested against De Matteo's direction of the office (*Sono Irrevocabili le Dimissioni del Procuratore Capo De Matteo* 1980). These protests led De Matteo to resign early and the Council to appoint a new chief prosecutor, Achille Gallucci. However, chief prosecutor Gallucci did not significantly change the informal hierarchical structure regulating the relationships with his subordinates. For instance, Gallucci created an informal ranking of prosecutors and surrounded himself with a group of loyalists that would dutifully follow his orders (*Per Gallucci Critiche e Riconoscimenti dei Magistrati Romani* 1980).

Gallucci and this narrow group of loyal prosecutors looked through cases, deciding which ones to move forward and which ones were not worth pursuing (*Per Gallucci Critiche e Riconoscimenti dei Magistrati Romani* 1980). Thus, instead of establishing collegial decision-making within his office, as the High Council had mandated, Gallucci instituted an informal structure that strengthened his control. Gallucci's reliance on a group of loyalists sheltered his decision-making from collective negotiations that might occur in regular office meetings.

Gallucci's hierarchical direction of his office also sparked several complaints among his subordinates. In 1983, a group of Roman prosecutors drafted a report to the High Council, in which they presented complaints about Gallucci's leadership. With this document, Roman prosecutors formally asked the High Council to open an inquiry into Gallucci's leadership (Bolzoni 1985). The possibility for prosecutors and judges to request the High Council's intervention had been part of the Council's efforts to empower lower ranks vis-à-vis their superiors, as I explained in chapter 2. Far from accepting his subordinates' complaints, however, chief prosecutor Gallucci chose an aggressive response to the accusations, which set him on a collision course with the High Council. While the latter was reviewing the complaint, chief prosecutor Gallucci prompted one of his loyal subordinates to press charges against Council representatives over the possible illicit use of Council's funds (Mazzocchi 1985, 1987). The institutional conflict between the Roman chief prosecutor's office and the High Council only came to a resolution thanks to the President of the Republic's intervention as the head of this institution (*La Scelta del CSM* 1996).

The harsh institutional conflict between chief Gallucci and the High Council was probably one reason for appointing a seemingly "bipartisan" personality as his successor. Marco Boschi's appointment attracted almost unanimous consensus among Council members. However, Boschi was not less conservative than his predecessors, and during his tenure, hierarchical structures did not disappear from the Roman office. For instance, Boschi did not dismantle the informal hierarchy that Gallucci had created, which placed a group of "loyalists" at the top. On the contrary, Boschi used this informal institution to handle sensitive investigations.

This was the case with the investigation involving neofascist terrorist Stefano Delle Chiaie. Delle Chiaie had been the subject of an arrest warrant for years and had just been extradited to Italy from Venezuela. Boschi ordered one of Gallucci's former loyal subordinates, Luciano Infelisi, to have an unofficial conversation with Delle Chiaie (Coppola 1992*a*). In addition, Boschi asked Infelisi to collect an informal record of Delle Chiaie's answers, ensuring that this information would not end up in an official file to be used at trial. This decision raised serious suspicions of a cover-up (M. Ne. 1987), especially given that Boschi defied official rules to entrust Infelisi with these tasks. According to the office's formal rules, Infelisi should not have been the prosecutor in charge of collecting Delle Chiaie' testimony. On top of this, Infelisi had no apparent expertise in terrorism investigations. Thus, Boschi could not appeal to Infelisi's expertise as a justification to bypass official rules (M. Ne. 1987).

Overall, although Boschi shied away from pursuing the same "authoritarian" leadership style as Gallucci, he nevertheless took advantage of the informal hierarchy established by his predecessor. Furthermore, Boschi's behavior in dealing with Delle Chiaie shows, once again, that the attitudinal model is ill-suited to explain Roman chief prosecutors' decisions. Political reactions to Boschi's handling of Delle Chiaie's testimony suggest that there was ample support for the prosecution of neofascist elements among political parties.

Giudiceandrea's appointment also initially seemed to usher in a change in the organizational structure of the Roman office. Chief prosecutor Giudiceandrea seemed eager to modernize the office's handling of investigations by applying new technologies to case distribution (D'Avanzo 1992). The use of new computer technology prevented Giudiceandrea from interfering with the assignment of cases, seemingly undermining any informal hierarchy that might have been in place. However, Giudiceandrea was swift to abandon this assignment method with sensitive investigations, particularly those involving state agents and elected officials.

During Giudiceandrea's tenure, prosecutors in Florence, Bologna, and Venice discovered a secret organization called *Gladio* (Cecchetti 1991). *Gladio* was identified as a "stay-behind" operation, meant to become operative if left-wing elements, either domestically or from neighboring Eastern bloc countries, should attempt to overthrow democracy and establish a Soviet-friendly regime. The secret organization enlisted high-ranking Italian military personnel and secret service members (Cecchetti 1991). Investigations conducted by prosecutors across several jurisdictions, particularly in Venice, suggested *Gladio*'s possible involvement in illegal activities. Giudiceandrea decided to use prosecutorial gatekeeping to have the entire case transferred to Rome. Therefore, he raised a jurisdictional claim over the *Gladio* investigation (*A Roma I Documenti di Gladio* 1990). Once the Roman prosecutor's office acquired the case, chief prosecutor Giudiceandrea did not use the usual method of randomized assignment to entrust his subordinates with the investigation. Instead, he chose subordinates with specific expertise to assemble an investigative unit working on the *Gladio* cases (*'Il Super Pool Necessario alle Indagini'* 1990).

The creation of a special unit investigating *Gladio* was an unusual decision on the part of the Roman chief prosecutor. As I explain in the following section, Roman chief prosecutors had carefully avoided creating special investigative units, even in the presence of complex criminal issues, such as terrorism investigations. Therefore, Giudiceandrea's decision seemed, once more, to dismantle previous hierarchical structures in favor of a more egalitarian approach to investigative work within the office. However, Giudiceandrea would soon defy these optimistic expectations. The chief prosecutor picked four prosecutors with expertise in the prosecution of criminal organizations to work together on all cases concerning *Gladio*'s alleged activities (*'Il Super Pool Necessario alle Indagini'* 1990). According to Giudiceandrea, the establishment of this team was necessary because of the scope of the *Gladio* investigation and its workload (*'Il Super Pool Necessario alle Indagini'* 1990). However, the work of the special unit turned out to be extremely ineffective.

The investigation concluded with the dismissal of all the charges against *Gladio* members. In 1992, chief prosecutor Giudiceandrea officially dismissed all charges against the secret organization (Scottoni 1992*a*). However, none of chief Giudiceandrea's subordinates joined him in signing the dismissal, a clear indication that his subordinates did not agree with the decision (Scottoni 1992*a*). This noticeable fact underscores the nature of the investigative unit: far from being a sincere attempt to implement egalitarian decision-making, this organizational structure did not replace the chief prosecutor's absolute control over his subordinates' work.

With the end of the conservative judicial community's control over the Roman office, Giudiceandrea's successors moved to significantly restructure the nature of professional relationships within their office. The appointment of Vittorio Mele, although short, brought significant changes in this respect. At the outset of his tenure, Mele promised to create special investigative units focusing on corruption investigations (Sarzanini 1992). Chief prosecutor Mele was initially hesitant to create these special units, whose establishment he delayed until December 1992 (Hav. F. 1992). Eventually, Mele consented to the numerous requests coming from his subordinates (Mastrogiacomo 1993).

The special anti-corruption units that formed within the Roman prosecutor's office resulted from a significant change in the latter's organizational structure. For the first time, work distribution and case assignment resulted from collective consultation with lower-ranked prosecutors, rather than from the chief prosecutor's initiative. Therefore, the decision-making process that led to the establishment of special units marked a shift from a strictly hierarchical approach to a more egalitarian model. Moreover, the very existence of special units reinforced this step toward an egalitarian structure. Special investigative units rely on the equal distribution of labor among their members, who share each other's findings and treat each other as peers. As the *Gladio* investigation shows, even special units that appear to be formally egalitarian can assume a more hierarchical organization under the influence of powerful officials. However, Mele's decision to establish these units seemed genuinely oriented at empowering his subordinates, who, for the first time in the history of this office, showed their support for the chief prosecutor in a letter signed by fifty-two of them (Mastrogiacomo 1994).

The organizational trends that chief Mele inaugurated continued under his successor, Michele Coiro, the first Roman chief prosecutor with a clear affiliation to a progressive judicial association, MD. Coiro established his leadership over the Roman prosecutor's office with a focus on fairness and equality. For instance, chief Coiro introduced a computer-based case assignment method, which prevented him from interfering with this process, where he inclined to favor one subordinate over another (Mastrogiacomo 1996*a*).

In addition, chief Coiro continued maintaining special investigative units to focus on salient criminal issues, like corruption. In an attempt to contribute to the Clean Hands operation, chief Coiro established a special investigative unit to examine the illegal assignment of public housing in exchange for bribes (*Un Pool per Affittopoli* 1995). He also established similar units for investigations involving elected officials' abuse of their power and privileges in relation to public pensions (E. V. 1995). For this reason, despite the controversies that led to Coiro's resignation in 1996, which I discuss later in this chapter, the progressive chief prosecutor maintained significant support among his subordinates (Hav. F. 1996).

THE ROMAN OFFICE AND PROSECUTORIAL GATEKEEPING

The *Gladio*'s case, which I briefly outlined in the previous section, shows how Roman chief prosecutors could use prosecutorial gatekeeping to appropriate cases from other jurisdictions. In chapter 1, I defined prosecutorial gatekeeping as a prosecutorial institution's ability to raise jurisdictional issues strategically for the purpose of having a case transferred under its jurisdiction and controlling its outcome. Prosecutorial institutions may deploy gatekeeping to undermine criminal accountability. They can do so by either dismissing the case after appropriation or by building a failing case—overcharging the defendant, for instance. Prosecutorial gatekeeping, however, is only available to those institutions that enjoy a "jurisdictional advantage" over specific types of crime. The Roman prosecutor's office clearly represents a prosecutorial gatekeeper, thanks to its physical proximity to all national political institutions and political parties' main branches. Due to its geographical position, the Roman prosecutor's office could raise a plausible jurisdictional claim over any crime involving elected officials or national politicians. As I explained earlier in this chapter, both judicial and political actors were keenly aware of the Roman office's gatekeeping powers.

As I explained in chapter 1, the purpose of prosecutorial gatekeeping will depend on legal actors' main preferences. Prosecutorial gatekeeping allowed Roman chief prosecutors to appropriate and control the outcome of sensitive investigations, especially those involving elected officials and state agents. Oftentimes, these investigations resulted in lenient sentences or the dismissal of most charges. As a result, prosecutorial gatekeeping effectively prevented corruption investigations from uncovering the full scale of elected officials' involvement in bribery and embezzlement schemes.

To illustrate this point, in this section, I explore in detail the Roman office's intervention in the so-called P2 case. The P2 investigation is particularly significant, as part of it revolved around a Swiss bank account called *Conto Protezione.* For decades, members of the Italian Socialist Party, including its leadership, used this Swiss bank account to transfer illegal contributions from a varied array of businessmen and company managers. According to then instructing judge Gherardo Colombo, Roman prosecutorial authorities' use of gatekeeping powers delayed the occurrence of the Clean Hands operation by at least ten years (Colombo 2010, 101).

In 1981, during chief prosecutor Achille Gallucci's tenure, Milanese judicial officials pursued a complex investigation into a web of corruption and political subversion. The so-called *Propaganda 2* case, or P2 case, developed from an investigation into corrupt businessman Michele Sindona (Colombo 2010, 39). While digging into Sindona's involvement in illegal activities, a team of Milanese instructing judges managed to uncover the existence of a subversive organization.[3] The web of individuals moving around Sindona belonged to a deviant Masonic lodge called *Propaganda 2* (39), which enlisted prominent politicians, military personnel, secret service members, among others, in a scheme to change Italy's democratic institutions (Colombo 2010, 49–50). Among the documents seized during the inquiry was proof of a Swiss bank account, the so-called *Conto Protezione*. The Italian Socialist Party national leadership had used the account to wire illegal funds (Colombo 2010, 100). Therefore, uncovering the nature of the *Conto Protezione* would have shed light on one of the corruption system's many ramifications. Milanese prosecutors petitioned Swiss authorities for more information about the bank account (Colombo 2010, 99). However, this information would never reach the Milanese team due to the Roman prosecutors' gatekeeping strategy.

As soon as the Milanese investigation became known to the public, the Roman prosecutor's office swiftly started paving the way for the use of prosecutorial gatekeeping. Chief prosecutor Gallucci began taking several trips to Milan with his most loyal subordinates, Domenico Sica and Luciano Infelisi (Colombo 2010, 96–97). The two prosecutors belonged to that inner circle of loyalists that the Roman chief prosecutor had formed around himself (*Per Gallucci Critiche e Riconoscimenti dei Magistrati Romani* 1980). While Roman prosecutors meant for these trips to appear as an offer of help, Milanese judicial professionals perceived them as the start of undue interference (Colombo 2010, 96–97). Indeed, prosecutorial gatekeeping soon followed: the Roman prosecutor's office eventually petitioned the Court of Cassation, the criminal court of last resort and the one in charge of jurisdictional conflicts, to transfer the entire investigation to the Roman jurisdiction (97). This would enable Roman prosecutors to control the handling of the case.

Even before Roman prosecutors would raise the jurisdictional issue, some Cassation judges had already been paying close attention to the P2 investigation. In his memoir, instructing judge Gherardo Colombo (2010) recalls one of his colleagues approaching him to discuss a comment he had received from the Court of Cassation chief judge. The latter had complained about Milanese judges' excessive activism in the P2 investigation. He had harsh comments specifically for Colombo, who, in the judge's opinion, acted as if he was "in charge of choosing the next President of the Republic" (109).[4] The Court of Cassation eventually approved the transfer of the P2 investigation in its entirety to the Roman jurisdiction (97–98).

Once the Roman prosecutor's office appropriated the case, it moved the P2 investigation forward at a different pace than their Milanese counterparts. Under chief Gallucci's supervision, Roman prosecutors concluded that the P2's subversive plan was hardly as threatening as Milanese judges had thought. The result was a weak prosecutorial framework, which depicted *Propaganda 2* more as an innocuous "club" rather than a subversive organization (Colombo 2010, 101). Furthermore, Roman prosecutors built this weak prosecutorial framework on a lack of evidence. When Swiss authorities made information about the bank account *Conto Protezione* readily available to Roman prosecutors, the latter carried out a scant and superficial analysis of the documentation, according to then instructing judge Colombo (2010, 99). This left the transactions occurring via the *Conto Protezione* in the dark.

Furthermore, the Roman prosecutor's office showed little collaboration with the parliamentary commission that was concurrently inquiring into the same facts (Mazzocchi 1985). To address the potentially subversive goals of the P2 lodge, Parliament established a bipartisan commission with ample powers to lead investigations into this secret organization. The parliamentary commission included members from all political parties. Despite ample bipartisan support for the parliamentary commission's work, chief Gallucci demonstrated "scarce cooperation" (Mazzocchi 1985) with this institutional body's efforts. Gallucci's behavior in this instance also rules out political preferences as the main driver of the chief prosecutor's decisions regarding the P2 case. If that were the case, it is unclear why chief Gallucci would oppose a bipartisan inquiry including several conservative political forces, such as the Italian Christian Democracy. Therefore, the attitudinal model (Segal and Spaeth 2002) hardly explains Gallucci's behavior. Rather, Gallucci's uncooperative attitude with parliamentary proceedings clearly speaks to traditional legal conservatism's inherent hostility toward criminal accountability against state agents.

The P2 case represents a significant instance of successful prosecutorial gatekeeping: the Roman prosecutor's office acquired control over a politically sensitive investigation, which became legally innocuous for most of the defendants through a weak case built on lacking evidence. More importantly, this gatekeeping instance guaranteed the enduring survival of the corruption system permeating Italian politics. As one of the Milanese instructing judges leading the P2 investigation, who would later also participate in the Clean Hands operation, argued:

> If [the P2 investigation] had continued unfolding in Milan, it would have anticipated the start of the Clean Hands operation by ten years. (Colombo 2010, 101)

THE ROMAN OFFICE'S HIERARCHY AND ITS EFFECTS ON LEFT-WING TERRORISM PROSECUTIONS

As I showed in the previous sections of this chapter, conservative dominance over the Roman prosecutor's office entailed the establishment of an informal hierarchy between chief prosecutors and their subordinates. Only the appointment of a moderate chief prosecutor in Vittorio Mele and, later on, a progressive chief prosecutor, Michele Coiro, brought to the introduction of a more egalitarian structure within the Roman prosecutor's office. However, the long-standing existence of a hierarchical organization had lasting consequences on prosecutorial independence and effectiveness, even after its dismantling. This hierarchical structure allowed conservative chief prosecutors to scrutinize their subordinates' work closely. It also allowed them to deploy prosecutorial gatekeeping easily, as in the *Gladio* and P2 investigations. In addition, the lasting presence of a hierarchical structure within the Roman office affected the emergence and diffusion of legal innovations to this jurisdiction. This informal hierarchical structure made it extremely difficult, if not impossible, for prosecutors to introduce the same legal innovations as their peers in other jurisdictions.

In this section, I show how the Roman prosecutor's office's impermeability to legal innovations created a long-lasting dearth of expertise among its prosecutors. My analysis focuses particularly on left-wing terrorism cases. Investigations into left-wing terrorism afforded prosecutors in Milan with a chance to develop new investigative methods and a novel interpretation of criminal rules. Despite the presence of the same criminal phenomenon within the Roman jurisdiction, Roman prosecutors did not adopt the investigative novelties previously elaborated by their Milanese peers. Instead, Roman prosecutors remained insulated from the emerging judicial network forming around terrorism investigations. As a result, Roman prosecutors continued applying an ineffective approach to this set of cases.

The effects of this long-lasting insulation were visible even after the shift to a more egalitarian model. In 1992, when Roman prosecutors could finally imitate their peers in the prosecution of systemic corruption, the former lacked the necessary expertise to do so. Years of insulation from other jurisdictions left Roman prosecutors lacking the required knowledge of new investigative techniques and legal interpretation to prosecute corruption effectively. For this reason, despite the increasing independence enjoyed by lower-ranked prosecutors under chief Mele and chief Coiro, the wave of accountability unleashed by the Clean Hands operation barely affected the Roman jurisdiction. Despite the evident centrality of Rome to most corruption schemes, as the center of political power, Roman prosecutors fell short of achieving the same degree of success against systemic corruption as their peers in the Milan jurisdiction. Thus, the hierarchical structure of the Roman prosecutor's office continued severely impacting prosecutorial effectiveness even after its dismantling.

Along with other urban centers, such as Milan, Turin, and Genoa, Rome also suffered terrorist attacks perpetrated by the Red Brigades during the 1970s. Moreover, Rome witnessed terrorist organizations' direct attacks on national politicians, most of which resided in the capital city. In 1978, a Red Brigades terrorist unit kidnapped and killed Christian Democratic leader Aldo Moro. This represented the peak of terrorist violence against the Italian political class. The killing of Aldo Moro prompted law enforcement's mobilization against the terrorist threat. Roman prosecutors and instructing judges followed in this mobilization, which took place at the same time as the first trial against Red Brigades members was starting in Turin.

The coordination among terrorist units was evident: during the Turin trial, the Red Brigades defendants declared that their organization was responsible for the terrorist attack against Aldo Moro (Violante 2018). As I will show in chapter 4, the apparent interconnections between cases sparked the creation of an equivalent network among judicial authorities, bringing together prosecutors and instructing judges from across several Italian jurisdictions. However, Roman prosecutors remained fairly insulated from these coordinated efforts. As a result, Roman prosecutors did not learn nor adopt the same legal innovations as their peers working in other jurisdictions.

The insulation of the Roman prosecutor's office is visible in how the investigations into Aldo Moro's killing, the so-called Moro 1, Moro-bis, and Moro-ter cases, unfolded. Roman instructing judges played a vital role in these investigations, along with their prosecutorial counterparts. For this reason, these cases also offer an interesting comparison between two offices with similar investigative functions within the same jurisdiction, dealing with the same criminal issue in radically different ways. Roman prosecutors did not join in the efforts of the emerging judicial network. Therefore, they did not have a chance to learn and apply new investigative techniques to terrorism cases. On the other hand, Roman instructing judges fully participated in this informal network. Therefore, the Moro cases show the increasing assertiveness of Roman instructing judges, as opposed to the passivity of their fellow prosecutors working on the same investigations. This behavioral difference was a product of the different organizational structure at work in the instructing judge's office, as opposed to the Roman prosecutor's office. These cases also show that the emergence of legal innovations depends on the nature of professional relationships within a local prosecutorial institution.

After Aldo Moro's killing, in May 1978, it took police forces and judicial actors one year to apprehend the terrorists responsible for this heinous act. The Roman prosecutor's office was initially shunned out of this investigation by order of the General Prosecutor at the Roman Court of Appeals.[5] This meant that a higher-ranked prosecutorial authority[6] who was perceived by some to be unethically close to the Minister of the Interior, Francesco Cossiga (Imposimato and Provvisionato 2018, 50), would be taking over one of the most sensitive and crucial investigations into a major terrorist attack. Furthermore, by appropriating the case, the General Prosecutor at the Roman Court of Appeals ensured that no other instructing judge or lower-ranked prosecutor could help with the investigation. By taking over the case, the Roman General Prosecutor ensured that he would be the only legal professional conducting the investigation, in isolation from any other (Imposimato and Provvisionato 2018, 336–337).

Moreover, the Roman General Prosecutor worked on the case in almost complete isolation from the network of prosecutors and instructing judges slowly developing across Italian jurisdictions to defeat the same terrorist organization. Even though prosecutorial authorities in other jurisdictions were amassing an increasing amount of information on the Red Brigades,[7] the so-called Moro 1 case focused solely on the events surrounding Aldo Moro's kidnapping and execution. In other words, the Roman General Prosecutor at the Court of Appeals decided not to extend the investigative focus to the whole scope of Red Brigades' activities in the capital city (Commissione Parlamentare d'Inchiesta sulla Strage di Via Fani, sul Sequestro e l'Assassinio di aldo Moro, e sul Terrorismo in Italia 1990).[8] This was in line with the lack of resources and personnel at the appellate level, where the General Prosecutor was the only individual in charge of investigations (Imposimato and Provvisionato 2018, 337).

The ineffectiveness of Roman prosecutorial authorities' approach to terrorist investigations stands in stark contrast to the work of the Roman instructing judge's office. The latter soon became the driving force behind the successful prosecution of Red Brigades' activities in Rome. This success derived from the different approach that Roman instructing judges applied to terrorism cases in the so-called Moro-bis. Instructing judge Ferdinando Imposimato initiated the latter in 1982, with the intention to extend the scope of the investigation beyond the finding of the Moro 1 case to all Red Brigades terrorist acts in Rome, including Aldo Moro's execution.[9] Prosecutorial authorities in Turin and Milan had adopted this investigative approach first, which conceived of one case as part of a broader operation into a vast criminal phenomenon. This investigative framework represented a huge break from the bureaucratic approach to criminal investigations. As a result, the "Moro-bis" case concerned all Red Brigades criminal activities in Rome from 1976 through 1980,[10] while the following case, the so-called Moro-Ter, examined the whole scope of Red Brigades' activities in Rome from 1978 to 1982 (Scottoni 1988*a*).

Moreover, instructing judge Imposimato shared the investigative and judicial work with his colleague Rosario Priore, therefore creating a small special investigative unit into the Moro cases with another instructing judge. From that moment on, Imposimato and Priore would work cooperatively on all cases into the Red Brigades' activities in Rome, including all five investigations and trials into Moro's killing. The creation of a special investigative unit focusing solely on terrorism cases was also one of the novelties adopted from Milanese prosecutors. The adoption of these new and more effective investigative techniques probably came from Imposimato and Priore's inclusion into the judicial network that had been forming since 1979. Both Turin's prosecutors Gian Carlo Caselli and Milan prosecutor Armando Spataro report the frequent interactions with their Roman colleagues, who regularly attended the meetings held by judicial network participants (Spataro 2016).

As prosecutor Gian Carlo Caselli recalls, interactions promoted information exchanges between Roman judges and the other judicial teams in the network. For instance, the Turin judicial team immediately shared any contribution from confidential informant Patrizio Peci that could be helpful to the Roman judges' investigation into the Red Brigades (Commissione Parlamentare di Inchiesta sul Rapimento e la Morte di Aldo Moro 2015*a*). At the same time, Roman judges in the network provided the Turin team with any relevant information that could complement Peci's account of the Red Brigades' actions in Turin (Commissione Parlamentare di Inchiesta sul Rapimento e la Morte di Aldo Moro 2015*a*). Furthermore, along with the other judicial teams in the network, Roman instructing judges took part in the December 1979 operation against *Autonomia Operaia* that would reveal the existence of a coordinated judicial effort against left-wing terrorist groups to the public (Spataro 2011, 161).

The result of these networking dynamics was the diffusion to the Roman instructing office of those legal and investigative innovations that had already emerged in other Italian jurisdictions. For instance, the so-called Moro-Ter case relied extensively on confidential informants' contributions, which sketched a complex picture of terrorist activities in Rome (Corte di Assise di Roma, October 12, 1988). Through these contributions, instructing judges Imposimato and Priore, with the collaboration of Roman prosecutor Sica, managed to outline the Red Brigades' internal organization (Corte di Assise di Roma, October 12, 1988). As a result, similar to their colleagues working in Milan and Turin, Imposimato and Priore did not limit themselves to identifying the terrorists responsible for Moro's killing, but also the Red Brigades' "directive committee" that commissioned this criminal action.

These astonishing results, however, were confined to the Roman instructing office. In addition to being initially shunned out of terrorism investigations, the Roman prosecutor's office remained essentially insulated from the larger judicial network forming across Italian jurisdictions. Therefore, legal and investigative innovations that could have improved prosecutorial work did not make roots inside the Roman prosecutor's office. This was a consequence of conservative chief prosecutors' preference for a rigid hierarchy within their office. Even if Roman prosecutors had wished to join the judicial network, they could not have done so out of their own initiative. Furthermore, this hierarchical structure stood in stark contrast with the instructing judge's office's internal organization. In his testimony to a Parliamentary Commission, instructing judge Imposimato described his office as "very different from the prosecutor's office" (Commissione Parlamentare di Indagine sul Caso Moro 2015*b*).

More evidence that the prosecutor's office internal hierarchy led to the former's insulation comes from the few tentative interactions with judicial network members. Turin prosecutor Gian Carlo Caselli recalls often interacting with instructing judges Imposimato and Priore, in addition to prosecutor Domenico Sica. Prosecutor Sica enjoyed a place of special prominence within the Roman prosecutor's office. He was a member of that elite circle of prosecutors that had pledged loyalty to chief Gallucci. However, Sica's participation in the judicial network did not lead to the diffusion of legal innovations, such as the creation of special investigative units. The latter, which rely on an equal distribution of labor and equality among peers, were incompatible with the prevalence of a hierarchy among Roman prosecutors.

Moreover, prosecutor Sica's participation in the judicial network did not lead to the diffusion of other novel legal and investigative approaches, which had instead reached the Roman instructing office. This is visible in how Roman prosecutors handled Carlo Fioroni's contributions. A former *Autonomia Operaia* member (158), a left-wing terrorist group, Fioroni was the first one to willingly offer information about the organization to prosecutorial authorities (Spataro 2011, 161). Fioroni provided the information necessary to the December 1979 coordinated operation among judicial network members against the terrorist group. Despite Milanese prosecutors' fruitful use of Fioroni's contributions, in February 1980, Milanese chief prosecutor Gresti decided to hand over Fioroni's case to the Roman prosecutor's office (Spataro 2011, 162). The special investigative unit members opposed their superior's decision. Although the Roman chief prosecutor had not raised jurisdictional issues over this case, it had nonetheless started investigating the same defendants. Gresti decided to hand over the entirety of the investigation to Rome to pre-emptively avoid possible jurisdictional controversies with the Roman office (Spataro 2011, 162).

The subsequent handling of the Fioroni case shows Roman prosecutors' lack of knowledge in the use of legal innovations, such as plea bargaining, which Milanese prosecutors had instead deployed successfully, as I show in chapter 4. Most of the trial stemming from Fioroni's contributions revolved around the latter's trustworthiness, which defendants' legal counsel brought into question (see *Giudici, I Pentiti Non Sono Credibili* 1984; *Per l'Omicidio Saronio Dovete Assolvere Negri con la Formula Piena* 1984). Moreover, on appeal, key defendants in the case received a significant reduction in their final sentences, therefore weakening the overall judicial effort against the Red Brigades and *Autonomia Operaia* (Spataro 2011, 163). Thus, the transfer of the case from Milan to Rome may have resulted in this investigation's failure, due to Roman prosecutors' inability to implement important legal innovations, such as plea bargaining.

The hierarchical structure regulating professional relationships within the Roman prosecutor's office blocked the diffusion of legal innovations among its members. This insulation had profound effects on the development of prosecutorial work not only on terrorism cases but also on later investigations into corruption. While prosecutors in Milan and Palermo were developing essential skills to tackle complex corruption cases, Roman prosecutors were lagging behind in their understanding of investigative techniques such as plea bargaining, joint investigations, and special investigation units. This lack of expertise fundamentally weakened Roman prosecutorial authorities' contribution to Clean Hands. Even when Roman prosecutors could finally join in this anti-corruption campaign, their lack of expertise undermined their efforts to prosecute systemic corruption successfully.

In the following sections, I examine the Roman prosecutor's office reaction to the Clean Hands operation. First, I show that Roman authorities' suspension of prosecutorial gatekeeping allowed the Clean Hands investigation to move forward. Second, I show that the enduring lack of expertise among Roman prosecutors hindered the successful emulation of the Clean Hands operation within their jurisdiction.

THE CLEAN HANDS OPERATION AND THE SUSPENSION OF PROSECUTORIAL GATEKEEPING

The beginning of the 1990s marked the end of the conservative legal community's control over the Roman chief prosecutor's office. As I previously showed, the appointment of a moderate chief prosecutor, Vittorio Mele, and then a progressive chief prosecutor, Michele Coiro, brought to the reorganization of the Roman office. Crucially, Mele's appointment also brought to the suspension of prosecutorial gatekeeping at a vital moment for the fate of corruption prosecutions: the start of the Clean Hands operation. Therefore, the appointment of prosecutorial authorities without any loyalty to legal conservatism led to significant institutional changes that removed the obstacles to corruption prosecutions.

Mele's association with UniCost set him apart from the interests and preferences of the conservative community. As I discussed earlier, conservative chief prosecutors had been using prosecutorial gatekeeping to have salient investigations into political actors and state agents transferred to their jurisdiction. In this section, I show that Mele's suspension of prosecutorial gatekeeping effectively allowed the Clean Hands operation to unfold without interference from the Roman office. Thus, the suspension of prosecutorial gatekeeping explains why the effective prosecution of systemic prosecution could finally occur in 1992.

The suspension of prosecutorial gatekeeping did not entail the absolute absence of jurisdictional disputes. The latter, however, resulted from the lack of legal expertise among Roman prosecutors and their inability to emulate their peers in the application of new investigative techniques and legal interpretation. Roman prosecutors' traditional understanding of corruption crimes and criminal procedure rules set the Roman jurisdiction on a collision course with their Milanese peers leading the Clean Hands operation. Nevertheless, chief prosecutor Mele's favorable attitude toward criminal accountability made it possible to resolve these jurisdictional issues through cooperation rather than prosecutorial gatekeeping.

Chief Mele's unwillingness to appropriate corruption cases via prosecutorial gatekeeping caught defendants and legal actors by surprise, given the

Roman office's previous interventions in similar investigations. In August 1992, for instance, Mele refused to claim jurisdiction over the ongoing corruption investigation against prominent members of the Italian Socialist Party unfolding in Venice (*De Michelis e Bernini Roma Non Avochera'* 1992), as part of what has been labeled the "Venetian Mani Pulite," or the equivalent local version of the Clean Hands operation. Lawyers for the defendants had raised the jurisdictional issue, claiming that the Roman prosecutor's office should oversee the investigation (*De Michelis e Bernini Roma Non Avochera'* 1992). This was probably a strategic choice on the part of the defendants' legal counsel. Given Roman prosecutors' established pattern of interventions in politically salient investigations, lawyers in the case were hoping for the use of prosecutorial gatekeeping. However, Mele rejected the defense counsel's arguments and affirmed the Venetian prosecutors' jurisdiction over the case (*De Michelis e Bernini Roma Non Avochera'* 1992).[11]

More importantly, Mele also refused to pursue prosecutorial gatekeeping against the ongoing Clean Hands operation. As I explain in the following chapter, through an impressive chain of incriminating testimonies by company managers and corrupt politicians, the scope of the Milanese investigation rapidly broadened beyond its original jurisdiction. Local bribe exchanges between different actors gradually appeared to be part of a national corruption scheme, involving party leaders and cabinet members as much as companies working across Italian regions. The gradual discovery of pervasive and systemic corruption transcending single regions or cities prompted prosecutorial authorities in other jurisdictions than Milan to initiate similar corruption investigations (Di Pietro 2017). This inevitably raised potential jurisdictional issues.

Defendants and lawyers in the Clean Hands investigation saw in this jurisdictional issue an opportunity to invite the intervention of the Roman prosecutor's office. For this reason, in September 1992, legal counsel for the defendants accused of bribe exchanges for the Rome metro system's construction raised the jurisdictional issue. Although evidence of these criminal exchanges had emerged in the context of the Clean Hands operation, defendants were alleged to have taken part in these illicit exchanges in the capital city (*Sulle Mazzette Romane Non Deve Indagare Di Pietro* 1992). Therefore, the defense argued that only the Roman prosecutor's office held jurisdiction over this investigation (*Sulle Mazzette Romane Non Deve Indagare Di Pietro* 1992).

Faced with the request to examine this issue, however, chief prosecutor Mele did not reply with a clear assertion of Rome's jurisdictional primacy over the case. Instead, he fostered informal collaboration between the two jurisdictions. Prosecutor Di Pietro, the leading prosecutor in the Clean Hands team, first visited Rome in October 1992. During his visit to the capital, Di

Pietro met with local law enforcement and had arrested seven individuals under investigation in the Clean Hands operation (*Da ieri Di Pietro Indaga a Roma* 1992). Di Pietro was scheduled to meet with chief prosecutor Mele and his subordinates (*Da ieri Di Pietro Indaga a Roma* 1992). As a result of this and other meetings, Rome and Milan started showing a cooperative attitude on several corruption cases as a result of a tacit deal on jurisdictional matters between the two offices (Colaprico and Fazzo 1992). This new cooperative attitude stood in contrast with past practices between Rome and Milan. As opposed to previous instances in which Roman authorities formally raised jurisdictional claims against Milanese prosecutors, the two offices were now refusing to follow this legal procedure over possible dissents and instead opting to resolve their jurisdictional conflicts via informal communications (Neppi Modona 1993).

An alternative explanation to the emergence of cooperation between Milan and Rome could be the introduction of the new code of criminal procedure in 1989. One could argue that this vast criminal procedure reform might have introduced new incentives to cooperation among prosecutors' offices. However, past interactions between Rome and other jurisdictions demonstrate otherwise. For instance, the *Gladio* case, which unfolded immediately after the introduction of the new code of criminal procedure, did not show any increase in cooperation between Rome and the other jurisdictions leading this investigation. On the contrary, as I previously showed, chief Giudiceandrea did not hesitate to deploy prosecutorial gatekeeping to appropriate the *Gladio* case, despite the new norms in the code of criminal procedure. Thus, it was chief prosecutor Mele's favorable attitude toward cooperation that brought to the coordinated efforts between Milanese and Roman prosecutors.

Chief Mele's decision to suspend prosecutorial gatekeeping was therefore crucial to the success of the Clean Hands operation. Without the Roman prosecutor's office raising jurisdictional issues in order to appropriate investigations, Milanese prosecutors could move forward with their work and uncover critical nodes in the corruption system that had remained in the dark for decades. This is particularly visible in the inquiries surrounding, once again, the Swiss bank account known as *Conto Protezione*. With the suspension of prosecutorial gatekeeping, favorable conditions were now in place for Milanese prosecutors to shed light on this node in the corruption scheme.

One of the many cases included in the Clean Hands operation concerned bribe exchanges for the Milan metro system's construction and revolved around Silvano Larini's collaboration. The latter had worked as a civil servant within the Milan city administration and had a clear affiliation with the Italian Socialist Party. After offering his cooperation to the Clean Hands prosecutorial team, Larini went well beyond describing the bribe exchanges connected to the Milan metro system. Larini provided a complete account of the nature and purposes of the Swiss bank account *Conto Protezione* (Colaprico and Fazzo 1993). As a result of Larini's testimony, in May 1993, the Clean Hands prosecutorial team finally managed to uncover how Socialist Party members had been wiring illegal payments through the *Conto Protezione* for decades (Colombo 2010, 100).

Larini's confession supplied the information that Milanese prosecutors could have obtained ten years earlier from Swiss authorities, had it not been for the Roman prosecutor's office use of prosecutorial gatekeeping. Ten years later, and this time under Vittorio Mele's direction, the Roman prosecutor's office did not show any willingness to pursue the same strategy against the Clean Hands operation. Larini's confession, along with any other documentary proof concerning the nature of the *Conto Protezione*, remained firmly under the control of Milanese prosecutors.

Further evidence that chief prosecutor Mele intended to suspend prosecutorial gatekeeping was his handling of the *Enimont* case. This case represented a relevant portion of the Clean Hands investigation, involving politicians from all political parties (including new formations, such as the Northern League Party) and a multi-billion merger between a publicly owned company, *Montedison*, and the private company *Eni* (Barbacetto, Gomez and Travaglio 2012, 177). As for many other cases involving high-scale corruption, defendants in the *Enimont* case resided in different jurisdictions, and the crimes (namely the agreement on and factual exchange of bribes) had also occurred across jurisdictions. The *Enimont* case exemplifies Mele's attitude toward relationships with other offices. Rather than affirming Rome's primacy over the case, Mele willingly delivered the whole file of evidence collected by Roman prosecutors to Milan, at the request of Milan's chief prosecutor Borrelli (D'Avanzo 1993). This decision came as a complete reversal of previous trends, particularly given the salience of the *Enimont* case.

As these examples detail, Mele's attitude cleared the way for the *Mani Pulite* prosecutorial team to pursue the full scope of their investigation unobstructed. As one of the *Mani Pulite* prosecutors remarked:

> Why did the Rome chief prosecutor's office not take action [against us] when we pursued the *Mani Pulite* investigation? Undoubtedly it was because there had been a change of personnel within this office. (Interview with Clean Hands prosecutor, phone, April 24, 2016).

Mele's behavior also contradicts the expectations of the attitudinal model. Based on his affiliation with a moderately progressive, "centrist" judicial association, UniCost (Coppola 1992*b*), we should expect Mele to deploy his gatekeeping powers to appropriate and control the unfolding of the Clean

Hands operation, which overwhelmingly targeted center-left political forces. On the contrary, Mele actively cooperated with Milanese prosecutors.

Although Mele ceased to pursue prosecutorial gatekeeping, the long-lasting lack of legal expertise among his subordinates still led the Roman office into a jurisdictional controversy with their Milanese peers. In the following section, I explore the effects of this lack of expertise among Roman prosecutors on their attempted emulation of the Clean Hands operation.

LACK OF EXPERTISE AND INEFFECTIVE CORRUPTION PROSECUTIONS IN ROME

As I previously mentioned, chief Mele's suspension of prosecutorial gatekeeping, which paved the way for the unencumbered unfolding of the Clean Hands investigation, might remain the most significant contribution of the Roman office to this anti-corruption effort. The lack of expertise among Roman prosecutors created by the office's previous hierarchical organization undermined their efforts to emulate Clean Hands prosecutors' work. Even when Roman prosecutors could finally pursue corruption investigations undeterred from their superior, previous hierarchical control had left them without the legal expertise necessary to handle complex corruption prosecutions. As a result, the number of corruption convictions within the Roman jurisdiction remained significantly lower than those in Milan.

The first corruption investigation to occur in Rome after the start of the Clean Hands operation unfolded almost by accident: a civil lawsuit over an inheritance uncovered documents detailing the payment of bribes to the Ministry of Finance over the selling of real estate properties (Scuteri 1992). Soon thereafter, police reports uncovered false accounting and fraud occurring at a publicly owned company, Safim (Scottoni 1992*b*). Both investigations had the potential to open similar lines of inquiry as those in the Clean Hands operation. The payment of bribes in exchange for public contracts and the selling of goods to government entities were at the center of the Milanese prosecutors' investigative efforts.

Chief prosecutor Mele was initially hesitant toward creating special investigative units working exclusively on corruption cases, and this resulted in an initial delay in these units' formation (Sarzanini 1992). However, Mele soon changed direction and decided to form special investigative units similar to the Clean Hands team in response to his subordinates' requests (Mastrogiacomo 1993). Mele eventually established a team of fifteen prosecutors to investigate all cases related to bribe exchanges for public contracts with the publicly owned company ANAS (*Anas, Una Nuova 'Bomba' Scoppia su Tangentopoli* 1993). This represented a meaningful change from the past. Chief

Mele established the investigative unit in response to pressure coming from his subordinates, who wished to focus on corruption cases (Mastrogiacomo 1993). Therefore, the establishment of a special investigative unit within the Roman prosecutor's office shows how the diffusion of legal innovations follows from an egalitarian approach to professional relationships.

Nevertheless, chief Mele was hesitant to present this development as an attempt to emulate Milanese investigative practices. Rather, the purpose of this investigative unit was to "set uniform rules" for prosecutors working jointly on corruption cases (Sarzanini 1992). Regardless of his actual intentions, chief Mele's favorable disposition toward a more egalitarian organization of his office paved the way to emulation: Roman prosecutors were finally allowed to adopt the same investigative structure currently in use in the Clean Hands operation. However, the establishment of a special investigative unit was not enough to make up for the enduring lack of legal expertise among Roman prosecutors brought about by the office's past insulation from the judicial network. This is visible in Roman prosecutors' legal approach to corruption cases, which differed greatly from their Milanese peers in the Clean Hands operation.

The most fundamental differences in legal interpretation between Rome and Milan revolved around the nature of the corruption system itself. The Clean Hands investigation relied on an understanding of corruption as an "environmental condition." This novel conceptualization implied that both sides in a bribe exchange were equally guilty and that possible coercion into a corrupt exchange did not alleviate the participants' criminal responsibility. As I explain in chapter 4, this interpretation of criminal rules facilitated the informal adoption of plea bargains in corruption cases. On the other hand, Roman prosecutors disagreed with this interpretation of criminal rules. They continued considering businessmen and company managers, the bribe-givers in the exchange, as "victims" of the system, forcefully dragged into illicit tradeoffs by the political class. As a result, in most cases, Roman prosecutors pressed charges of *concussione*, the Italian legal term for forceful participation in corruption on the part of the bribe-giver.

This traditional understanding of corruption fundamentally undermined the effectiveness of prosecutions within the Roman jurisdiction. Milanese prosecutors' innovative conceptualization of corruption crimes had helped them obtain plea deals and incriminating testimonies, becoming the driving force behind the Clean Hands operation's success. On the contrary, Roman prosecutors' choice to apply the traditional interpretation of criminal norms resulted in a lack of cooperating defendants. Therefore, while the Clean Hands investigation rapidly expanded because of the revelations from the actors involved, Roman investigations into corruption remained fairly limited. As a compounding factor, Roman prosecutors lacked the legal expertise necessary to exploit plea bargains and testimonies' contributions effectively, as demonstrated by their handling of previous terrorism cases.

Furthermore, Roman prosecutors' lack of expertise sometimes put them on a collision course with their Milanese peers, due to their differing interpretation of criminal rules. As I previously showed, Roman prosecutors considered bribe givers' participation in corrupt exchanges to be the result of coercion. For this reason, Roman prosecutors would often call businessmen and company managers to testify at trial as victims with relevant knowledge of the crime, rather than treating them as defendants (Ravelli 1993). However, the Clean Hands team would often investigate the same individuals as co-perpetrators of a crime (Ravelli 1993). Therefore, differences in the application of criminal rules could create discrepancies that might endanger the development of one or the other investigation. The chain of incriminating testimonies that helped Clean Hands prosecutors uncover the corruption system resulted from a classic "prisoner's dilemma" (Sberna and Vannucci 2013, 576). The possibility that the same individuals might be considered witnesses rather than co-perpetrators in another jurisdiction could endanger the sequence of interactions between defendants and prosecutorial authorities that produced this chain of testimonies.

The different applications of criminal rules between Milan and Rome revitalized jurisdictional controversies between these offices. Milanese prosecutors argued that all cases and investigations concerning different parts of the corruption system should fall within the Milan jurisdiction. Clean Hands prosecutors built their argument around the existence of one complex criminal scheme, holding together different corruption instances. On the other hand, Roman prosecutors continued considering bribe-givers as victims of corruption rather than co-perpetrators. Therefore, they argued that these individuals' involvement in bribery lacked that "conspiratorial" element necessary for the existence of one grand criminal scheme connecting all corruption instances.

The conflict between these opposing views is visible in the ANAS cases, involving bribes to the publicly owned company overseeing infrastructure projects. Milan prosecutors argued that their jurisdiction extended to all investigations concerning the offer of bribes to ANAS, since they all pertained to the same "criminal scheme" (Scottoni 1993). On the other hand, Roman prosecutors argued that the guiding principle to decide jurisdiction should be the "connection to the most serious crime." This principle would have moved all or most investigations to Rome (Scottoni 1993).

Once more, however, Mele appeared to behave differently than his predecessors in relation to jurisdictional matters. Chief prosecutor Mele sought to address the jurisdictional issue in the ANAS case through cooperation with Milan judicial actors (Scottoni 1993). Despite the manifest attempts at collaboration, however, the institutional conflict eventually ended up before the Court of Cassation. The latter assigned jurisdiction over a couple of major cases to the Roman jurisdiction. Commenting on the Court of Cassation's decision, Mele argued that Milan's position, which the Court had rejected, was based on the "subjective connection" between corruption cases (D'Avanzo 1993). In other words, Milanese prosecutors and judges had based their jurisdictional claim on the involvement of the same individuals across investigations, which suggested the existence of a grand corruption scheme. On the contrary, Rome's interpretation, which the Court of Cassation affirmed in the case, was premised on the place in which the single occurrence of a bribe exchange occurred (D'Avanzo 1993).

Despite the resolution of the issue in favor of the Roman office, this conflict did not represent a new instance of prosecutorial gatekeeping. Instead, this partial setback to the Clean Hands operation resulted from Milanese prosecutors' novel interpretation of criminal rules and Roman prosecutors' corresponding attachment to the traditional interpretation of the same provisions. The Court of Cassation was not ready to receive and formalize Milanese prosecutors' new understanding of jurisdictional issues in its jurisprudence. When discussing this jurisdictional conflict between Rome and Milan, prosecutor Di Pietro recognized that Roman authorities were not pursuing prosecutorial gatekeeping, but rather acting on a traditional understanding of criminal procedure. On the other hand, he also underscored how legal counsel for the defendants might have pushed this jurisdictional issue for strategic reasons:

> The criminal procedure code establishes that trials should be held in the place where the crime took place. However, the code also foresees the possibility of "interconnected crimes" whereby the connection is the presence of the same defendant across places [. . .] Rome raised a procedural issue because the crimes were committed within its jurisdiction, the defendants exchanged bribes within its jurisdiction. There was no jealousy, no anger, or malice on the part of Roman prosecutorial authorities raising this issue. Instead, they pursued a legal matter that the defendants' legal counsels had first raised in an attempt to prolong the length of trials and reach the statute of limitations. I have to be honest, in procedural terms, [Roman authorities] were right. At a practical level, however, [this legal issue] had negative consequences. (Di Pietro 2017)[12]

Overall, under the leadership of chief Mele first and chief Coiro later, the Roman prosecutor's office did not attempt to interfere with the Clean Hands investigation. Rather, the Roman office tried to emulate its Milanese counterpart in the fight against corruption without achieving the same level of effectiveness. Nevertheless, one cannot deny the presence of a few "rotten apples" who actively worked against anti-corruption efforts within their own office. Some Roman prosecutors deployed a traditional understanding of corruption not out of genuine belief but "strategically" to derail and sabotage ongoing investigations.

Prosecutor Antonino Vinci and prosecutor Orazio Savia had played a major role in leading the inquiries into real estate property sales to the Ministry of Finance, the so-called Golden Buildings case, as well as some corruption investigations into ANAS. Later, it became known that prosecutor Orazio Savia had received bribes to have salient investigations, like the *Enimont* case, transferred to Rome from Milan (*Savia nei Guai per Trecento Milioni della Tangente Enimont* 1997). Savia's attempt was futile, since, as I discussed earlier in this section, chief Mele decided to transfer the whole *Enimont* case to the Milan prosecutor's office. Vinci and Savia strongly argued that defendants in these cases, particularly company managers, were victims of the corruption system (Milella 1998*a*). Therefore, they pressed charges of *concussione* instead of *corruzione*, ensuring that some of the company managers and politicians in the case would be acquitted (Milella 1998*a*).[13] However, several of their attempts ended up in failure. For instance, the Roman prosecutor's office later decided to re-try the "Golden Buildings" case on charges of *corruzione* (Mastrogiacomo 1998), subverting Vinci's prosecutorial framework.

Even though prosecutors Vinci and Savia's efforts to undermine corruption investigations failed, their actions brought the end of chief Michele Coiro's tenure. Under Coiro's leadership, the Roman prosecutor's office continued its cooperation with the Clean Hands investigative unit. However, Coiro had also developed a trusted relationship with prosecutors Savia and Vinci and the latter had used this bond for the purpose of hindering specific corruption investigations. When the Caltagirone brothers, powerful businessmen secretly funding prosecutors Savia and Vinci (Milella 1998*b*), became the subject of a corruption investigation in Milan, Vinci convinced his superior to use the office's gatekeeping powers to appropriate the investigation (Barbacetto, Gomez and Travaglio 2012, 679). Coiro eventually raised a jurisdictional claim, and the case was transferred to Rome (Barbacetto, Gomez and Travaglio 2012, 679). Although no criminal proceedings were opened against chief Coiro, the High Council initiated an inquiry for possible violations of ethical rules (Mastrogiacomo 1996*b*). Before the Council could make a decision, Coiro received a promotion to a different judicial post, therefore avoiding a formal removal order (Bellu 1996).

CONCLUSION

The case study of the Roman prosecutor's office allowed me to explore the effect of different organizational structures on prosecutorial independence and effectiveness. Conservative prosecutorial authorities implemented a hierarchical structure of professional relationships within the Roman office for decades. Through this hierarchical structure, they could closely oversee their subordinates and direct their work. This informal hierarchy deprived lower-ranked prosecutors of a say in the handling of cases. Furthermore, hierarchical structures left a long-lasting legacy. Above all, they insulated Roman prosecutors from the diffusion of legal innovations via informal judicial networks. As a result, Roman prosecutors lacked the necessary preparation to join in the rising wave of corruption cases sparked by the Clean Hands operation. Consequently, despite the several interactions between Milanese and Roman prosecutors, this cooperation did not translate into a comparable number of appellate corruption convictions within the Roman jurisdiction, one of the central nodes in the corruption system.

Furthermore, via prosecutorial gatekeeping, Roman chief prosecutors managed to appropriate several investigations targeting public officials' wrongdoing in other jurisdictions, such as Milan and Venice. Several of these investigations concluded with few convictions. Thus, conservative chief prosecutors' control of this crucial node in the Italian criminal justice system helps explain the absence of effective corruption investigations until 1992. As I showed in this chapter, the appointment of moderate and progressive prosecutors to the Roman office eventually brought to the suspension of prosecutorial gatekeeping. The latter removed a key obstacle to the effective deployment of prosecutorial powers against public officials, namely the Roman office's intervention. The suspension of prosecutorial gatekeeping allowed the Clean Hands operation to unfold undisturbed and finally uncover the corruption system. Thus, the case study of the Roman prosecutor's office powerfully demonstrates the effect of prosecutorial gatekeeping on corruption prosecutions.

While the Roman prosecutor's office shows the effects of hierarchical structures over prosecutorial institutions, in the following chapter, I explore the effects of egalitarian structures over a different prosecutorial institution: the Milan prosecutor's office. The latter's interactions with the Roman office, which I reported in this chapter, show Milanese prosecutors to be very different in comparison to their Roman counterparts in terms of prosecutorial assertiveness and legal expertise. In the following chapter, I explore the conditions that brought the Milan prosecutor's office to the center of the fight against systemic corruption.

NOTES

1. It is well known that some Christian Democrats had attempted to create a channel of influence over the Roman prosecutor's office. Roman judge Claudio Vitalone,

for instance, used any means of influence, including unethical and illicit ones, to sway legal proceedings in favor of his political patron, senator Giulio Andreotti, one of the most influential Christian Democratic leaders (Della Porta 2001, 8).

2. Table 3.2 highlights the role of elected Council members and politically appointed Council members in choosing chief prosecutors. The Council also includes, by law, the President of the Republic and the General Prosecutor at the Roman Court of Appeals.

3. In most civil law countries, like Italy, instructing judges perform similar functions as prosecutors. More specifically, they supervise investigations and contribute to assembling the evidence that the prosecution will use at trial to make its case.

4. The comment sounds odd, given Italy's parliamentary system and the designation of the prime minister (commonly called "premier" in Italian political jargon) as the head of the executive branch. At the same time, the President of the Republic is the official head of state, and the judge presumably meant to highlight Milanese judges' alleged self-importance and inappropriateness in interfering with matters outside their institutional purview. Author's translation.

5. The development of the first Moro investigation is visible in its legal documents, which have been collected and made accessible by the Parliamentary Commission set up to examine the Moro cases. Volume LII contains the documents formally transferring the investigation to the General Prosecutor at the Court of Appeals (Commissione Parlamentare d'Inchiesta sulla Strage di Via Fani, sul Sequestro e l'Assassinio di aldo Moro, e sul Terrorismo in Italia 1990).

6. As I illustrated in chapter 1, in Italy every level of judicial review is coupled with a prosecutor's office.

7. Turin prosecutor Gian Carlo Caselli explained that his special investigative unit had obtained critical information about the Red Brigades from confidential informant and former Red Brigades leader Patrizio Peci (Commissione Parlamentare di Inchiesta sul Rapimento e sulla Morte di Aldo Moro 2015*a*).

8. Although the General Prosecutor did examine the Red Brigades' ideological profile and organizational evolution in his inquiry, the latter did not extend to criminal activities beyond Aldo Moro's killing.

9. This approach is visible in the Court of Appeal's ruling on the first two Moro cases, the so-called Moro 1 and Moro-bis. The appellate ruling mentions the Red Brigades' activities in Rome before and after the Moro killing, from 1976 to 1980, which Priore and Imposimato described thanks to former terrorists' contributions (Corte di Assise di Appello di Roma March 14, 1985, p. 42).

10. The scope of the case is visible at the outset of the Court of Appeals ruling on the Moro bis case (Corte di Assise di Appello di Roma March 14, 1985, p. 42).

11. Furthermore, the case represented an even more accurate parallel with opposite decisions previously made by Mele's predecessors. The team of Venetian prosecutors investigating Socialist Party members included some of the same prosecutors working on the *Gladio* case years before.

12. Di Pietro argued that the fragmentation and transfer of some cases to the Rome jurisdiction negatively impacted the overall prosecutorial effort against corruption (Di Pietro 2017).

13. Both prosecutors had strong ties with some of the most prominent businessmen in Rome, particularly the powerful real estate broker (and owner of the most important Roman newspaper, *Il Messaggero*) Francesco Gaetano Caltagirone and his brother Leonardo. Along with businessman Domenico Bonifaci, the Caltagirone brothers used their money and influence to buy prosecutors Vinci and Savia's loyalty (Milella 1998*b*).

Chapter 4

A New Model of Criminal Justice

The Milan Prosecutor's Office

In the previous chapter, I discussed the effects of hierarchical structures over the Roman prosecutor's office and the prosecution of systemic corruption. The Milan prosecutor's office, on the other hand, shows how the early adoption of egalitarian organizational structures created the conditions for the uncovering of complex criminal phenomena, from terrorism to pervasive corruption. In the years following re-democratization, the Milanese legal community, which had remained peripheral and marginal until then, mobilized in favor of profound institutional changes to the Italian judicial system. This mobilization revealed this legal community's profound adherence to a new democratic culture, rooted in the values of the new Constitution and standing in stark contrast to Italian legal positivism's hierarchical attitudes.

Milanese judicial professionals' vocal adherence to new constitutional values had significant implications for this jurisdiction's prosecutorial institution. First of all, it translated into the appointments of chief prosecutors respectful of this community's legal preferences for the whole period considered in this chapter, from 1975 to 1996. Milanese chief prosecutors consistently structured professional relationships with their subordinates along egalitarian lines. The introduction of egalitarian decision-making enhanced lower-ranked prosecutors' independence, allowing them to pursue bold legal and investigative novelties. For instance, during investigations into left-wing terrorist groups, such as the Red Brigades and First Line, at the end of the 1970s, Milanese prosecutors helped develop the first attempt at plea bargaining within the Italian legal system. Furthermore, the presence of an egalitarian structure allowed Milanese prosecutors to transfer the use of this and other legal innovations to another pressing criminal phenomenon, namely corruption. The P2 investigation was a first test of several legal tools and investigative methods that would lead to the uncovering of systemic corruption ten years later, in the *Mani Pulite* operation.

Milanese prosecutors' enhanced independence, fostered by an egalitarian structure of professional relationships, led to several attempts at uncovering pervasive corruption over the years. However, as I showed in chapter 3, the Roman office's use of prosecutorial gatekeeping stood in the way of its Milanese counterpart's efforts on this issue. Eventually, the enduring presence of corruption and the repeated failed attempts at uncovering it led Milanese prosecutors to embrace a new form of judicial activism, which I explore in this chapter. Through a novel interpretation of extant criminal rules and the creation of a new legal concept, *dazione ambientale*, Clean Hands prosecutors created an informal plea-bargaining process around corruption charges that lacked textual support in the criminal procedure code. As I explain in this chapter, this represents a clear instance of judicial activism where judicial professionals filled a legislative vacuum via a creative interpretation of extant rules (Kmiec 2004). The latter resulted in the creation of new, judicially made legal procedures.

In this chapter, I show how judicial activism against corruption emerged among Milanese prosecutors. This also allows me to explore the development of a new judicial ethos among Milanese judicial professionals, with a stronger focus on ethical conduct and civic duty toward the public. This new ethos derived from judicial involvement in anti-corruption mobilization among local civil society, whose driving force was an organization by the name of *Società Civile*. This organization's focus on anti-corruption mobilization provided Milanese prosecutors with a venue to present their new activist interpretation of criminal rules regarding corruption. Furthermore, Milanese judicial professionals' interactions with *Società Civile* also led to the formation of a new judicial association, called *Movimento per la Giustizia*. Thus, in this chapter, I show how Milanese judicial professionals' relationship with *Società Civile* led to a renewed sense of civic commitment and a more radical understanding of their independence from political influences.

In what follows, I first examine the Milanese judicial community's legal culture immediately after re-democratization. I show that the local progressive legal community grew so rapidly in its strength that it obtained the appointment of sympathetic chief prosecutors to the Milanese office in the mid-1970s. I then explore how these prosecutorial appointments led to the establishment of egalitarian decision-making within the Milan office. My analysis proceeds to show how this egalitarian structure promoted both the emergence and diffusion of investigative innovations among Milanese prosecutors, first on terrorism cases and later on corruption investigations. I then analyze Milanese prosecutors' involvement in local civil society organizations and how the latter promoted the emergence of a new sense of civic duty among judicial professionals. Finally, I examine how a new, activist interpretation of criminal rules, along with Milanese prosecutors' accumulated expertise and significant independence, were at the root of the *Mani Pulite* operation's unprecedented success. In doing so, throughout this chapter, I also address an alternative hypothesis to my argument, specifically the application of the attitudinal model (Segal and Spaeth 2002) to corruption investigations.

THE PROGRESSIVE LEGAL CULTURE OF THE MILANESE JUDICIARY

In the years following the end of World War II, the Milanese legal community showed a strong adherence to the democratic legal culture that would inform the new constitutional text. While the Constituent Assembly worked on the text of the new founding document, Milanese judges and prosecutors decided to issue a document detailing what they considered to be the most critical institutional reforms to the Italian judicial system. This short "manifesto," issued in 1946, provides precious insights into the Milanese judiciary's legal culture. In their declaration, Milanese judicial professionals asked the National Judicial Association (ANM) to dismantle the system of evaluations that regulated promotions and appointments, allowing higher-court judges to rule over the lower ranks (Moriondo 1967, 266).

This declaration presented the new and invigorated democratic culture that had taken hold in this peripheral jurisdiction, which stood in stark contrast to the ANM's persistent legal positivism. By petitioning the ANM to remove the system of evaluations, Milanese prosecutors were advocating for an end to the hierarchical principle and higher-court judges' control. This institutional reform, which would only occur in the 1970s, entailed the redistribution of power downward – or decentralization – as I called this process in chapters 1 and 2. In other words, this type of institutional restructuring would allow lower-ranked judges more leeway and independence from their superiors' scrutiny. Thus, the Milanese judicial community's proposal manifested a new understanding of the judicial profession, counter to legal positivism's rigid emphasis on hierarchical control.

This short manifesto clearly outlined the significant ideational changes that had taken place in the Milanese judicial community. While the national leadership of the ANM stood by legal positivism's central tenets, including a hierarchical approach to the structure of the judicial system, Milanese judges manifested a new inclination toward more democratic principles. The content of the Milanese proposal to the ANM echoed a more egalitarian understanding of the judicial profession, where lower-ranked professionals enjoyed increasing independence from their superiors. The Milanese proposal was only one of many peripheral judicial communities' petitions for a more egalitarian justice system. In a couple of years, what had started as a simple spark turned into a fire that the ANM could hardly put out. The Milanese judicial community played a central role in the mounting wave of protests against the dominant legal conservative faction and the latter's vision for the judicial institution.

This judicial mobilization gained strength with the 1956 ANM General Assembly, which took place in Milan. The ANM met with the Minister of Justice to discuss new legislative provisions that would improve judicial professionals' economic status as state employees (Moriondo 1967, 275–276). The government's refusal to adjust judicial salaries to current inflation rates was hitting younger judicial professionals harder than their senior counterparts (1967, 277). The 1956 ANM Assembly brought fuel to this controversy. In this instance, the Milanese judicial community attempted to pass a resolution that would put the judiciary and the current Italian government at odds with each other on the issue (1967, 280). The ANM leadership, where conservative judicial professionals were still the majority, prevented this resolution from ever becoming public (1967, 280). This did not stop the Milanese community from becoming the leading force behind the mounting judicial protests.

As I explained in chapter 2, the institutional reforms necessary to implement decentralization would only occur in the mid-1970s. However, the Milanese judicial community's role in this mobilization speaks to the increasing consensus around a new democratic culture within this jurisdiction. When decentralization finally came to completion in 1975 and the principles first advocated by Milanese judicial professionals became a reality, even the appointments to the Milanese chief prosecutor's office started reflecting this community's legal culture.

As opposed to the Roman prosecutor's office, the Milan office remained relatively peripheral in terms of its political relevance. Despite local judicial professionals' mobilization, the Milan prosecutor's office remained mostly unimportant in the eyes of national politicians and members of the judicial profession, given its lack of gatekeeping powers. Therefore, as opposed to appointments to the Roman prosecutor's office, the selection of Milanese chief prosecutors did not attract the same attention, nor was it as contentious as the selection to the Roman office. As a result, starting in 1975, Milanese chief prosecutors closely reflected the preferences of the local legal community they had been called to work in.

The close alignment between the Milanese chief prosecutor's office and the local legal community's preferences is visible in this office's remarkable stability. From 1974 to 1996, the Milan prosecutor's office changed its head only three times. Table 4.1 provides information on Milanese chief prosecutors' background and affiliation with judicial associations.

While Giuseppe Micale and Mauro Gresti did not openly belong to any judicial association, their previous appointments speak to their legal background and deeply held legal convictions. Before being appointed to the Milan chief prosecutor's office in 1972, Giuseppe Micale had been an appellate judge in Trento. Therefore, Micale had held the status of higher-court judge at a moment in which judicial professionals belonging to this elite group still showed a persistent sense of loyalty toward Italian legal positivism. The *Unione Magistrati Italiani* (UMI), the judicial association representing higher-court judges, had formed in 1961 to defend the justice system's hierarchical structure and the privileged status of higher-court judges (Guarnieri 2003, 103). Although Micale was not affiliated with UMI, his previous role as a higher-court judge is indicative of his plausible adherence to the traditionally conservative mindset shared by a majority of his peers.

Indeed, Micale's strong adherence to Italian legal positivism prompted vocal protests among his Milanese subordinates, protests that eventually brought to his ousting in 1976. In a note issued by the Milanese branch of the ANM in 1974, Milanese prosecutors lamented the state of the office under Micale, which reflected the enduring presence of authoritarian practices: "Thirty years after the end of the Fascist regime, the Fascist judicial system (*ordinamento giudiziario fascista*) is still in place" (*I Magistrati Accusano il Procuratore Micale* 1974, 7). Micale, who had entered the judicial profession in 1935 (*La "Guerra" tra Micale e i Suoi Sostituti* 1975, 8), did not question the legacy of these authoritarian practices, such as chief prosecutors' absolute control over their subordinates' work and career. Instead, he worked to implement this authoritarian legacy within the Milan prosecutor's office, as I discuss later in this chapter.

As it appears from table 4.1, Mauro Gresti also did not belong to any judicial association, although he seemed to show some proximity to MI, the legally conservative association (*Il Dottor Mauro Gresti Nominato*

Table 4.1 Milan Chief Prosecutors' Profiles

	Giuseppe Micale (1972)	*Mauro Gresti (1975)*	*Francesco Saverio Borrelli (1988)*
Associational Affiliation	None	Proximity to *Magistratura Indipendente* (MI)	Former member of *Magistratura Democratica* (MD)
Previous Appointment	Appellate judge in Trento	Prosecutor at the Milan General Prosecutor's office (Milan Court of Appeals)	Prosecutor at the Milan General Prosecutor's office (Milan Court of Appeals)

Source: Information from *Il Corriere della Sera*, *La Repubblica*. Author's elaboration.

Procuratore Capo della Repubblica 1976, 8). Before being appointed as Milan chief prosecutor, Gresti had worked at the Milan General Prosecutor's office, namely the prosecutor's office for the Milan Court of Appeals (*Dopo 40 Anni la Procura E' Diretta da un Milanese* 1976, 17). As a result of his appointment to the chief prosecutor's office in 1975, Gresti became the first member of the Milanese legal community to lead this key institution (*Dopo 40 Anni la Procura E' Diretta da un Milanese* 1976, 17). In this sense, Gresti's appointment truly represented an attempt to appease the Milanese judicial community after Micale's ousting. Gresti seemed to possess the typical background of a conservative judicial professional. Nevertheless, some of Gresti's past experiences distinguished him from more traditionally conservative legal figures.

Gresti entered the judicial branch in 1943, around the time of Mussolini's ouster from power (Pelizzari 1976, 8). However, Gresti had to delay taking office in Milan as a lower-ranked prosecutor due to military service (Pelizzari 1976, 8). During that time, Gresti was forcibly moved to Germany as a prisoner of war (Pelizzari 1976, 8). Although never a "revolutionary" (Pelizzari 1976, 8), over the course of his professional career, Gresti developed a reputation as an open-minded judicial professional capable of mediation and impartiality (Pelizzari 1976, 8). During his tenure at the Milan prosecutor's office, Gresti would be described by his subordinates as an "enlightened conservative" (Spataro 2011, 16). As such, Gresti strongly supported an egalitarian organization of relationships with his subordinates, as I discuss later.

Of the three Milan chief prosecutors who held this office from 1974 to 1996, Francesco Saverio Borrelli was the only one with a clear past affiliation with a judicial association. Borrelli had been a founding member of *Magistratura Democratica*, MD, the progressive judicial association (*Milano, Borrelli E' da Ieri il Nuovo Procuratore Capo* 1988). However, Borrelli soon distanced himself from MD (*Milano, Borrelli E' da Ieri il Nuovo Procuratore Capo* 1988) and briefly joined UniCost, the moderate centrist judicial association, before opting out of associational life entirely (*Milano, Borrelli E' da Ieri il Nuovo Procuratore Capo* 1988). Thus, Borrelli's associational trajectory clearly manifested his proximity to the progressive legal movement.

As a result, Borrelli's appointment satisfied a unique set of conditions. On the one hand, his professional profile did not seem to represent too big of a disruption with the past. Borrelli's lack of a clear membership in a judicial association made his candidacy appear in continuity with Gresti's enlightened and impartial leadership. On the other hand, Borrelli's past affiliation with MD and continued ideological distance from conservative groups strongly appealed to the Milanese progressive judicial community. The latter had significantly gained strength by the time of Borrelli's appointment. While in the early 1980s, MD had won between 15% and 30% of the votes to the High

Council of the Judiciary within the Milan jurisdiction, it jumped to more than 45% in 1992 (Ceron and Mainenti 2015, 227), therefore achieving a significant increase in membership over the decade. Thus, Borrelli's appointment to the Milan chief prosecutor's office constituted a relevant victory for the local progressive judicial community.

In the following section, I explore how each chief prosecutor mentioned above shaped his office's organization and the professional relationships with his subordinates. This analysis is key to understanding the remarkable progress in the prosecution of complex criminal phenomena, including corruption, that the Milanese office achieved in the decades leading to the *Mani Pulite* operation.

THE MILAN PROSECUTOR'S OFFICE'S ORGANIZATIONAL STRUCTURE

The appointment of chief prosecutors in line with Milanese judicial professionals' legal ideals deeply affected the structure of professional relationships within this prosecutor's office. Under chief prosecutor Gresti first and chief Borrelli later, the Milan prosecutor's office adopted an egalitarian organizational structure. This structure, which remained in place without too many alterations since the mid-1970s, strengthened prosecutorial independence, fostered the emergence of critical legal innovations, and promoted the Milan office's inclusion into a broader judicial network. Thus, early organizational choices and their gradual consolidation laid the foundations for the effective prosecution of systemic corruption in the Clean Hands operation. In this section, I examine the organizational structures that chief prosecutors Micale, Gresti, and Borrelli implemented within their office.

Until 1976, the Milan prosecutor's office followed a clear hierarchical organization of the professional relationships between chief prosecutor and subordinates. In line with his traditional legal conservatism, chief prosecutor Micale implemented a strict hierarchy that completely excluded his subordinates from the office's decision-making process. Milanese prosecutors' testimonies offer a detailed account of Micale's hierarchical attitudes. In February 1974, a gathering of the local ANM branch brought together 250 Milanese judges and prosecutors to draft a document denouncing Micale's handling of his office (*La "Guerra" tra Micale e i Suoi Sostituti* 1975, 8). According to the document, the office presented "a hierarchical-bureaucratic and centralized decision-making process" (*La "Guerra" tra Micale e i Suoi Sostituti* 1975, 8). Micale closely oversaw every single decision in the office and left no room for autonomous decision-making on the part of his subordinates. Micale's hierarchical control found expression in direct orders to lower-ranked prosecutors, including on how to read and apply the law, and sometimes in the reassignment of cases and prosecutors with no explicit rationale (*La "Guerra" tra Micale e i Suoi Sostituti* 1975, 8).

The document perfectly describes the hierarchical mindset typical of traditional legal conservatism, which chief Micale applied to the relationships with his subordinates. Two-thirds of all Milanese prosecutors agreed to add their names to the document (*I Magistrati Accusano il Procuratore Micale* 1974, 7). This group included members of MI, who subscribed to a reformed understanding of legal conservatism, in line with the new constitutional values, and opposed Micale's authoritarian tendencies (*I Magistrati Accusano il Procuratore Micale* 1974, 7). According to his subordinates, Micale manifested unquestionable "incompatibility" with the Milan prosecutor's office (*La "Guerra" tra Micale e i Suoi Sostituti* 1975, 8). The document was only the latest manifestation of Milanese prosecutors' dissatisfaction with their superior. During Micale's tenure, as many as thirteen prosecutors had decided to leave the office (Solazzo 1976, 8), possibly further evidence of a hostile working environment.

As a result of the ongoing controversy between his subordinates and chief Micale, the High Council decided the latter's reassignment to a different office (*Il Consiglio Superiore Decide Oggi il Trasferimento del Procuratore Capo Micale* 1975, 7). Overall, this dynamic embodies an important development: it shows that the judicial system's recent decentralization had partially succeeded in empowering lower-ranked judicial professionals. The possibility for lower-ranked prosecutors to raise issues about their superiors represented a vital aspect of the decentralization process. Its deployment in chief Micale's ousting demonstrates that institutional reforms had afforded lower-ranked judicial professionals new and useful tools to stand up to oppressive superiors.

Given the dynamics surrounding Micale's resignation, chief Gresti immediately understood the necessity to restructure professional relationships within the Milan prosecutor's office. From the very beginning, the newly appointed chief prosecutor demonstrated to be much more open to an egalitarian relationship with his subordinates. Gresti started his tenure by holding informal conversations with prosecutors (something that could have never happened under Micale's leadership), in which he promised their inclusion in the office's decision-making process (Pelizzari 1976, 8). Gresti would soon deliver on his promise: during his tenure, he held regular meetings with his subordinates whose results would then inform Gresti's direction of the office, to the point that he almost considered this type of collegial decision-making "binding" (Spataro 2011, 16). Furthermore, Gresti often invited his subordinates' suggestions outside these regular meetings (Spataro 2011, 16).

Gresti's moderate conservatism won him the support and admiration of lower-ranked prosecutors and led to a long period of stability within the Milan prosecutor's office. Gresti's tenure lasted for twelve years without much turmoil. More importantly, Gresti's tenure laid the foundations for the Milan office to become the center of anti-corruption investigations with the Clean Hands operation, thanks to Milanese prosecutors' increasing independence and growing expertise. The possibility for lower-ranked prosecutors to bring their proposals to chief Gresti's attention paved the way for the emergence of legal novelties and the accumulation of legal expertise in the prosecution of complex criminal phenomena. This is visible in the creation of the first investigative unit specializing in terrorism investigations, which Gresti established following one of these subordinates' suggestions. I explore this development in detail in the following section of this chapter.

These positive trends in prosecutorial independence and effectiveness continued under Gresti's successor, chief prosecutor Francesco Saverio Borrelli. As I previously mentioned, Borrelli was the first Milan chief prosecutor with a clear associational affiliation. As a former member of *Magistratura Democratica* (MD), Borrelli had developed decent progressive credentials, in addition to maintaining significant distance from conservative elements within the Italian judicial profession. During his tenure, Borrelli preserved the egalitarian decision-making practices that his predecessor had established, such as regular consultations with lower-ranked prosecutors, which were fundamental to the Clean Hands operation's success, as I explain later in this chapter. Furthermore, Borrelli's legal progressivism lacked any deference toward judicial hierarchies and state agents outside the justice system when it came to salient investigations. This would become a key feature of Borrelli's leadership during the *Mani Pulite* operation.

LEGAL INNOVATIONS AND MILAN'S INCLUSION IN THE ANTI-TERRORISM JUDICIAL NETWORK

Starting in 1975, Milanese chief prosecutors restructured their office's internal organization from a rigid hierarchy to a more egalitarian organization. These changes paved the way for the emergence of legal innovations and the significant accumulation of legal expertise among Milanese prosecutors. These organizational changes empowered lower-ranked prosecutors to adopt legal innovations not only of their own making but also some that had originated in other jurisdictions. The latter came along with Milanese prosecutors' inclusion into a broader judicial network cutting across jurisdictions. In this section, I explore the emergence and diffusion of legal innovations to the Milan jurisdiction and the increases in Milanese prosecutors' legal expertise on complex criminal phenomena, such as terrorism and corruption. I show how these developments created the conditions for the effective prosecution of systemic corruption in the Clean Hands operation.

In the previous section, I mentioned how Gresti's openness to suggestions from his subordinates led to the creation of the first investigative unit on terrorism cases. The establishment of this special investigative unit demonstrates the link between an egalitarian organizational structure and the emergence of legal innovations via a bottom-up approach—namely, thanks to lower-ranked prosecutors' initiatives. As I argued in chapter 1, hierarchical structures enhance chief prosecutors' scrutiny over their subordinates and compress the latter's independence in choosing investigative approaches. On *the other hand, egalitarian structures allow prosecutors to explore the variety of investigative and legal* approaches available and empower them to adopt novel legal tools out of their own initiative. The creation of a special terrorism unit within the Milan prosecutor's office illustrates this dynamic.

Special investigative units working on terrorism cases had emerged for the first time in the neighboring Turin jurisdiction in 1976; two years before, Milanese prosecutor Armando Spataro suggested their adoption to chief Gresti, in 1978 (Spataro 2016). Turin prosecutors had developed creative ways around the legal and procedural constraints to the formation of these groups of peers working jointly on a set of cases.[1] Gian Carlo Caselli, one of the first members of the Turin unit, recalls that its goals were to "increase our resources, bring together different sensitivities and experiences, and distribute tasks according to each judicial professional's inclination" (Caselli 2009, 30). From its inception, the Turin investigative team had enjoyed ample media coverage, thanks to its growing success in the fight against terrorist organizations. As a result, by 1978, Milanese prosecutors had a valid investigative model available for imitation, thanks to the Turin team's successes and the spread of information about its work.

However, the diffusion of special investigative units from Turin to Milan was only possible because of the egalitarian structure regulating professional relationships within the Milan prosecutor's office. Prosecutor Spataro, then a young, newly appointed member of the judiciary, had been working closely with instructing judge Guido Galli on left-wing terrorism investigations (Spataro 2011, 40–41). As a result of this work, Galli and Spataro became convinced that the formation of special investigative units would promote an effective prosecutorial response to this criminal phenomenon (Spataro 2011, 43). Thus, prosecutor Spataro asked his superior, chief prosecutor Gresti, for permission to form such a unit. Gresti granted such authorization (39).

The formation of the first investigative unit on terrorism cases underscores the importance of an egalitarian organizational structure for the emergence of investigative innovations. Gresti's decision to involve his subordinates in decision-making increased lower-ranked prosecutors' independence and paved the way for the adoption of new investigative techniques. This example also stands in stark contrast to the concurrent hierarchical dynamics visible in the Roman prosecutor's office, which I explored in chapter 3.

Without the inclusion of lower-ranked prosecutors in the local decision-making process, Spataro's suggestion would not have reached his superior, chief Gresti. The latter could still have acted on his own to import this innovation into his office. For instance, given Gresti's role as the head of a prosecutor's office, he could have instituted this special unit to comply with guidelines from the High Council or with rulings from the Court of Cassation. However, the High Council had issued no such directive, and the creation of the special terrorism investigative unit in Turin had not yet passed the test of appellate review.[2] Thus, there was no obligation or incentive on Gresti's part to adopt this new investigative tool. Instead, its diffusion to the Milan jurisdiction resulted from lower-ranked prosecutors' increased independence due to their inclusion in the office's decision-making process.

The presence of an egalitarian structure within the Milan office leads not only to the diffusion of this innovation but also to the formation of an informal judicial network between Milan and Turin. Prosecutor Spataro and chief prosecutor Gresti established the Milan special investigative unit for the explicit purpose of creating a regular collaboration with the equivalent team working in Turin (Spataro 2016). Soon, this network would extend to other jurisdictions across Italy (Spataro 2016). Interestingly, the creation of this judicial network did not result automatically from the interconnections between terrorist attacks. The terrorist groups Red Brigades and First Line, for instance, presented well-structured organizations with active cells in many Italian cities. However, several jurisdictions, like Rome,[3] Naples, Florence, and Bologna, joined the judicial network despite the absence of interconnected investigations between these jurisdictions (Spataro 2016). Later on, more prosecutors would join the judicial network while working on an entirely different criminal phenomenon, namely mafia organizations, as I explain in chapter 5.

The judicial network became an incredibly effective tool against left-wing terrorist organizations. The number of judges and prosecutors meeting regularly to exchange information on terrorism cases soon went from fifteen (Spataro 2016) to about twenty to twenty-five (Spataro 2011, 144). This cooperation led to a process of mutual learning. By sharing information and coordinating their work, prosecutors and judges in the judicial network learned how to apply new legal tools and coordinate large investigative operations across jurisdictions. Overall, this brought about the so-called "*cultura del coordinamento*" (Spataro 2016), which roughly translates to "predisposition for joint investigations," namely judicial professionals' ability to coordinate investigations across different jurisdictions. The most well-known example of this coordination is the 1979 operation against *Autonomia Operaia*, another left-wing terrorist group. Investigative units across several Italian jurisdictions moved together to arrest members of the terrorist organization in a joint operation that revealed the judicial network's existence to the public for the first time (Spataro 2011, 161).

The creation of special investigative units was not the only innovation that took root among Milanese prosecutors working on terrorism cases. The focus on this criminal issue and the autonomy guaranteed to Milanese prosecutors by their superior also led to a new interpretation of criminal rules and criminal procedure. Milanese prosecutors found themselves having to adapt old and inadequate criminal rules to a new and complex criminal phenomenon. The criminal code did not contain any explicit provision concerning terrorist organizations (Caselli 2009, 34–35).[4] For this reason, Milanese prosecutors developed and applied new legal concepts that would facilitate their prosecutorial efforts.

One such example is the concept of *concorso esterno*. This new legal concept identified the criminal responsibility of individuals who provided support for a criminal organization without being directly affiliated with it (Spataro 2016). The development of *concorso esterno* helped Milanese prosecutors deal with the sometimes-blurry lines of affiliation and support for terrorist organizations. However, Milanese prosecutors could only elaborate and adopt this new legal concept thanks to the independence that an egalitarian structure of professional relationships guaranteed within their office. It was only three years before that chief Micale sent directives to his subordinates with specific guidelines on how to interpret the law (*La "Guerra" tra Micale e i Suoi Sostituti* 1975, 8). On the contrary, chief Gresti's openness to his subordinates' initiatives had made the adoption of legal innovations finally possible, paving the way for the more effective prosecution of complex criminal issues.

The introduction of legal innovations via legislation also aided the accumulation of legal expertise among Milanese prosecutors. Given the rise in terrorist attacks over the 1970s and 1980s, the Italian government decided to help prosecutorial authorities by partially modernizing old criminal and procedural rules. With a 1979 law, Parliament established a series of conditions under which terrorists could receive more lenient sentences (Spataro 2016). Specifically, collaboration with judicial authorities, under the condition of having fully rejected affiliation with a terrorist organization, could open the door to lesser sentences. This set of rules closely recalled well-established plea-bargaining techniques familiar to law enforcement officials and prosecutors in the United States. This new legislation came to be called *diritto premiale*,[5] because of the "rewarding" mechanism that granted terrorists a chance to receive a less harsh punishment in exchange for their collaboration.

As prosecutor Spataro recalls, the passing of this law immediately produced the stepping forward of confidential informants among the defendants under arrest for their membership in left-wing terrorist organizations (Spataro 2016). Although Milanese judges and prosecutors did not invite the passing of such legislation (Spataro 2016), they nevertheless made the most out of it. Consequently, because of *diritto premiale*'s effectiveness in promoting collaboration among former terrorists, judges and prosecutors asked Parliament to pass additional legislation along similar lines. In 1982, Parliament passed another bill granting an even more significant lessening of final sentences for confidential informants from terrorist organizations, while at the same time setting a temporal limit for collaboration and the validity of the law itself (Spataro 2016). The final step in this legislative effort was the passing of a 1987 bill allowing significantly shorter sentences and pardons for those defendants who had already been convicted and only later decided to disavow their terrorist organization (Spataro 2016).

Milanese prosecutors mastered these innovations introduced by Parliament, and in the years following the introduction of this legislation, they skillfully applied it to the prosecution of terrorist organizations. This process created a vital reservoir of expertise, which Milanese prosecutors would later deploy on other criminal issues, above all systemic corruption. The development of this legal expertise was, once again, the result of the egalitarian framework in which Milanese prosecutors found themselves working and the independence that this organizational structure granted them. Even the High Council of the Judiciary recognized Milanese prosecutors' increasing knowledge of the investigative and legal innovations applicable to terrorism investigations. Every year, the High Council would organize workshops that provided continuous judicial training for members of the profession. Soon, the High Council started inviting Milanese prosecutors to give lectures during the workshops dedicated to the handling of terrorism cases. As prosecutor Spataro explained:

> The first workshops on joint investigations [*coordinamento*] and the use of confidential informants' contributions significantly drew from our experience in the field. It was as if we had written, in practice, a handbook on the correct investigative method. (Spataro 2016)

LEGAL INNOVATIONS IN THE PROSECUTION OF CORRUPTION

Chief prosecutor Gresti's decision to follow one of his subordinates' recommendations and establish a terrorism investigative unit had momentous consequences for investigative work within the Milan jurisdiction. Above all, it sparked an internal process of emulation, which brought the application of the same investigative innovation to other criminal issues beyond terrorism. The 1980s investigation of corrupt businessman Michele Sindona is one such example. Sindona was under investigation for corrupt business practices, including the harassment and killing of potential rivals (Colombo 2010, 39). Because of these crimes' interconnectedness, a group of three Milanese instructing judges talked with their immediate superior about using the organizational structure previously developed by their colleagues in the prosecutor's office to the inquiries into Sindona's activities (Colombo 2010, 39–40).

Therefore, the establishment of a special investigative unit within the Milan prosecutor's office led to the formation of a similar institution within the instructing judge's office. Although these offices were distinct units within the Milan courthouse at the time, both engaged in pretrial investigations. It is also important to notice that, as the *Sindona* cases show, the adoption of special investigative units within the Milan instructing office also derived from this office's egalitarian organization. Lower-ranked instructing judges felt empowered to bring suggestions to their superior, which swiftly complied with their request. Thus, once more, an egalitarian structure of professional relationships paved the way for the adoption of legal innovations.

In this section, I examine the application of investigative and legal innovations in the P2 case and subsequent corruption cases. The P2 case is particularly relevant, since, as I explained in chapter 3, it could have led to the uncovering of the corruption system ten years before the Clean Hands investigation (Colombo 2010, 101). Even though the Milan instructing judge's office handled most of the P2 case, the latter represents a key moment in the development of legal expertise among Milanese prosecutors. With the 1989 reform of the criminal procedure code, the instructing judge's office would merge with the Milan prosecutor's office. Several Milanese instructing judges became prosecutors at the turn of the 1990s. One of the leading instructing judges in the P2 investigation became part of the Clean Hands investigative unit. Thus, the development of significant expertise on corruption investigations among Milanese instructing judges turned into prosecutorial expertise when these two offices eventually merged. This dynamic helps explain how Milanese prosecutors acquired the legal knowledge necessary to handle the *Mani Pulite* investigation.

The *Sindona* cases led to the discovery of an intricate criminal scheme involving corrupt businessmen, a deviant Masonic lodge, and corruption at the Italian state's highest levels. Sindona had been a prominent businessman with investments both in Italy and in the United States. At the same time, his rise to the top of the financial world had resulted from his relationships with criminal personalities, such as the Gambino family members, one of the most powerful mafia families in New York City (Colombo 2010, 46). The team investigating Sindona consisted of three instructing judges: Gherardo Colombo, Gianni Galatti, and Giuliano Turone (Colombo 2010, 39). Instructing judge Colombo had previously worked alongside his colleague Guido Galli, who was working on terrorism cases, to design the internal structure of these special investigative units (Colombo 2010, 32). The creation of a special unit focusing exclusively on the *Sindona* investigation therefore would test the implementation of this organizational structure on other types of criminal cases.

The application of this investigative tool to the *Sindona* cases immediately highlighted its potential for uncovering corruption. By looking at different investigations as interconnected criminal activities within a larger scheme, the team of instructing judges not only found out about Sindona's illicit business but also discovered the larger criminal design in which Sindona's actions fit. For instance, the team of instructing judges, reduced to only two people after judge Galatti's departure (Colombo 2010, 40), uncovered the relationships between Sindona and *Cosa Nostra* members in Sicily and the United States (Colombo 2010, 46). More importantly, by looking into Sindona's corrupt business dealings and criminal actions, judge Colombo and judge Turone discovered the existence of a secret organization with subversive purposes to which Sindona, like hundreds of others, belonged. Thus, through the joint examination of several criminal cases, the judicial team deciphered the existence of a criminal design, in which a secret organization, the so-called P2 lodge, played an essential part.

The P2 was a secret Masonic lodge, disavowed by the Italian Masonry, that was actively pursuing a political agenda. The secret organization had been enlisting members among the highest-ranking law enforcement officials, in addition to influential businessmen, party officials, government ministries, journalists, intellectuals, and even members of the judiciary (Colombo 2010, 49–50). According to the findings of the judicial team's investigation, the secret organization had prepared a plan of action in case the Italian Communist Party were to defeat ruling political forces, especially the Christian Democratic Party, at the ballot box and democratically take control of the government (Colombo 2010, 62). This plan of action seemed to entail the heavy involvement of the armed forces against the possibility of such a scenario (Colombo 2010, 62). At the same time, the lodge had laid out a political agenda with clear policy points to enact through legislation, which would deeply impact the design of several institutions, including the prosecutorial system (Colombo 2010, 65). Therefore, via their investigation of Sindona's corrupt financial dealings and criminal activities, the judicial team found out much more than expected thanks to the joint examination of several criminal cases.

Despite its remarkable work, the judicial team fell short of holding those responsible for this political conspiracy accountable. In 1981, judge Colombo and judge Turone were forced to defer the entirety of their investigative work to the Roman prosecutor's office (Colombo 2010, 98). This was a brazen exercise of prosecutorial gatekeeping by Roman authorities, which concluded with a dismissal of the most serious charges against some of the prominent political personalities enlisted in the P2 lodge (Colombo 2010, 99). Furthermore, although the P2 investigation concluded with several convictions, both at trial and on appeal, the rulings understated the potentially subversive nature of the P2 lodge (Colombo 2010, 100–101). As I explained in chapter 3, this outcome was clearly affected by how Roman prosecutorial authorities pursued the case after appropriating it.

The outcome of the P2 investigation exemplified both the potential inherent in legal innovations and the persistent obstacles to effective corruption prosecutions. While new investigative approaches showed significant promise for uncovering complex criminal schemes, no investigation into political personalities and state agents could unfold undisturbed as long as the Roman prosecutor's office could deploy its gatekeeping powers against it. I examined the latter dynamic more in-depth in chapter 3. Furthermore, the presence of a legally conservative, though enlightened, Milanese chief prosecutor like Gresti did not help. Despite Gresti's openness to egalitarian decision-making within his office, he remained highly deferential toward conservative elements within the judiciary, especially toward the Roman chief prosecutor. At the height of the P2 investigation, Gresti welcomed Roman authorities' forceful intervention in the case (Colombo 2010, 95–96), which eventually resulted in its transfer to Rome

Nevertheless, the development and diffusion among Milanese judicial professionals of these new investigative methods laid the foundations for the uncovering of systemic corruption in the Clean Hands operation. The latter would rely on the same investigative techniques and legal tools first applied to terrorism cases and the P2 investigation. Furthermore, the link between the P2 case and the Clean Hands operation is directly observable in the same actor's participation in both. Instructing judge Gherardo Colombo, which led the investigative effort in the P2 case, would join the Clean Hands investigative team almost from its very start, therefore contributing his invaluable expertise to this new anti-corruption operation.

These preconditions came to fruition under the leadership of a new, progressive chief prosecutor for the Milan prosecutor's office, Saverio Borrelli. By the time Borrelli became Milan chief prosecutor, the instructing judge's office had been dismantled as a result of the 1989 reform of the code of criminal procedure. Therefore, Borrelli took the reins of an office that might have benefited from an infusion of personnel from the instructing judge's office.

Chief Borrelli encouraged and supported the application of the investigative practices that had emerged in previous terrorism and corruption investigations beyond these criminal issues.

Under Borrelli's leadership, for instance, the Milan prosecutor's office formed special investigative units on mafia investigations, which would uncover these criminal organizations' activities within the city of Milan in the so-called "Duomo Connection" investigation (Fazzo 1991). Chief Borrelli also continued the practice of creating special investigative units to investigate corruption cases. In 1988, Milanese prosecutors started investigating bribe exchanges between construction company manager Bruno De Mico and the Milan city administration for construction bids, after their counterparts in Genova first uncovered this corrupt scheme (*Un Pool di Giudici a Consulto sulle Maxitangente a Milano* 1988). The scandal, which was labeled "*Carceri d'Oro*" (Golden Prisons), since some of the construction bids were for penitentiary buildings, offered a glimpse of the corruption schemes the Clean Hands operation would soon uncover. To handle the investigation, the Milan prosecutor's office established a special investigative unit composed of three prosecutors: Filippo Grisolia, Piercamillo Davigo, and Antonio Di Pietro (Ravelli 1989). The latter two would eventually lead the Clean Hands operation.

However, other than for its use of special investigative units, the Golden Prisons investigation unfolded in accordance with well-established (and partially outdated) procedural and legal practices. For instance, following well-established jurisprudence, Milanese prosecutors charged all the defendants with *concussione*, rather than *corruzione* (Ravelli 1989), legal concepts on which I elaborate later in this chapter. Furthermore, the investigation did not deploy the informal plea-bargaining deals that would later become typical of the Clean Hands operation. For these reasons, while highly effective, prosecutorial efforts in the Golden Prisons investigation remained limited in their reach and left the corruption system weakened, but still in place.

Several important developments would occur between 1989 and 1992 that would set the final conditions for the Clean Hands investigation's unprecedented success. One of them was the appointment of a less conservative chief prosecutor to the Roman prosecutor's office in 1992. As I explained in chapter 3, this would lead to the suspension of prosecutorial gatekeeping during the Clean Hands operation. Above all, however, Milanese judicial professionals' growing engagement with local civil society would be key to explaining the success of the Clean Hands operation. In the following sections, I explore the Milanese judicial professionals' involvement with civil society, particularly with a local organization called *Società Civile*. The latter would rekindle a new sense of civic commitment in Milanese judicial professionals. As I explore later in the chapter, the relationship with *Società Civile* improved Milanese prosecutors' knowledge of corruption dynamics and provided a venue for them to present novel legal and investigative approaches to corruption prosecutions. Thus, the relationship between Milanese prosecutors and local civil society set the stage for the development of effective corruption prosecution in the Clean Hands operation.

MILANESE JUDICIAL PROFESSIONALS' INVOLVEMENT WITH CIVIL SOCIETY

In addition to increasing their prosecutorial expertise, Milanese judicial actors' engagement with complex criminal issues, like terrorism, had also led to their involvement with civil society organizations over time. The violence brought about by left-wing terrorist groups in the 1970s and 1980s prompted significant social mobilization in several urban contexts impacted by this criminal phenomenon, particularly Turin and Milan. Similarly, the pervasive presence of corruption, with its societal burden on fair political representation and civic equality, also sparked a response on the part of Milanese civil society, with the formation of new civic groups leading anti-corruption campaigns. Milanese prosecutors often became an active part of these social movements. In this section, I show how Milanese judicial professionals' involvement in this type of social mobilization promoted the emergence of a renewed sense of civic commitment among them.

The first relevant instance of judicial engagement with civil society did not occur in Milan, however, but in Turin, and on a different criminal issue than corruption. In 1979, in response to the rising political violence perpetrated by left-wing terrorist groups, such as the Red Brigades and First Line, the Turin city administration created a questionnaire which was handed out as widely as possible among city residents and civil society organizations (Boffano 2009). The questionnaire's purpose was to encourage individuals and organizations to identify possible suspicious activities related to left-wing terrorism (Caselli 2009, 40). The questionnaire's diffusion also marked a critical rejection of terrorist violence by the Italian Communist Party (Boffano 2009).

Several members of the Turin special investigative unit took part in this social mobilization against terrorist violence. Instructing judges and prosecutors working on terrorism cases often accompanied local politicians in their speeches and public lectures. They also wholeheartedly endorsed the diffusion of the questionnaire among civil society organizations (Boffano 2009). This social mobilization against terrorist violence soon came to include their Milanese colleagues as well and, more broadly, all judicial professionals participating in the judicial network. As prosecutor Armando Spataro, the founder of the Milan special investigative unit on terrorism cases, recalled:

> When I started working on terrorism cases in 1977 – 1978, I remember several people were skeptical about the actual roots of left-wing terrorism [. . .] There were even some intellectuals [. . .] who argued that we should neither stand with the State nor with the Red Brigades. During our gatherings with other judges and prosecutors, those gatherings in which we developed joint investigation methods [. . .] we realized it would be essential to give lectures in schools, neighborhood meetings, and labor union meetings, to defeat this passive attitude and general ignorance. I did so frequently at the time in order to share information on terrorism and push back against the idea of neutrality on such a serious issue, which is unacceptable in a democracy. (Spataro 2016)

Therefore, Milanese prosecutors, like their colleagues in Turin, actively engaged in social mobilization against left-wing terrorism. The purpose of such mobilization was to educate the public about the nature of this criminal phenomenon and promote the emergence of a genuinely democratic culture among citizens. Therefore, judicial engagement with criminal issues with profound social impact, like terrorism, fostered the emergence of a new civic commitment among members of the judicial profession.

The traditionally conservative understanding of the judicial profession relegated judges to the margins of civil society, given the high standard of "institutional impartiality" they were to embody as the "mouth of the law." On the other hand, judicial professionals' involvement in social mobilization squandered this idea and introduced a new model of professionalism. The latter entailed judicial commitment to democratic values' diffusion through direct engagement with civil society. This new commitment was definitely in line with the legal progressivism embodied by an association like MD, which had always supported judicial professionals' involvement with civil society to realize democratic constitutional values (Guarnieri 2003, 110). However, the judicial mobilization against left-wing terrorism brought this commitment to a new level, foisting new responsibilities in the defense of democracy on judicial professionals and enriching their understanding of the judicial mission.

Judicial mobilization alongside civil society would not remain limited to terrorism cases. A decade later, several Milanese judicial professionals would again engage in social activism on another salient social issue, namely corruption. In Milan, a new civil society organization, called *Società Civile*, became the leading force in the social mobilization against the corruption system pervading Italian politics.

Sociologist and university professor Nando Dalla Chiesa founded *Società Civile* in 1985. He created the organization for the purpose of increasing civil society's awareness and respect for the rule of law (*Ma Questi Cosa Vogliono Un Oggetto Misterioso nel Cielo di Milano* 1987). This was necessary, as a "passive" civil society often lent unintentional complicity to pervasive criminal phenomena. For this reason, the association's purpose was to promote the development of a widespread sense of civic duty (*Una Cicogna con Cento Ragioni* 1988). Furthermore, *Società Civile*'s mission found inspiration in the resurgence of social movements in Southern Italy, where mobilization against mafia organizations, the so-called "Palermo Spring" (Lentini 2011), had recently gained new strength. *Società Civile* established an ongoing relationship especially with the Palermo-native organization *Città per l'Uomo*. *Società Civile*'s journal often hosted articles authored by this organization's leadership (Pintacuda 1986; Orlando 1989). More importantly, the relationship between *Societa' Civile* and *Citta' per l'Uomo* contributed to the former's understanding of the social context in which mafia organizations could thrive. This type of knowledge, in turn, helped shape *Società Civile*'s understanding of corruption as well.

Società Civile was essentially composed of two entities: the circle and the journal, named after the organization itself. The journal was the vehicle through which *Società Civile* ran its aggressive investigative campaigns exposing corrupt activities within the Milan city government and public administration (Dalla Chiesa 2016). On the other hand, the organization's inner member circle included several local judges and prosecutors. *Società Civile*'s founder explicitly chose judicial professionals to join the organization based on their expertise, particularly expertise on terrorism, organized crime, and corruption investigations (Dalla Chiesa 2016). Therefore, most of these individuals had also been active participants in the judicial network connecting special investigative units across jurisdictions. For instance, prosecutor Armando Spataro, one of *Società Civile*'s circle members, had been the leading promoter of the terrorism investigative unit and one of the most active judicial network participants. Among the association's members were also prosecutors Gherardo Colombo and Giuliano Turone (Dalla Chiesa 2016), the instructing judges who had investigated Sindona's corrupt business affairs and the P2 lodge.

From its foundation, *Società Civile* declared its full-fledged rejection of traditional politics. This was visible in that any individual with a clear affiliation to a political party could not join the organization. This manifest aversion toward traditional politics was rooted in *Società Civile*'s understanding of the dynamics underpinning corruption. The organization identified in *partitocrazia*, or political parties' control of every public space, the primary source of systemic corruption (LaPalombara 1989). The decision to keep political parties and party members out of the association aimed to preserve a space for discussion free from partisanship (Dalla Chiesa 2016). By rejecting any tie to political parties, *Società Civile* also manifested its apparent belief that political change could only come from outside traditional channels of democratic representation.

Judicial professionals' engagement with *Società Civile* is relevant for several reasons. First of all, engagement with *Società Civile* brought about the emergence of a new professional ethos among Milanese judicial professionals. The latter found inspiration in *Società Civile*'s rejection of traditional politics and its "crime-generating" practices (Interview with *Società Civile* activist, Milan, June 23, 2016). Motivated by *Società Civile*'s rejection of current political practices, judicial members turned to their own institution to criticize it for adopting similarly corrupt methods in its self-government. Therefore, *Società Civile*'s radical understanding of independence from politics generated in judicial professionals a similar commitment to reforming their own institution in order to purge it of any unethical political influences. This had long-lasting consequences for the Italian judicial system, thanks to the formation of a new judicial association called *Movimento per la Giustizia*.

Second, via their membership in this organization, judicial professionals were exposed to *Società Civile*'s increasing knowledge of corruption features and dynamics. *Società Civile* worked endlessly to uncover the corruption system's features and diffuse knowledge about its internal functioning. The organization developed a complex sociological understanding of systemic corruption. This framework originated in activists' investigative reports and *Società Civile*'s relationship with Southern Italian grassroots organizations dedicated to the fight against the mafia. At the same time, judicial engagement with *Società Civile* created an ongoing mutual exchange of knowledge. On the one hand, Milanese judicial professionals significantly contributed to *Società Civile*'s understanding of corruption. On the other hand, *Società Civile*'s judicial members also benefited from the organization's knowledge and theoretical understanding of this criminal phenomenon.

Furthermore, *Società Civile* provided judicial professionals with a venue to present new legal concepts and investigative techniques, which would be central to the Clean Hands operation's success. As I show later in this chapter, Milanese prosecutors would adopt legal tools and investigative techniques consistent with a new understanding of corruption as a criminal phenomenon, which they presented on *Società Civile*'s journal.

In the following section, I examine how judicial engagement with *Società Civile* improved and shaped judicial professionals' understanding of corruption. Then, I explore how *Società Civile* promoted the emergence of a new professional ethos among its judicial members. Finally, I show how *Società Civile* provided a space for prosecutor Antonio Di Pietro to present a new activist approach to corruption prosecutions.

UNDERSTANDING SYSTEMIC CORRUPTION

To fully illustrate the effects of judicial professionals' involvement in *Società Civile*, it is first necessary to examine this organization's understanding of corruption as a criminal and societal issue. From its very beginning, *Società Civile* devoted much of its efforts to exposing suspicious malpractices within the Milan city administration. The first issue of its journal, titled "Società Civile" like the organization itself, opened in 1986 with an article about corrupt malpractices within local health care institutions (Severisio 1986). Later in the same year, *Società Civile* closely followed the scandal involving suspicious practices in the assignment of public contracts for several construction sites throughout the city of Milan (*Sottogovernare Milano* 1985).

In particular, *Società Civile* focused its attention on the informal "redistributive" practices pursued by party representatives in the Milan city council. The assignment of head offices within the city administration, including state-owned companies, followed informal rules of redistribution based on each party's seat share within the city council. Council members appointed civil servants according to the latter's political affiliation to guarantee party control over different branches of the public administration. This practice, called *lottizzazione*, was the basis of political clientelism: through their control of key offices within the public administration, political parties could distribute rewards to their constituencies in exchange for votes (LaPalombara 1989, 78).

Società Civile effectively uncovered the informal rules of redistribution followed by local political parties in the Milan city council. In 1987, the organization published documentary proof of the redistribution calculus performed by elected officials during a council session (Albini and Colombo 1987). Although not illegal, these practices lacked transparency. *Società Civile* argued that the redistribution of public offices among political parties was a "crime-generating factor [. . .] whose inevitable consequence was corruption" (Interview with former *Società Civile* activist, Milan, June 23, 2016). This practice along with the non-transparent assignments of public contracts to local businessmen were the symptoms of a well-structured corruption system (Interview with former *Società Civile* activist, Milan, June 23, 2016).

In addition to uncovering the corruption system's informal rules and visible symptoms, *Società Civile* also provided a sociological framework that could explain this complex criminal phenomenon. Specifically, the organization turned to its knowledge of mafias to make sense of pervasive corruption. In an article for the organization's journal, Corrado Stajano compared the development of illegal exchanges between local politicians and real estate managers (with the possible intervention of criminal organizations as well) to similar relations between mafia-backed company managers and local administrations in 1950s Sicily (Stajano 1986, 3). The similarities between mafia activities in Palermo and corrupt exchanges in Milan became the lens through which the city administration's local reality was interpreted. To substantiate its reports,

Società Civile collected several testimonies from local civil servants confirming that, within the Milan city administration, bribes had become an accepted means of work (Barbacetto 1987).

Società Civile's increasing knowledge of corruption practices had a significant effect on Milanese judicial professionals. As previously explained, *Società Civile* identified in *lottizzazione* the informal rule that regulated the system of illegal exchanges among political and economic actors. Party control of public administration branches also meant control over state-owned companies and the assignment of public contracts. As prosecutors would later discover, public administration was the key place in which political and economic actors could negotiate the assignment of business contracts in exchange for illegal financial support. Thus, *Società Civile*'s judicial members learned from the organization that some practices pointed to the likely occurrence of corrupt exchanges. As one of the prosecutors in the Clean Hands investigative unit explained:

> Overall, it was fairly clear that corruption was widespread. However, [*Società Civile*'s] inquiries contributed to revealing some of these corrupt practices' specificities. [. . .] judicial investigations moved along autonomously, as much as *Società Civile*'s young reporters and volunteers autonomously conducted their inquiries into these phenomena. However, at times it could well happen that *Società Civile* activists' reports would stimulate prosecutors' investigative efforts. (Interview with *Mani Pulite* prosecutor, phone, April 24, 2016)

Therefore, *Società Civile* provided Milanese judicial professionals with increased knowledge of corruption's specific features. In addition, the organization used its findings to encourage judicial action against corruption:

> What is the disease affecting the city of Milan, if journalists are incapable of saying the things that young, inexperienced reporters can see and expose, who discovered these illegalities before prosecutors did? [. . .] we did not resign ourselves to waiting for the judicial discovery of illegality. Rather, we encouraged the judiciary to achieve such discovery, always with full respect for its independence, while we also reported independently. (Dalla Chiesa 2016)

THE EMERGENCE OF A NEW JUDICIAL ETHOS: THE CREATION OF MOVIMENTO PER LA GIUSTIZIA

In addition to improving and shaping judicial professionals' understanding of systemic corruption, judicial engagement with *Società Civile* also brought about the emergence of a new professional ethos. As I detailed in chapter 2, the Italian judicial system's decentralization clearly enhanced the latter's independence at all levels. At the same time, decentralization empowered judicial associations. The latter became "quasi-political" (Nelken 1996*a*, 100) groupings and adopted practices such as *lottizzazione correntizia*, which closely mimicked political parties' *lottizzazione*. Judicial engagement with *Società Civile* helped rekindle a strong sense of civic commitment and prompted judicial professionals to act in order to reform their own institution. Furthermore, *Società Civile*'s absolute rejection of ordinary politics inspired its judicial members to adopt a similar posture and advocate in favor of a radical understanding of judicial independence from political influences.

As I previously showed, Milanese judicial professionals' previous involvement in anti-terrorism mobilization had already contributed to instilling in them a new commitment to the public good.[6] However, judicial professionals' engagement with *Società Civile* enhanced this sense of civic duty, sparking in judicial professionals a new urgency to public action. As prosecutor Spataro explained:

> I have learned a lot [from *Società Civile*]. [. . .] Through this experience, I came to realize that even a judge needs to show a sense of civic duty [. . .] before joining *Società Civile,* I only cared about doing my job as a prosecutor. I was not interested in participating in politics because, in addition to lacking any interest in it, I also did not have time for it. However, during my time [in the organization], I came to realize how important it was to bring the kind of knowledge we had acquired to the public, so that it may be available to the community. [. . .] I can trace the development of this sense of civic duty directly to my experience in *Società Civile*. (Spataro 2016)

Spataro's words demonstrate the emerging awareness that the judicial role, even when it involves the prosecution, has a "political" dimension. Judicial professionals have a "civic duty" to fulfill, which endows this institution with an obligation toward the public. This obligation cannot be considered in isolation from a renewed commitment to ethical professionalism among members of the judicial branch and radical judicial independence from political influences.

Both of these principles are visible in the creation of a new judicial association, which resulted directly from Milanese judicial professionals' involvement in *Società Civile*. As I previously explained, *Società Civile* had made the rejection of any allegiance or proximity to political parties one of its founding principles. This decision inspired its judicial members to replicate the same commitment within their professional environment. As *Società Civile*'s founder, Nando Dalla Chiesa, recalled:

> At some point, prosecutor Spataro left *Società Civile*'s directive committee. He told me: "*Società Civile* has taught me what needs to be done." [. . .] he founded a judicial association different from any other judicial association, the so-called

> "Greens." Several prosecutors who were actively involved in corruption and mafia investigations joined the association. [. . .] prosecutor Spataro always told me: "I have you to thank for making me realize what needs to be done." (Dalla Chiesa 2016)

In 1988, a few of the judges affiliated with *Società Civile* created *Movimento per la Giustizia*, a new judicial association whose members were also labeled the "Greens." Soon after its foundation, about fifty judges and prosecutors working within the Milan jurisdiction joined *Movimento per la Giustizia*, including Gerardo D'Ambrosio, who would later oversee the investigative team leading the Clean Hands investigation (*I Magistrati Vogliono Rompere l'Accerchiamento dei Partiti* 1988).[7] Among the judicial professionals who joined this new association from all over the country were also several personalities leading the fight against mafia organizations. For instance, almost all members of the Palermo special investigative unit that had achieved unprecedented successes against Cosa Nostra in the 1986 maxi trial joined *Movimento per la Giustizia* (*I Magistrati Vogliono Rompere l'Accerchiamento dei Partiti* 1988).

The reasons for the creation of *Movimento* closely echoed *Società Civile*'s disappointment with traditional politics. In the same way as *Società Civile* questioned the presence of widespread corrupt practices among elected officials and called for a new sense of civic duty among civil society, *Movimento per la Giustizia* called for judicial institutions' renewed focus on merit and professionalization, along with radical independence from political influences (Spataro 2016). Judicial associations' use of practices such as *lottizzazione correntizia* (Spataro 2016) had prevented professional advancements based on meritocratic criteria, such as significant prosecutorial achievements. *Movimento per la Giustizia* aimed to promote professionalization and meritocracy as the main principles regulating professional advancements and appointments within the Italian judicial system (Spataro 2016). This goal embodied a profound rejection of how the latter had regulated itself until then. Therefore, *Movimento per la Giustizia* manifested a profound convergence of interests and goals with *Società Civile*, visible in the explicit rejection of any traditional practices linked to corruption, like *lottizzazione correntizia*.

Movimento per la Giustizia's mission to revive the judiciary's ethical commitment also stemmed directly out of its ties to *Società Civile*:

> *Società Civile* was committed to sparking debate and diffusing knowledge among citizens in the same way as *Movimento per la Giustizia* was dedicated to the diffusion of those professional values that everyone should be mindful of, but often fails to uphold, among judicial professionals. (Spataro 2016)

For instance, *Movimento per la Giustizia* pointed at the questionable contacts between judicial professionals and Masonic lodges or between judicial professionals and economic elites, which seriously undermined judicial independence (Spataro 2016). In addition, *Movimento per la Giustizia* pointed to the problematic nature of judicial appointments to government agencies (Spataro 2016), which I discussed in chapter 3. *Movimento* denounced the widespread use of these judicial appointments to unduly influence the administration of justice.

Therefore, the new judicial association aimed to provide a space devoid of these unethical practices, which might empower judicial professionals in the pursuit of their duties. In order to do this, *Movimento per la Giustizia* embraced a radical understanding of judicial independence based on the absolute separation between this branch and other government branches. At the same time, judicial professionals' civic duty toward the public, as described by prosecutor Spataro, placed judicial professionals in an ongoing, dynamic, and direct relationship with the citizenry. Overall, *Movimento*'s goals clearly found inspiration in *Società Civile*'s fervor against politics and its degenerations. This led *Movimento* to confront complex dilemmas when deciding, for instance, whether to compete in High Council elections or not, or, in other words, whether to reform judicial institutions from within or avoid participating in their practices (Spataro 2016).

Judicial interactions with *Società Civile* are also crucial to understanding the development of the Clean Hands operation. However, an important caveat is warranted: responsibility for the Clean Hands operation falls solely with the judicial professionals who led this anti-corruption effort. While the empirical analysis that follows traces the effects of judicial professionals' engagement with *Società Civile*, it is not claiming that the latter organization somehow "directed" prosecutorial efforts in the Clean Hands operation. Rather, my empirical analysis uncovers an ideational process by which judicial professionals may gain new knowledge of social dynamics and develop a renewed understanding of their role via their involvement with local civil society. Such ideational processes do not represent "shady" attempts to direct the judiciary toward the prosecution of specific legal issues. Rather, similar processes are well-documented and empirically analyzable in other scenarios and on other legal issues, such as transitional justice (Lutz and Sikkink 2000; González-Ocantos 2014, 2016).

In the years leading to 1992, Clean Hands prosecutors had all been exposed to *Società Civile*'s anti-corruption campaign, either via their active membership in the organization, like prosecutors Gherardo Colombo and Piercamillo Davigo, or external collaboration with it, like prosecutor Antonio Di Pietro. Therefore, it is safe to assume that all these judicial actors had benefited from *Società Civile*'s in-depth study of corruption dynamics within the local city administration. It is also safe to assume that these judicial actors shared in the new judicial ethos forming around *Società Civile*. For instance, the Clean Hands special investigative unit direct supervisor, Gherardo D'Ambrosio, had been among the first Milanese judges to join *Movimento per la Giustizia*. More importantly, *Società Civile* had provided a venue for prosecutor Di Pietro to present the legal and investigative tools that would produce the Clean Hands operation's unprecedented success. These new investigative approaches were clearly in line with the organization's understanding of corruption, to which Di Pietro had actively contributed. At the same time, they also reflected a new ensuing activism among judicial professionals in their fight against corruption. In the following section, I examine the emergence of this activist approach to corruption prosecutions, visible in Di Pietro's interactions with *Società Civile*.

THE EMERGENCE OF JUDICIAL ACTIVISM AGAINST SYSTEMIC CORRUPTION

Earlier in this chapter, I outlined *Società Civile*'s new understanding of corruption dynamics. The organization's sociological framework for understanding this criminal issue emerged partially from the former's interactions with local prosecutors. In particular, local prosecutor Antonio Di Pietro significantly contributed to *Società Civile*'s knowledge of corruption dynamics. Although not an organization member, Di Pietro published several pieces in *Società Civile*'s journal. In his interview for the journal's 1990 issue, Di Pietro outlined the elaborate scheme economic and political actors had devised to make their illicit exchanges untraceable to law enforcement authorities (Colombo 1990). More importantly, *Società Civile*'s journal offered a venue for Di Pietro to present new investigative and legal approaches to corruption investigations. These reflected an understanding of corruption that was deeply aligned with *Società Civile*'s and, at the same time, embodied a new, activist approach to its prosecution.

In his 1991 article for *Società Civile*'s journal, Di Pietro argued that the distinction between individuals who pursued corruption willingly for their benefit and individuals who were forced into agreeing to a corrupt exchange under threat held little to no legal significance. Italian criminal rules had traditionally defined corruption as an exchange in which one actor coerced another into an illicit exchange. This created the legal category of *concussione*. According to Di Pietro, the nature of the relationship between economic and political actors in corrupt deals had evolved to the point of being systemic. Both parties to a corrupt exchange simply submitted to a systemic phenomenon's informal rules. Under these conditions, the legal distinction between an individual's forced participation in an illicit exchange under threat, embodied in the crime of *concussione*, and *corruzione*, or the willing participation of both parties in an illegal exchange, had become meaningless.

Instead, according to Di Pietro (1991), it would be more appropriate to describe corruption as an "environmental condition" (Di Pietro 1991, 8). By this, the prosecutor meant that bribe exchanges had become a mutually accepted informal norm, which regulated the interactions between individuals with converging interests, usually a businessman looking to win a government bid and a party-affiliated civil servant overseeing the latter. As a result of this socio-legal construction, Di Pietro created the concept of *dazione ambientale* (Di Pietro 1991, 8) which equated both participants' responsibilities in illegal exchanges, the bribe-giver and the bribe-receiver.

On the one hand, equating the bribe-giver and bribe-receiver's responsibilities based on their participation in a systemic phenomenon provided a more accurate description of this criminal reality. On the other hand, this legal interpretation also provided prosecutors with increased discretion when considering how to charge individuals for their participation in corrupt exchanges. This, in turn, opened up opportunities for defendants' cooperation with legal authorities in exchange for leniency. In other words, the concept of *dazione ambientale* provided Italian prosecutors with an informal plea-bargaining process. As Di Pietro argues in the article:

> Within a similar social context, it seems to me that a novel and more functional way of ascertaining the facts in a case would consist in re-qualifying the bribe-giver's legal responsibility. This might perhaps open the door to more leniency at trial, were the defendant willing to provide information about the crime under investigation in a timely fashion. (Di Pietro 1991, 9)

Di Pietro's elaboration of the concept of *dazione ambientale* and his use of extant legal concepts like *corruzione* and *concussione* were geared toward obtaining a specific outcome: defendants' collaboration in uncovering the corruption system. While the new legal concept of *dazione ambientale* accurately reflected corruption's systemic features, at the same time, it lent itself to being used strategically to incentivize collaboration on the part of the defendant. Therefore, *dazione ambientale* was a powerful new legal tool that allowed prosecutors to craft informal plea bargains with defendants involved in corrupt exchanges.

Di Pietro's use of the concept of *dazione ambientale* for the purpose of introducing an informal plea-bargaining process represents the true novelty that would fuel the Clean Hands operation. It also embodies a clear example of what scholars have normally labeled "judicial activism" (Kmiec 2004). As I explained in chapter 1, this term usually refers to instances of judicial "law-making," whereby judicial professionals introduce new rules via a creative interpretation of extant legal texts. The introduction of the concept of *dazione ambientale* clearly falls into this category. At the time of Di Pietro's article in *Società Civile*'s journal, this legal concept was absent from the body of rules regulating corruption prosecutions. Therefore, *dazione ambientale* was a "judge-made" concept with no foundation in written texts.

Furthermore, the use of *dazione ambientale* to pursue informal plea bargaining also found no support in extant legal rules. As I explained in chapter 1, Italian criminal procedure, even after the 1989 reform, did not provide the prosecution with the power to negotiate criminal charges (Pizzi and Mirafioti 1992, 22).[8] Therefore, the pursuit of informal plea bargaining, based on a discretionary use of *concussione* or *corruzione* charges dependent on a defendant's collaboration, was also a judge-made novelty with no foundation in the criminal procedure code, even after the 1989 reform. Thus, Di Pietro's novel approach to corruption investigations clearly represented an instance of judicial "law-making" with the informal introduction of new legal concepts and the creation of an informal plea-bargaining process.

Often, judicial activism implies an understanding of the judicial role that extends the latter's responsibilities way beyond its usual confines. In other words, when judges (and prosecutors, in the Italian case) pursue a creative interpretation of extant legal rules, they might do so under the impression that it is their responsibility to fill a legislative vacuum. The Clean Hands prosecutors adopted the legal and procedural novelties described in Di Pietro's 1991 article out of their perceived responsibility to enforce accountability against other branches' systemic failure to do so. One of the Clean Hands prosecutors articulated this understanding of their professional mission in the following way:

> If politicians took care of expelling corrupt party members before we have to do it, there would be no tension between politics and the judiciary. (Interview with *Mani Pulite* prosecutor, Milan, July 5, 2016)

This statement embodies the awareness of a new professional mission rooted in the idea of "role substitution" (Della Porta 2001, 4). This idea calls for members of the judicial profession to step up against the pervasive presence of corruption and fill the void resulting from other branches' dereliction of duty regarding political accountability. In other words, this new orientation sees the prosecutorial system as the only institution capable of enforcing accountability against corrupt elected officials or government bureaucrats (Della Porta 2001, 4). Della Porta (2001) links this new understanding of the judicial profession directly to judges' "search for support in public opinion" (16). As she explains: "when the political class appears to have failed, many of the judges tend to perceive themselves as the last line of defense for the community" (16).

Della Porta suggests that this new understanding of the judicial mission motivated the actors leading the Clean Hands operation (16). She also argues that earlier manifestations of this new professional ethics may have appeared in the prosecution of terrorist and mafia organizations during the 1970s and the 1980s (16). As opposed to the earlier prosecution of left-wing terrorism by the same prosecutor's office, however, the Clean Hands operation clearly represented an instance of judicial activism in its interpretation of extant legal rules concerning *corruzione* and *concussione*. The difference with previous efforts by Milanese prosecutors to combat left-wing terrorism is fairly clear: in that instance, plea bargaining was introduced via legislation, which the judiciary endorsed, but it had no direct role in shaping. On the other hand, the new approach to corruption investigations that Clean Hands prosecutors pursued represented a novelty of their own making.

As Kmiec (2004) points out, although usually associated with negative connotations, judicial activism may also support morally desirable outcomes (1451). The Clean Hands operation illustrates both sides of this debate. On the one hand, the use of new judge-made legal approaches to corruption investigations entailed inevitable tensions with defendants' rights. On the other hand, the Clean Hands Operation also resulted in an unprecedented and long-awaited judicial breakthrough against systemic corruption. I discuss both dimensions in the following section.

THE MANI PULITE OPERATION

The unprecedented judicial breakthrough in the Clean Hands operation might appear, at first, as an entirely serendipitous event. In this chapter, however, I examined the gradual development of the conditions that would lead to the operation's success. Throughout this chapter, I showed how the early establishment of egalitarian structures within the Milan prosecutor's office led to increasing prosecutorial independence and the accumulation of legal expertise over time. Thanks to the high degree of independence they enjoyed within their office, Milanese prosecutors could develop a new activist understanding of criminal rules on corruption that would be crucial to the Clean Hands operation's success. Furthermore, Milanese prosecutors' interactions with a local anti-corruption organization, *Società Civile*, improved the former's understanding of corruption dynamics and rekindled a sense of civic duty among them. Finally, the end of conservative control over the Roman prosecutor's office in 1992, which I discussed in the previous chapter, led to the suspension of prosecutorial gatekeeping. The latter paved the way for the unfolding of the Clean Hands operation undeterred from undue influences by Roman prosecutorial authorities. In this section, I outline how all these conditions contributed to the Clean Hands operation's unprecedented breakthrough.

The Clean Hands operation originated from an investigation into one of the almost daily corruption instances taking place within the Milan administration. In February 1992, company manager Luca Magni decided to ask law enforcement for help against the local civil servant and Socialist Party affiliate Mario Chiesa (Barbacetto, Gomez and Travaglio 2012, 5). The latter had requested the company manager pay a substantial bribe in exchange for a contract with the retirement services of which he was in charge (Barbacetto, Gomez and Travaglio 2012, 5–6). Prosecutor Di Pietro decided to ask for Magni's collaboration in arresting Mario Chiesa. As a result of this sting operation, the civil servant was caught red-handed in the act of accepting a bribe (Barbacetto, Gomez and Travaglio 2012, 5–6). This legally warranted pretrial detention for the accused.

Mario Chiesa's arrest could have resulted in just one more isolated corruption investigation like many others before. Instead, Di Pietro's application of a new interpretation of criminal rules, the so-called *dazione ambientale*, against key actors in the corruption network[9] sparked a chain reaction of incriminating testimonies. During his pretrial detention, Chiesa decided to provide information about several important nodes within the corruption network. Chiesa explained from which companies he had been receiving bribes, in addition to mentioning several Socialist Party politicians to whom he had delivered these illegal contributions. Furthermore, Chiesa outlined several other instances where companies had been paying bribes to other civil servants across the most varied branches of public administration (Barbacetto, Gomez and Travaglio 2012, 11–14). Thus, Chiesa's testimony effectively described the internal rules and functioning of the corruption system, in addition to incriminating several of its members.

Chiesa's testimony provided prosecutor Di Pietro with a chance to apply his understanding of political corruption as an "environmental condition." Prosecutor Di Pietro filed formal requests to put several company managers under pretrial detention, on the grounds that they had willingly participated in the bribe exchanges described by Chiesa (Barbacetto, Gomez and Travaglio 2012, 16). The choice of charging businessmen with corruption (*corruzione*) and not with forceful collaboration in corruption (*concussione*) was another important novelty in the Clean Hands operation (Interview with a journalist, Milan, May 9, 2016). No judicial authority had ever charged any bribe-givers with accusations that would go beyond their forceful (therefore, unwilling) participation in these exchanges. The initial charges of *corruzione* and false accounting against businessmen in the corruption network were instrumental to a more complex game of incentives, which relied on the concept of *dazione ambientale*.

According to prosecutor Di Pietro, corruption entailed forming a criminal association for the purpose of an illegal exchange. This informal association implied the structuring of criminal activities along a two-tiered structure, which included both "means crimes" and "end crimes" (Di Pietro 2017). The former were crimes that bribe-givers committed to pursue the end crime, namely the illegal exchange of bribes for public contracts. The distinction between means crimes and end crimes had previously emerged within the context of mafia investigations and served to describe mafia activities' multi-tiered structure (Falcone and Turone 2015). Therefore, by using this distinction, prosecutor Di Pietro was adopting an interpretive framework based on the similarities between systemic corruption and organized crime.

This approach aligned closely with *Società Civile*'s understanding of systemic corruption. After all, Di Pietro's 1991 article for *Società Civile*'s journal opened with a comparison between businessmen's complicity with mafia organizations in Sicily and corruption investigations in Milan (8). Besides being an accurate description of criminal behavior, the distinction between means crimes and end crimes was also functional to obtaining defendants' cooperation:

> The *Mani Pulite* investigation was not about corruption; Mani Pulite was about false accounting. [. . .] I wondered: if [a businessman] needs to pay a bribe, where will they draw the money from? The money has to come from their own business activities. But if this is the case, they cannot report these expenses in their books, so they have to commit false accounting. [. . .] I pressed charges of false accounting against these company managers and I told them: "there is a six-year sentence for false accounting, while a sentence for *corruzione* or *concussione* can last up to five years." However, considering the "environmental" features of the corruption system [. . .] it is possible that the person might have been "forced" into this system. So, if the person was willing to tell me why they committed false accounting, I might have been able to conclude that the businessman was forced into giving a bribe. As a result, I did not charge the company manager with false accounting [. . .] but he was not charged with *corruzione* either, since that person was forced into paying a bribe by the environmental conditions they faced, and of which that person was a victim. In this way, I broke the oath of silence (*patto di omertà*) between bribe-givers and bribe-receivers. (Di Pietro 2017)[10]

The initial charges of false accounting, a means crime, and *corruzione*, an end crime, served the purpose of breaking the bond of loyalty among individuals in the corruption system and forcing them into collaboration with judicial authorities. The use of *dazione ambientale* then afforded prosecutor Di Pietro some bargaining leverage to persuade defendants to cooperate. In other words, the concept of *dazione ambientale* allowed Di Pietro to offer leniency in exchange for information, where the defendant was willing to admit (and to describe) the system's dynamics. As I showed earlier in this chapter, the use of *diritto premiale* had been key to the effective prosecution of left-wing terrorist organizations in the 1970s. Similarly, during the Clean Hands investigation, prosecutors consistently rewarded cooperation (Interview with a lawyer, March 21st, Milan, 2016). Judicial actors elaborated informal rules that afforded defendants pleading guilty fewer years of prison the more information they provided about the corruption network (Interview with a lawyer, Milan, March 23, 2016).

Prosecutor Di Pietro's strategy highlights the instrumental use of criminal norms for the purpose of obtaining cooperation from the defendants. When first discussing corruption as an environmental condition in his 1991 article, Di Pietro had argued that legal differences between bribe-givers and bribe-receivers were meaningless, because they equally accepted the informal rules regulating corrupt behavior. Therefore, Di Pietro's use of *concussione* and *corruzione* charges, as described above, did not aim to reflect actual differences in defendants' criminal responsibilities. Rather, the goal of shifting from one type of charge to another was to informally reward cooperation, offering the defendant a lesser charge based on the "systemic" or "environmental" nature of corruption.

As a result, Di Pietro set in motion a chain of incriminating testimonies among defendants. The first group of company managers put under pretrial detention soon started collaborating with judicial authorities (Barbacetto, Gomez and Travaglio 2012, 16). Thanks to their collaboration, Di Pietro obtained an even more detailed picture of the corruption scheme involving politicians, civil servants, and company managers. This criminal system extended to essential services such as retirement services, hospitals, local public transportation, state-owned energy companies, and even airport services (Barbacetto, Gomez and Travaglio 2012, 19). This led to further charges and more offers of cooperation, as the investigation gradually included an increasing number of defendants. Scholars have identified in Di Pietro's investigative strategy a classic example of prisoner's dilemma (Della Porta 2001, 14–15; Sberna and Vannucci 2013, 576). Faced with the possibility that their co-perpetrators might expose their activities or might do so in the near future, politicians and businessmen started volunteering information to improve their chances of avoiding corruption charges. This resulted in a race to testify, with potential defendants lining up in front of Di Pietro's office at all hours of the day to provide testimony in exchange for leniency.

While this prosecutorial strategy was highly effective, it was also prone to abuses. The widespread use of pretrial detentions, for instance, put a deep emotional strain on several defendants. Defendants charged with *corruzione* were put into pretrial detention on the basis that they held an active role in the corruption network. On the other hand, *concussione*, technically, reflected "coercion" into a corrupt exchange and therefore did not warrant the same treatment. However, the instrumental use of these charges to obtain cooperation suggests that pretrial detention might also have served the purpose of putting pressure on the defendants, in addition to preventing defendants' flight or attempts at destroying evidence.

The use of pretrial detentions, along with heightened public scrutiny and media coverage of the Clean Hands operation, created a public shaming effect that led a few defendants to take their own lives. Giglioli (1996) explored the nature of media coverage over the years of the operation. By the end of 1992, national newspapers were filling their first pages with chronicles from the operation, including the content of defendants' confessions to prosecutorial authorities. The close contact that several reporters had established with local police forces in previous years often allowed them to easily obtain transcripts of defendants' confessions (Interview with journalist, May 31, 2016). As a result, the use of pretrial detention and the ample media coverage of the operation created a massive self-reinforcing system of public shaming of the political and economic class, which led some individuals to extreme reactions, such as taking their lives.

As I mentioned before, judicial activism holds different normative connotations depending on its purpose. This is because, as Kmiec (2004) points out, judicial activism is essentially "result-oriented" (1447). Prosecutor Di Pietro's activist interpretation of criminal procedure for the purpose of obtaining defendants' cooperation was geared toward a normatively desirable outcome, namely accountability against corruption. In doing so, however, this activist interpretation of extant rules also created inevitable tensions with well-established legal principles fundamental to the democratic rule of law, namely defendants' rights. In the past, Italian criminal procedure had avoided introducing plea bargaining due to concerns with defendants' protection—to prevent a defendant from bargaining their innocence away in exchange for a lesser sentence. The introduction of this informal negotiation of charges, while extremely effective in uncovering corruption, created clear tensions with defendants' rights that were not explicitly addressed or regulated in the criminal procedure code. The frequent use of pretrial detentions, which put a lot of pressure on defendants to enter this bargaining process, also created strong tensions with defendants' rights.

The dynamic driving the chain of incriminating testimonies kept repeating itself until the final moments of the investigation: one defendant's confession would lead to somebody else's pretrial detention and, then again, prompt somebody else's incriminating testimony. Documentary investigations would precede and follow every testimony in the case (Colombo 1994,

477). Nevertheless, the "engine" behind the operation's continuous expansion was the flow of testimonies from individuals in the corruption network (Colombo 1994, 477). The increasing number of testimonies also allowed for the extension of the investigation beyond the local level. While initial findings revealed the permeating presence of corrupt practices within the Milan city administration, several testimonies pointed at the involvement of national politicians (Colombo 1994, 469–470). Therefore, the flow of testimonies soon extended the scope of judicial proceedings from the local level to the national level, with the involvement of political parties' national treasurers first and national secretaries later.

In order to handle the amount of work and pursue the joint examination of cases, judicial authorities in Milan decided to create a special investigative unit focusing only on the corruption inquiries stemming from Di Pietro's original investigation into Mario Chiesa (Colombo 2010, 132–133). Chief prosecutor Francesco Saverio Borrelli and deputy chief prosecutor Gerardo D'ambrosio decided to bring together lower-ranked prosecutors with significant expertise on this criminal issue. One month after Chiesa's confession, Borrelli and D'Ambrosio persuaded prosecutor Di Pietro to work alongside prosecutor Gherardo Colombo (Colombo 2010, 132). Another month into the investigation, prosecutor Piercamillo Davigo also joined the special unit (133). Both Colombo and Davigo held remarkable expertise in this type of inquiry. The former had led the P2 case, and the latter had been working on recent corruption cases alongside Di Pietro. Thus, both the availability of expert prosecutors and their previous experience working in special investigative units were beneficial to the unfolding of the Clean Hands operation.

The composition of the investigative unit, which spearheaded and continued leading the prosecutorial efforts from 1992 to 1996, debunks attitudinal arguments that identify in political ideology the driving force behind corruption prosecutions (Segal and Spaeth 2002; Ceron and Mainenti 2015). The Clean Hands unit included judicial professionals who had in the past professed affiliation with very different judicial associations. For instance, both Gherardo D'Ambrosio, deputy chief prosecutor and direct supervisor to the special investigative unit, and prosecutor Gherardo Colombo used to be affiliated with MD (Colombo 2010, 27; Nelken 1996*a*, 106), while prosecutor Piercamillo Davigo used to be a member of MI (Milella 2016). As I articulated in chapter 2, these two associations held radically different legal ideologies, with MD taking a more legally progressive stance and MI espousing a reformed version of legal conservatism. Ceron and Mainenti (2015) use individual affiliation as a proxy for judicial professionals' ideology. From this standpoint, the Clean Hands operation can hardly be coded as either a "left-wing" or "right-wing" prosecutorial effort. If political ideology were the driving force behind corruption prosecutions, it would be hard to identify exactly which political ideology motivated Clean Hands prosecutors.

Furthermore, both chief prosecutor Borrelli and prosecutor Di Pietro, the leading member of the special investigative unit, lacked a clear associational affiliation (Nelken 1996*a*, 106). In addition, Nelken (1996*a*) explains that Clean Hands prosecutors always maintained a lenient attitude toward one of the most prominent political personalities under investigation, then head of the Italian Socialist Party Bettino Craxi (106). According to Nelken (1996*a*), Di Pietro's strategic goal in doing so was to encourage cooperation on the part of the Socialist politician, in the hope that this would produce access to more incriminating evidence (106). However, this behavior hardly falls in line with the attitudinal model. Di Pietro's strategy in this instance shows more preoccupation with the operation's overall effectiveness than fervor to punish specific members of the political class. At the same time, this does not mean that the Clean Hands operation did not have political consequences. As I mentioned in chapter 1, Nelken (1996*a*) argues that the Clean Hands operation created a favorable political environment for left-wing political forces such as the Italian Communist Party (which rebranded itself "PDS"—Democratic Party of the Left) (106). It also paved the way for Silvio Berlusconi's political ascendancy, and the alternation in power of left-wing and right-wing coalitions. I explore these developments in the conclusion.

The creation of a special investigative unit was crucial to prosecutorial effectiveness in Clean Hands operation. The formation of a unit handling all interrelated corruption cases entailed the sharing of information and a very efficient division of labor among its three members. Prosecutor Di Pietro focused on gathering confessions from cooperating defendants, while Colombo focused on looking into financial documentation corroborating confidential informants' accounts. Finally, prosecutor Davigo drafted hundreds of requests to Parliament to press charges against MPs (Colombo 2010, 134). Once again, the reservoir of expertise accumulated among Milanese prosecutors thanks to their past experience in special investigative units allowed the Clean Hands operation to achieve unprecedented success.

Overall, the operation resulted in 1,254 convictions, of which 609[11] were reached at the pretrial stage via criminal procedures called "*patteggiamento*" and "*rito abbreviato*" (Di Nicola 2003, 121).[12] Though structured like a trial, the latter is based on the defendant's cooperation and was at the time the closest equivalent of plea bargains within the Italian legal system. The high number of convictions based on *rito abbreviato* underscores the Clean Hands team's ability to reach informal plea deals with defendants. The latter was the result of Di Pietro's novel understanding of corruption as an "environmental condition" and the strategic use of *corruzione* and *concussione* charges to reward defendants' cooperation. Thus, these numbers clearly show that the use of informal plea bargaining was one of the main reasons for the success of the Clean Hands Operation. Furthermore, the high number of appellate corruption convictions[13] that followed first-instance trials also speaks to the effectiveness of the investigative method deployed.

In addition to the deployment of an activist approach to corruption prosecutions, the Milan jurisdiction's lasting inclusion into the judicial network since the 1970s also contributed to the Clean Hands operation's success. Besides contributing to Milanese prosecutors' expertise, inclusion in the judicial network provided the Milanese investigative unit with access to strategic resources. Defendants' testimonies gradually uncovered a corruption system that extended well beyond the Italian borders. In order to transfer huge amounts of money, individuals in the corruption network had taken advantage of slush funds abroad, many of which were located in Switzerland. However, following the money and getting access to Swiss bank accounts were a long and cumbersome bureaucratic process involving local judicial authorities, the Ministry of Justice, and the Ministry of Foreign Affairs, among others (Di Pietro 2017). The involvement of so many veto players decreased the odds of success, given that any of the institutional actors involved might have an interest in preventing the uncovering of illicit exchanges.

To overcome these obstacles, prosecutor Di Pietro appealed to former prosecutor Giovanni Falcone. Falcone had played a vital role in the prosecution of mafia organizations in Palermo, as I will explain in chapter 5. Falcone had also been an active member of the judicial network, whose investigative techniques he had learned to apply to mafia investigations. After leaving the Palermo prosecutor's office, Falcone took up a position at the Ministry of Justice. Early in the Clean Hands operation, prosecutor Di Pietro met with Falcone in the latter's role as a government representative. The two discussed how to obtain documentary evidence of international money transfers (Barbacetto, Gomez and Travaglio 2012, 30), something Falcone had become particularly acquainted with in his investigations into mafia activities. As prosecutor Di Pietro explained:

> After Falcone started working for the Ministry of Justice Penal Affairs General Direction, and because he had stayed in touch with a Swiss prosecutor, prosecutor Del Ponte, who at the time was working in Lugano, Switzerland, Falcone tried to modify the procedure [to request access to Swiss bank accounts for investigative purposes]: [. . .] when urgent circumstances called for it, prosecutors could coordinate among each other [without the Ministry of Justice's intervention]. Hence, what did I do? I filed all the required paperwork, but, at the same time, I would also regularly meet with Swiss prosecutor Del Ponte over a cup of coffee in Chiasso, during which somebody gave me the documentation I needed. (Di Pietro 2017)

Thanks to the Milan jurisdiction's inclusion in the judicial network and Falcone's participation in the latter, the Clean Hands operation could unfold free of red tape and undue interferences from additional veto players. The informal cooperation between Milanese and Swiss prosecutors provided the Milanese special investigative unit with access to the so-called "*Conto Protezione*." As I explained in chapter 3, the latter was a slush fund that the Italian Socialist Party's national leadership had set up and used to transfer bribes (Colombo 2010, 99). Milanese judicial actors had already discovered this slush fund ten years before, during the P2 case (Colombo 2010, 98–99). However, at the time, prosecutorial gatekeeping by the Roman office had prevented the effective prosecution of financial crimes in the P2 case (Colombo 2010, 101). On the contrary, all conditions were now in place for Clean Hands prosecutors to finally uncover this as much as other nodes in the corruption network. Despite changes in the composition of the Clean Hands investigative unit over time, Milanese prosecutors' anti-corruption work concluded in 1996 after having brought to light a massive corruption system and having achieved several convictions against its participants.

CONCLUSION

In this chapter, I examined the development of prosecutorial independence and prosecutorial effectiveness within the Milan prosecutor's office over the years from 1975 to the *Mani Pulite* operation. Even though the latter seemed a sudden and complete disruption of past practices at the time of its unfolding, my analysis shows that the conditions for this massive anti-corruption campaign had long been in the making. The roots of the *Mani Pulite* operation's success lie in the early introduction and enduring presence of egalitarian organizational structures within the Milan prosecutor's office.

The Milanese legal community manifested early its adherence to new constitutional values, and the diffusion of power enacted by the Italian prosecutorial system's decentralization allowed local prosecutors to call for local leadership to align with the new democratic setting. The appointment to the Milan prosecutor's office of "enlightened" conservatives and moderate progressives brought about the restructuring of its internal organization along egalitarian lines. As I showed in this chapter, an egalitarian structure of professional relationships, in turn, allowed Milanese prosecutors to pursue the adoption of investigative and legal novelties. It also allowed them to network with their peers from other jurisdictions and exchange investigative findings and legal knowledge. The same egalitarian structure facilitated the adoption of legal novelties in the prosecution of corruption. Thus, Milanese prosecutors' enhanced independence and increased legal expertise laid the foundation for the effective prosecution of systemic corruption in the *Mani Pulite* operation.

The *Mani Pulite* operation did not remain confined within the Milan jurisdiction. Rather, the Milan investigative unit's work seemed to produce a wave of similar corruption investigations that propagated across several, though not all, Italian jurisdictions. One of the jurisdictions that appeared to join in this anti-corruption campaign, after some hesitation, was Palermo, Sicily's regional capital. After much hesitation and struggle, and at high cost, the Palermo prosecutor's office eventually deployed all its resources in the fight against corruption. The latter intersected closely with the fight against the local mafia organization, *Cosa Nostra*. In the following chapter, I examine the development of prosecutorial independence and effectiveness within the Palermo prosecutor's office. To better understand this case study, I pair it with a case study of the Reggio Calabria prosecutor's office, where unfavorable conditions prevented the development of prosecutorial independence and expertise and therefore the effective prosecution of systemic corruption during the Clean Hands operation.

NOTES

1. The code of criminal procedure established that each investigation should be assigned to one prosecutor. To overcome this formal obstacle to collegial work, chief prosecutor Mario Carassi decided to assign all terrorism investigations to himself formally and then "delegate" each investigation to one of the investigative team members (Caselli 2009, 31–32). In this way, the chief prosecutor became "first among peers," without formally violating the hierarchical principle.

2. The first trial based on the work of the Turn investigative unit took place within the same jurisdiction in 1979, only one year after the adoption of a similar unit by Milanese judicial professionals.

3. As I explained in chapter 3, the Roman instructing judge's office became part of this judicial network, while the prosecutor's office barely participated in this coordinated effort.

4. To overcome this obstacle, prosecutors and instructing judges working on terrorism in Turin relied on a criminal code provision describing groups illegally carrying weapons and adapted this provision to terrorist organizations. As prosecutor Gian Carlo Caselli explains: "It was up to us, to our investigations, to revitalize a legal provision that Antolisei [one of most prominent jurists contributing to criminal law jurisprudence in Turin during the 1960s] thought was dead and buried for good. We had to interpret it in a way that would match the internal organizations of groups such as the Red Brigades and First Line. Of course, we had to do so in a way that was also respectful of the letter of the law." Quote in Caselli (2009, 35). Author's translation

5. "Premiale" in Italian contains the same root as the word "premio," which means "prize."

6. See prosecutor Spataro's testimony (2016) in the previous section, where he elaborated on his newly found commitment to educating the public about the nature of terrorist organizations and the threat to democracy.

7. In chapter 5, I elaborate on the work of the special investigative unit against mafia organizations in Palermo.

8. Plea bargains had only been applied to terrorism cases before, and for a limited time prescribed by legislation, as I explained earlier in this chapter.

9. As the head of a publicly-owned company and member of the Socialist Party, Chiesa was likely to be an important node within a broader network of illegal exchanges (interview with a journalist, Milan, May 4, 2016).

10. It is noticeable that Di Pietro calls the mutual agreement on silence about illegal exchanges "*patto di omertà*," an expression that has come to describe mafia organizations' effort to intimidate into silence anyone who came in contact, willingly or under threat, with their activities. In addition to describing corruption as a criminal system comprising "means crimes" and "end crimes," a description first applied to mafia organizations (Turone and Falcone 2015), Di Pietro is explicitly referencing terms used in the context of mafia organizations.

11. These numbers are the author's elaboration on the data offered by Di Nicola (2003, 121).

12. Di Nicola presents the number of "persone 'condannate' dal GuP," which roughly translates to "convictions issued by the GuP" (121). These convictions in turn can be broken down into those achieved "con patteggiamento" and "con rito abbreviato." The former are 506 and the latter are 103 (121). Therefore, the total number of convictions reached at the pre-trial stage is 609. Di Nicola (2003) also presents a category for "Persone condannate dal tribunale" (individuals convicted at trial) (121). This category is broken down into two further groups: "con patteggiamento" and "al dibattimento." The former lists 341 convictions, the latter 304 (121). Thus, the total number of individuals convicted at trial is 645. As a result of adding 609 pre-trial convictions to 645 convictions at trial, the total number of individuals convicted in the Clean Hands operation was 1,254.

13. I presented the number of appellate corruption convictions in chapter 1.

Chapter 5

Tackling *Omertà*

The Prosecutors' Offices in Palermo and Reggio Calabria

In the previous chapters, I explored the effects of hierarchical and egalitarian structures within the prosecutors' offices in Rome and Milan on prosecutorial independence and effectiveness. Ultimately, chief prosecutors' choices about their offices' internal organization determined the outcome of corruption prosecutions before and during the Clean Hands operation. The case studies of Palermo and Reggio Calabria also offer important insights into the role of organizational structures in fostering the conditions for effective corruption prosecution over time. These cases further illustrate the role of informal as well as formal institutions in shaping a prosecutor's office's internal organization.

The predominant legal culture among lower-ranked prosecutors in Palermo and Reggio Calabria remained highly bureaucratic and traditionally conservative well into the 1980s, as opposed to growing trends toward enlightened conservatism or legal progressivism in other jurisdictions. This represents a significant difference in prosecutors' offices in Milan and Rome. Milanese prosecutors had been at the forefront of the fight for decentralization after re-democratization. In Rome, conservative chief prosecutors were faced with a growing insurgence among their lower ranks, who often complained about their superiors' hierarchical attitudes. On the contrary, a large group of lower-ranked prosecutors in Palermo and Reggio Calabria seemed to welcome their superiors' traditional legal conservatism, especially in its bureaucratic understanding of the judicial mission and its insistence on hierarchical control.

For this reason, these case studies offer a more nuanced picture of the relationship between prosecutorial leadership, organizational structures, and the prosecution of corruption. The Palermo case study, in particular, shows that lower ranks' opposition to egalitarian structures may have practically invalidated the latter's formal introduction in its early years. In Palermo, progressive chief prosecutors at times found extreme resistance to their investigative and organizational methods among their subordinates, who held a more traditional understanding of their profession. Therefore, this case study highlights the importance of examining both formal and informal institutions within a prosecutor's office.

As I show in this chapter, it was the presence of an instructing judge's office with less traditionalist legal views among its lower ranks that offered a lifeline to progressive and enlightened conservative prosecutors in Palermo. The tight inter-office collaboration between Palermo instructing judges and prosecutors under an enlightened conservative leadership in both offices brought about unprecedented results in the prosecution of local mafia organizations. The 1986 Palermo maxi trial against more than 300 mafia members resulted from the egalitarian relationship between this enlightened leadership and its lower ranks, which allowed prosecutors and instructing judges to pursue significant innovations in the prosecution of mafia organizations. In turn, this facilitated the expertise accumulation that would allow Palermo prosecutors and instructing judges to prosecute systemic corruption effectively during the Clean Hands operation.

Nevertheless, the Palermo prosecutor's office also offers significant longitudinal variation in its prosecutorial leadership and organizational structures, which I leverage to understand these variables' impact on the prosecution of mafia organizations first and systemic corruption later. Until the 1990s, every advancement toward egalitarianism faced incredible resistance within the Palermo prosecutor's office and the instructing judge's office. Traditionally conservative chief prosecutors and chief instructing judges dismantled the organizational structures and investigative innovations that had led to the 1986 maxi trial, with some help from judicial associations in the High Council. Thus, the Palermo prosecutor's office also exemplifies the fight between different legal factions within the Italian judiciary.

Despite the struggle between different legal factions within the Palermo prosecutor's office, changes in prosecutorial leadership right at the start of the Clean Hands operation allowed Palermo prosecutors to bring their previously accumulated expertise to this anti-corruption effort. On the other hand, for the whole period of time considered in this analysis, the Reggio Calabria prosecutor's office maintained a traditionally hierarchical organization. This resulted in the creation of an extremely hostile working environment for young prosecutors, who left the Reggio Calabria office as soon as possible. The high personnel turnover also undermined any effort to resist or protest this organizational approach among lower-ranked prosecutors. Thus, over time, the persistence of a hierarchical organization in the Reggio Calabria office led to a dearth of personnel and expertise. This explains this office's inability to effectively join in the anti-corruption efforts spearheaded by the Clean Hands operation.

Furthermore, the case studies of Palermo and Reggio Calabria allow me to control for differences in the nature of the local corruption network as potential alternative reasons behind the success of the Clean Hands operation. The corruption system that Milanese prosecutors uncovered included businessmen, civil servants, and elected officials. While the main features of this corruption network remained the same across most Northern and central regions of Italy, in Southern regions, this network also included mafia organizations (Della Porta and Vannucci 2012, 220–221). The involvement of criminal organizations like *Cosa Nostra* in Sicily and the *'Ndrangheta* in Calabria profoundly affected the corruption network's structure and internal dynamics.

Despite the presence of a similar criminal framework, the prosecutors' offices in Palermo and Reggio Calabria showed significant differences in the prosecution of mafia organizations and systemic corruption. Palermo prosecutorial authorities successfully joined in the wave of corruption prosecutions following the Clean Hands operation, after some hesitation. On the other hand, Reggio Calabria prosecutorial authorities showed little effectiveness in their efforts to do the same. Thus, the comparison between Palermo and Reggio Calabria further illustrates the importance of local egalitarian structures in producing an effective response to systemic corruption, regardless of this criminal phenomenon's local features.

In this chapter, I first explore the case study of the Palermo prosecutor's office and then the Reggio Calabria prosecutor's office. For both case studies, I examine chief prosecutors' profiles and behavior from the mid-1970s to the time of the Clean Hands operation. I explore how chief prosecutors organized the relationships with their subordinates and how these offices' internal organization affected the development of investigative and legal innovations in the prosecution of local mafias. In doing so, I take into account the contributions of instructing judges' offices to the work of their prosecutorial counterparts, where necessary. Finally, I show how the early development of prosecutorial expertise in the fight against mafia organizations helped Palermo prosecutors join in the Clean Hands operation's anti-corruption efforts. At the same time, the hostile working conditions within the Reggio Calabria prosecutor's office and the lack of accumulated expertise in the prosecution of mafia organizations explain this office's failure to prosecute systemic corruption effectively.

PALERMO CHIEF PROSECUTORS

The appointment of chief prosecutors to the Palermo office seems to indicate the long-lasting prevalence of the conservative legal faction. As it is visible from table 5.1, for almost a decade, from 1981 to 1990, Palermo chief prosecutors manifested a clear affiliation with the conservative judicial group

Table 5.1 Palermo Chief Prosecutors' Profiles

	Gaetano Costa (1978)	*Vincenzo Pajno (1981)*	*Salvatore Curti Giardina (1987)*	*Pietro Giammanco (1990)*	*Gian Carlo Caselli (1992)*
Associational Affiliation	No affiliation	MI	MI	No affiliation	MD
Previous Appointment	Caltanissetta chief prosecutor	Lower-ranked prosecutor at the General Prosecutor's Office	Catania chief prosecutor	Lower-ranked prosecutor in Palermo	Turin Appellate Court President

Source: Information from *Il Corriere della Sera, La Repubblica*. Author's elaboration.

Magistratura Indipendente (MI). However, this straightforward observation does not convey the full complexity of appointments to this office. In decades prior to the 1980s, the Palermo prosecutor's office often appeared as a challenging post, troubled by systemic criminal issues such as the presence of a still powerful *Cosa Nostra.* In the 1960s and 1970s, Parliament took the lead in the fight against mafia organizations, much more than local prosecutor's offices. The so-called *Commissioni Parlamentari d'Inchiesta*, parliamentary investigative committees, were set up to investigate mafia presence over the Sicilian territory and the judicial system's response to it. These parliamentary committees thoroughly examined mafia organizations' historical development and the current state of their activities.

The committee's reports praised aggressive judicial action against this criminal phenomenon, but still found the latter essentially ineffective. Too often, mafia trials with hundreds of defendants would end in an abysmal number of convictions, due to "lack of evidence" (Commissione Parlamentare d'Inchiesta sul Fenomeno della Mafia in Sicilia 1976, 159). This resulted from the use of traditional prosecutorial practices ill-fit to tackle mafia organizations. I elaborate on this flawed approach to mafia prosecutions later in the chapter. Thus, the Palermo prosecutor's office lacked an effective response to this systemic criminal issue.

At the same time, the Palermo office represented one of the most dangerous prosecutorial posts. *Cosa Nostra* had not hesitated to kill prosecutorial authorities in the past, like chief prosecutor Pietro Scaglione (Madeo 1971). While the prosecutorial methods used in past investigations may have proved ineffective against *Cosa Nostra*, these efforts demonstrated local actors' willingness to fight criminal dominance over the territory. The killing of chief prosecutor Scaglione and his personal guard in 1971 (Madeo 1971) inaugurated the war between *Cosa Nostra* and local judicial authorities, which would continue in the years to come with more casualties among law enforcement and judicial personnel.

In addition, the Palermo prosecutor's office could be quite a hostile environment for some chief prosecutors. Chief prosecutor Gaetano Costa, for instance, experienced deep resistance from both his subordinates and his superiors within the Palermo jurisdiction. Hostility to Costa's new appointment immediately manifested itself in the delay with which he was granted his new position. Rather than delivering the office to Costa immediately after the latter's formal appointment by the High Council, the Palermo General Prosecutor at the Court of Appeals allowed one of the office's lower-ranked prosecutors to continue serving as the interim chief for at least another month (Bartoli Costa 2001, 33–34). This was highly unusual, since other appointments to judicial offices in the Sicilian region had not incurred the same delay (33–34).

The intervention of a higher-ranked prosecutor to prevent the timely appointment of the new Palermo chief prosecutor appears as a clearly hostile intervention from a higher judicial official against a lower-ranked one. This hostility might have resulted from Costa's unusual political background: chief prosecutor Costa was an active member of the Italian Communist Party (Lodato 2012, 42). This political affiliation stood in stark contrast with the general environment within the Palermo prosecutor's office, where progressive associations like MD struggled to gather consensus in the 1970s (Ceron and Mainenti 2015, 227). Chief prosecutor Costa continued facing a highly hostile environment within his office during his tenure, as I detail in the following section of this chapter.

Costa's tenure ended with his killing by *Costa Nostra* in 1981, another casualty in the war between the local mafia and state authorities. Both his successors, Vincenzo Pajno and Salvatore Curti Giardina, presented a very different background, given their affiliation with the conservative judicial association MI. Both Pajno and Curti Giardina seemed to reflect the generally conservative environment in which they found themselves working. However, at the same time, Pajno and Curti Giardina espoused two different understandings of legal conservatism at odds with each other.

During his tenure, chief prosecutor Pajno would turn out to be an enlightened conservative, while Curti Giardina would demonstrate a more traditionalist understanding of legal conservatism. The latter became visible especially in Curti Giardina's relationship with the press. In order to protect his office, Curti Giardina did not hesitate to prosecute and jail two journalists for their investigative work into ongoing mafia investigations (Marroni 1988). Curti Giardina's repressive measures against freedom of the press were so extreme and reactionary that, allegedly, the High Council initiated disciplinary proceedings against him following a suggestion from Curti Giardina's predecessor, Vincenzo Pajno, now Palermo General Prosecutor (Bolzoni 1988). Pajno's intervention in this case highlights the differences in these two judicial professionals' legal conservatism.

Curti Giardina's appointment, as much as his successor Pietro Giammanco's, reflects the struggle between legal factions within the Palermo prosecutor's office. Curti Giardina's appointment created significant divisions between the progressive association *Magistratura Democratica* (MD) and the alliance between more conservative elements, namely MI and a part of UniCost (Rosso 1987). Despite having passed the High Council's internal committee selection, Curti Giardina did not immediately receive enough votes to be confirmed (*Fumata Nera per il PM di Palermo* 1987). Even during the final vote, MD members opposed Curti Giardina's appointment to signal their disapproval of the agreement around his nomination reached by other associations (Rosso 1987). Overall, Curti Giardina's appointment seemed to represent a "corrective" to previous progress achieved by enlightened conservative leadership in the Palermo office. As I discuss later in this chapter, Curti Giardina's appointment paved the way for a significant restructuring of the Palermo prosecutor's office's internal organization.

In a similar fashion, Pietro Giammanco's appointment to the Palermo prosecutor's office resulted from a harsh fight between judicial associations within the High Council. Giammanco's appointment came at the end of significant internal struggle between Palermo prosecutors, partially encouraged by chief prosecutor Curti Giardina (Bolzoni 1989). By the end of the latter's tenure, prosecutors' successes against *Cosa Nostra* had provoked a harsh response by their peers not specializing in mafia investigations. This feud between prosecutors had paralyzed the work of the office, thanks to anonymous letters that contained unfounded allegations against the judicial professionals leading anti-mafia efforts (Rosa and Zilocchi 2021). Chief prosecutor Curti Giardina had failed to reconcile differences among his subordinates (*Fumata Nera per il PM di Palermo* 1987), Giammanco being one of them. Thus, Giammanco' appointment was supposed to "bring peace" in the war between different prosecutorial factions (Bolzoni 1990*b*).

However, this appointment also came with significant allegations, which clouded Giammanco's tenure. While Giammanco held no affiliation with judicial associations, he was known to be very close to prominent local Christian Democratic politicians (Mazzocchi 1990). For this reason, Giammanco's appointment, once again, divided High Council members between conservative and moderate judicial associations (MI and UniCost, except for one of the latter's members) on the side of Giammanco, vis-à-vis MD members (Mazzocchi 1990), who opposed him. Interestingly, members of the new judicial association, *Movimento per la Giustizia*, which I discussed in chapter 4, supported Giammanco's appointment (Mazzocchi 1990). This might have been a reward for Giammanco's work to reconcile differences among Palermo prosecutors (Mazzocchi 1990). At the same time, important voices close to *Movimento* condemned Giammanco's appointment because of his relationship with the Christian Democratic party (Mazzocchi 1990).[1]

Giammanco's tenure exacerbated tensions even more and resulted in a very short term in office. In May 1992, a few months after the start of the Clean Hands investigation, Giovanni Falcone, who had been one of the instructing judges in the 1986 maxi trial, died in a brutal mafia attack. Fifty days later, his former colleague, chief prosecutor Borsellino, was also brutally killed by *Cosa Nostra*. Falcone and Borsellino's killings represented the mafia's revenge for the maxi trial, whose final convictions on appeal came in 1992. These killings provoked an immediate surge of outrage against chief prosecutor Giammanco among his subordinates (Rosso 1992). Palermo prosecutors threatened to leave their jobs if Giammanco did not resign and if they were not granted heightened protection against mafia attacks (Rosso 1992).

Giammanco eventually decided to leave (*'Via Giammanco, Ma Non Basta'* 1992), and the Council appointed Gian Carlo Caselli as his successor. Caselli possessed clear progressive credentials (Coppola 1992*c*). Furthermore, he had been among the Turin instructing judges at the forefront of the fight against left-wing terrorism in the 1970s (Coppola 1992*c*). As a member of the first special anti-terrorism unit in Turin, Caselli had helped build that expertise that would later facilitate the emergence of effective mafia and corruption investigations. Caselli had also been one of the founding members of the judicial network through which special investigative units would share their investigative and legal novelties. Furthermore, Caselli had an even closer connection to Palermo. In the years leading to the Palermo maxi trial, Caselli had helped former chief instructing judge Nino Caponnetto to formalize the creation of the Palermo special investigative unit (Caselli 2009, 31–32), as I explain later in this chapter.

Therefore, Caselli's appointment concluded a long struggle among prosecutorial factions within the Palermo office. While outsiders like Costa and an enlightened conservative like Pajno had organized the relationship with their subordinates along egalitarian lines, more traditionally conservative elements, both among lower-ranked and chief prosecutors, had met any such change with harsh pushback. Caselli's appointment, the first chief prosecutor clearly affiliated with a progressive association, brought an end to this fight. The progressive legal faction could claim a victory at a high cost, since Caselli's appointment resulted from the aftershock to Falcone and Borsellino's killings.

THE PALERMO PROSECUTOR'S OFFICE'S INTERNAL ORGANIZATION

The alternation between prosecutorial authorities with vastly different legal preferences produced similar alternations in the Palermo office's organizational structure. Progressive chief prosecutors and enlightened conservatives like Pajno attempted to shape the relationship with their subordinates along egalitarian lines, therefore promoting the emergence of prosecutorial expertise and innovations. On the other hand, conservative chief prosecutors like Curti Giardina and controversial personalities like Giammanco implemented a highly hierarchical understanding of their role in relation to their subordinates, often opposing the use of legal novelties. This aversion to investigative innovations produced increasing factionalism among prosecutors. In this section, I briefly discuss how each Palermo chief prosecutor organized the relationship with his subordinates.

Mirroring his status as an ideological outsider, Costa's style of leadership and organizational preferences represented a significant break in past practices within the Palermo office. Above all, Costa was willing to reshape the relationship with his subordinates to include them in the office's decision-making even when it involved salient decisions about mafia investigations. In May 1980, Costa reviewed a police report that outlined the relationships between Sicilian *Cosa Nostra* families and *Cosa Nostra* families in the United States. Costa invited his subordinates to a collegial discussion about prosecutorial actions to take based on the report (Bartoli Costa 2001, 35–36).

Unfortunately, he found significant resistance among his subordinates. Costa's subordinates refused to co-sign the arrest warrants that the chief prosecutor issued based on the evidence in the police report (Bartoli Costa 2001, 35–36). Thus, Costa's attempt to include his subordinates in decision-making on important mafia investigations resulted in the chief prosecutor's isolation within his office. Furthermore, this was not the only instance in which the progressive chief prosecutor found himself facing a hostile working environment. In one of his personal notes, Costa wrote that one of these subordinates, prosecutor Gaetano Martorana, was a domineering presence hovering over his work:

> He [Martorana] handles every issue and seems to want to preserve his prerogatives entirely. In his view, I should only take action on his behalf, and he has so far succeeded (at least until now) in isolating me. He has managed to leave only a few issues within my reach. He is the first one to receive any individual, including prominent figures and police chiefs, to acquire their contributions, and only afterwards he introduces them to my attention. He checks all the mail, which only gets distributed to everyone after his careful review. He commands his subordinates.[2]

What Costa is describing is the existence of an alternative, informal organizational structure within his office. Far from embracing the new chief prosecutor's egalitarian attitudes, Palermo prosecutors rather continued operating within an informally hierarchical environment in which Martorana acted as *de facto* chief prosecutor. In this informal role, Martorana managed to isolate the *de jure* prosecutorial authority.

On the other hand, chief prosecutor Pajno might have faced a more favorable environment than his predecessor. First of all, Pajno presented himself as an enlightened conservative, therefore more attuned to his lower ranks' general preferences. However, since Pajno's tenure lasted longer than Costa's, he might have also witnessed some significant changes in his subordinates' ideological outlook over the years, possibly moving away from more traditional forms of conservatism, in line with broader trends among young prosecutors in the 1980s (Della Porta 2001, 5–6). Regardless of the surrounding environment, chief prosecutor Pajno's conservative attitudes did not prevent him from being an enlightened reformer.

This is immediately visible in Pajno's support for his subordinates' willingness to pursue aggressive prosecutorial action against the mafia. During Pajno's tenure, the Palermo instructing judge's office was pursuing new investigative methods to tackle mafia crimes by informally creating a special investigative unit on mafia cases. The latter introduced a new model for mafia investigations that attracted the attention of a few prosecutors under Pajno's supervision. When prosecutors Di Pisa and Geraci received a new, massive police report into mafia activities in Palermo, the two prosecutors did everything they could to make sure that the special investigative unit in the instructing judge's office would join them on the case (Recanatesi 1986).

Pajno's enlightened reformist attitude is clearly visible in his willingness to go along with his subordinates' initiative, rather than imposing a course of action of his own. In this instance, prosecutors decided that it would be highly beneficial to collaborate with the new special investigative unit in the instructing judge's office, and chief prosecutor Pajno allowed this cooperation to occur. Furthermore, the chief prosecutor soon decided to imitate the practices of the Palermo instructing office. Pajno therefore established a similar special investigative unit within his office (Stille 1995, 89). Pajno's decisions clearly indicate his openness to innovations and initiatives coming from the lower ranks.

Pajno's attitude was in stark contrast to his superiors' attitudes toward the same type of investigative innovations. The instructing judge's office had already received harsh criticism from the Palermo judiciary's higher ranks for its aggressive use of investigative innovations in the prosecution of mafia organizations (La Licata 1993, 92–93). The Palermo Court of Appeals president had been particularly receptive to local banks and financial investors' complaints that investigations into financial transactions and money laundering represented an "undue intervention" (La Licata 1993, 92–93). As reported by chief instructing judge Chinnici in his personal diary, the president of the Palermo Court of Appeals personally summoned him to recommend that Chinnici only assigned simple, uncontroversial cases to his subordinate, judge Falcone, so that "he would avoid trying to find out anything, because instructing judges have never found out anything" (La Licata 1993, 73).

Chief prosecutor Pajno's openness to adopting the same investigative methods as the Palermo instructing judge's office stands in stark contrast with the Court of Appeals president's aversion to these same innovations. Thus, Pajno's enlightened conservative attitudes provided crucial support to the diffusion of investigative innovations that would enhance prosecutorial effectiveness against mafia organizations. These same reformist attitudes would contribute to creating an important reservoir of prosecutorial expertise in the long run.

On the other hand, the progress that Pajno made in reshaping professional relationships along egalitarian lines within his office suffered serious pushback under the new chief prosecutor, Salvatore Curti Giardina. As previously mentioned, Curti Giardina was a different type of legal conservative than Pajno. This was visible in how Curti Giardina handled the relationship with his subordinates. The prosecutors involved in the special mafia investigative units represented a minority within the office, and the unit's work had not met unanimous support. These tensions, whether genuinely focused on legal issues or hiding shadier motives and interests, would create huge divisions among Palermo prosecutors (Rosa and Zilocchi 2021). Curti Giardina exacerbated these tensions by walking back his predecessor's egalitarian decision-making and openness to lower-ranked prosecutors' suggestions and instead encouraging one faction in this fight.

In 1988, the High Council of the Judiciary "invit[ed] all prosecutorial authorities in Palermo (but also, in other Sicilian jurisdictions as well) to submit recommendations on how to strengthen prosecutorial and judicial institutions involved in the fight against mafia organizations" (Bolzoni 1988). To comply with this directive, Curti Giardina did not pursue collegial forms of decision-making. Rather, by order of the chief prosecutor, the task to evaluate prosecutorial institutions fell on two of Curti Giardina's subordinates with limited experience in the fight against organized crime (Bolzoni 1988). Furthermore, these two prosecutors operated in complete isolation from their colleagues, therefore neglecting to include investigative units' prosecutors in this assessment process (Bolzoni 1988).

Only when the two prosecutors delivered their report to Curti Giardina, their peers became aware of its existence and forced their superior into an animated discussion about the content of the final document (Bolzoni 1988). The tensions between different factions within the Palermo office (essentially, special unit prosecutors on one side and the rest of the office on the other) derived from the report content. Apparently, the two prosecutors had modeled their report after the chief instructing judge's report, which argued that "a special investigative unit was not necessary to prosecute mafia organizations" and advised assigning single prosecutors to mafia cases, in the traditional way (Bolzoni 1988).

This instance perfectly describes how a return to a more hierarchical organization of the relationships among Palermo prosecutors had detrimental effects on investigative innovations and exacerbated divisions within the office. Curti Giardina's decision to assign the assessment process to two subordinates, instead of involving all prosecutors in a collegial discussion, delivered a document with clearly one-sided argument. Even though this effort did not end the way the chief prosecutor had probably hoped, its effects deeply impacted the office's work. This episode created divisions and further exacerbated tensions between prosecutorial factions. As I show later in the chapter, these divisions would cripple prosecutors' work against mafia organizations during Curti Giardina and chief Giammanco's tenure.

Chief Giammanco's tenure had a similar impact on the office's internal organization. Giammanco was the first Palermo chief prosecutor after the 1989 reform that disbanded instructing judges' offices and probably favored a personnel migration to prosecutors' offices. Therefore, chief Giammanco found himself overseeing a group of prosecutors and former instructing judges who had previously led the fight against mafia organizations collaboratively, though in formally separate tracks. Giammanco's appointment came with high hopes among his subordinates. When the High Council was considering replacements to Curti Giardina, Giammanco received former instructing judge Falcone's endorsement. Falcone, the most prominent member of the special investigative unit, hoped that Giammanco would manifest less hierarchical attitudes than his former superior, chief instructing judge Vittorio Meli (Stille 1995, 317).

However, Giammanco soon betrayed Falcone's expectations. After taking office, Giammanco made it clear with his behavior that he did not see Falcone, now a lower-ranked prosecutor, as a peer. Rather than creating space for collegial consultations with his subordinates, Giammanco created his own group of loyalists within the office (Stille 1995, 329). As a result, he excluded Falcone from some key decision-making moments regarding important investigations into the relationship between the mafia and politics (Stille 1995, 329–330). Giammanco's hierarchical attitude isolated Falcone, who decided to leave his role as anti-mafia prosecutor because of his frustration with his superior (Stille 1995, 332).

Falcone's death in a terrible mafia attack brought Giammanco's tenure to an end (Rosso 1992). This paved the way for Gian Carlo Caselli's tenure, as the result of Palermo prosecutors' insurgence against chief Giammanco. The High Council specifically chose Caselli for his previous experiences working with special investigative units on left-wing terrorism (Coppola 1992*c*). Therefore, Caselli's appointment reflected Palermo prosecutors' preference for a superior that would facilitate the adoption of investigative novelties and that would abandon his predecessors' hierarchical style of leadership.

These expectations were correct. Gian Carlo Caselli not only empowered the special investigative unit on mafia cases but also contributed to bringing back collegial consultations within the office. This was especially visible in salient investigations, like the one into Christian Democratic leader Giulio Andreotti. Chief Caselli led the investigation alongside several other prosecutors, who worked collegially to build the case against Andreotti and his involvement with mafia organizations (Stille 1995, 391–394). This egalitarian structure of relationships and the strengthening of the special investigative unit brought significant results in the prosecution of corruption as well, as I explain later in this chapter.

In order to understand Palermo's contribution to the Clean Hands investigation, it is first necessary to examine how different organizational structures contributed to or hindered the development of expertise among Palermo prosecutors over the years. In the following section, I discuss the emergence of prosecutorial effectiveness as a function of egalitarian structures in the Palermo prosecutor's and instructing judge's office. Egalitarian structures allowed lower-ranked prosecutors and instructing judges to pursue significant legal innovations against mafia organizations. On the other hand, I also discuss the setbacks to prosecutorial effectiveness that followed the reinstatement of hierarchical structures within both offices.

BUILDING EXPERTISE IN THE PROSECUTION OF MAFIA ORGANIZATIONS: THE MAXI TRIAL

Palermo chief prosecutors' organizational choices had momentous effects on the development of prosecutorial expertise within their office. Enlightened conservative and progressive chief prosecutors introduced collegial forms of decision-making, which allowed their subordinates to pursue legal innovations and strengthen the prosecutorial response to mafia organizations. However, the Palermo case also shows that lower ranks' resistance to egalitarian structures may guarantee the informal survival of hierarchy, with significant effects on prosecutorial effectiveness. Chief Costa's example sheds light on the role of informal institutions. The delayed introduction of egalitarian structures within the Palermo office, however, found a remedy in the Palermo instructing office's embrace of this collegial organization. Thus, in this section, I devote ample space to explaining the development of egalitarian structures and investigative expertise among instructing judges as well, given the important pattern of interactions between the latter and their prosecutorial counterparts.

The persistence of an informal hierarchy within the Palermo prosecutor's office during Costa's tenure crippled the early development of innovations in the prosecution of mafia organizations, despite novel findings showing the latter's increasing complexity due to its coordinated drug trafficking operations between the United States and Sicily (Chinnici 1990, 12–13). On the other hand, the presence of a parallel investigative institution, the instructing judge's office, filled the vacuum resulting from the lack of prosecutorial action and laid the foundations for a resurgence of prosecutorial effectiveness in the future. Chief Costa was not the only judicial authority who had taken note of the mafia's changing features. Chief instructing judge Chinnici had also been studying the same police reports that had alerted Costa. As one of Chinnici's subordinates explained, based on these reports:

> He [Chinnici] believed that only a massive judicial effort to look at this criminal phenomenon comprehensively, trying to make sense of the connections among all most relevant crimes, would shed light on the criminal scheme underlying mafia activities, and on their authors. This judicial effort was in turn a necessary response to the investigative inertia of the previous decade, which created a vacuum [Chinnici] and his judges were called to fill.[3]

Therefore, this new understanding of the criminal phenomenon called for a different investigative method than the traditional bureaucratic approach to criminal inquiries. More importantly, Chinnici's egalitarian attitudes allowed him to establish the conditions for the effective prosecution of mafia organizations, based on the chief instructing judge's improved understanding of this criminal phenomenon. Chinnici, who held progressive legal views (Stille 1995, 31), strongly supported his subordinates' independence (La Licata 1993, 59). For this reason, Chinnici entrusted his subordinates to work together on interconnected mafia cases, creating the foundation for what would later formally become the special investigative unit into mafia cases. Chinnici's egalitarian attitudes afforded his subordinates the freedom to pursue investigative novelties that would revolutionize the prosecution of mafia organizations.

At the beginning of the 1980s, prosecutorial successes against left-wing terrorism had received public commendation and ample coverage on Italian newspapers. This attracted the attention of Chinnici's subordinates. As one Milanese prosecutor recalled:

> Because at some point news spread of the work we were conducting and of the results we achieved. I recall a newspaper article by Montanelli,[4] published immediately after a coordinated operation against *Autonomia Operaia*[5] on December 21st, 1979. The operation brought to arrests all over Italy, and Montanelli wrote an article [. . .] in which he evaluated our work along these lines, if I recall correctly: "We praise these judges who have gathered to work in collaboration with each other, while nobody was aware of their work and without letting any news of it spread to the media. They have showed that it is possible to commit to the prosecution of grave crimes such as terrorism with excellent results." [. . .] From that point on, our joint investigation methods[6] diffused across the judiciary. For this reason, Falcone as well as others started taking part in our gatherings from time to time. (Spataro 2016)

Instructing judge Falcone and instructing judge Borsellino, whom chief Chinnici had entrusted with some of the most salient mafia investigations, started meeting regularly with the network of prosecutors working on terrorism cases and learning from them:

> How we coordinated with police forces, how we interpreted legal rules so as to hold accountable individuals who were not formally affiliated with terrorist organizations, but who had provided "external support" for their criminal actions. Finally, they [the Palermo judicial professionals] wanted to learn how we handled confidential informants' testimonies, and how these testimonies directed our investigative work. (Spataro 2016)

Chinnici's egalitarian attitudes created space for his subordinates to follow their interests in new investigative approaches. Thus, the introduction of an egalitarian organizational approach within the instructing office facilitated the adoption of significant investigative and legal innovations in the prosecution of mafia organizations.

After Chinnici's violent death in a mafia attack in 1983 (Caselli 2009, 31), his successor, Antonino Caponnetto, persevered in a similar style of leadership, working to formalize Chinnici's intuitions about collegial work. Once he assumed the role of Palermo chief instructing judge, Caponnetto sought to formalize the existence of the special investigative unit on mafia cases (Caselli 2009, 31–32). To do this, Caponnetto reached out to one of the instructing judges who had developed this innovation in the first place, former Turin instructing judge Gian Carlo Caselli, to learn from his expertise (Caselli 2009, 31–32).

The creation of the special investigative unit in the Palermo instructing judge's office also provides an interesting test of attitudinal arguments (Segal and Spaeth 2002). To the extent that attitudinal arguments may help explain judicial and prosecutorial actors' aggressiveness against mafia organizations, the composition of the special investigative unit in the Palermo instructing judge's office disproves these arguments. Its members held radically different political views, with judge Falcone's political sympathies leaning left (Stille 1995: 24) and judge Borsellino's leaning decidedly right (Stille 1995, 25). The cooperation between ideologically opposed judicial professionals in the same investigative unit dispels attitudinal hypotheses that might link aggressive mafia prosecution to specific political attitudes.

Chief Chinnici and chief Caponnetto's egalitarian attitudes, along with their openness to their subordinates' adoption of investigative novelties, immensely benefited the Palermo prosecutor's office as well. As I previously mentioned, chief Costa found unwavering opposition to his egalitarianism among his subordinates. However, by the time Pajno became chief prosecutor, a small minority of prosecutors with very different attitudes had emerged within the prosecutor's office. The creation of an informal group of instructing judges working together on mafia cases attracted the attention of these lower-ranked prosecutors who wished to tackle mafia crime more aggressively. As I previously mentioned, these prosecutors did everything they could to work with the special investigative unit on mafia cases in the instructing office (Recanatesi 1986). Chief prosecutor Pajno not only consented to this but also soon moved toward forming a similar group of specialized prosecutors within his office (Stille 1995, 89).

Chief Pajno's openness to his subordinates' initiatives set the Palermo prosecutor's office on a course toward achieving unprecedented success in the prosecution of *Cosa Nostra* with the so-called Palermo maxi trial. The 1986 Palermo maxi trial was the result of the collaborative work between the special investigative units on mafia cases in the prosecutor's and in the instructing judge's offices. Together, these groups brought to trial 452 individuals with charges of mafia affiliation (Suro 1987). The trial started in 1986 and concluded in 1987, after months of secret deliberations among the judges and jurors adjudicating the case, which brought to 338 convictions (Suro 1987).

The Palermo maxi trial was not the first instance in which prosecutorial authorities had indicted hundreds of defendants on mafia-related charges. However, as opposed to previous trials, charges in the maxi trial resulted in a massive number of convictions. The 1968 "trial of the 114," for instance, had started with the indictment of 114 individuals and led to a dismal number of convictions (Falcone and Turone 2015, 120). The reasons for the maxi trial's success, which survived the final level of appeal (Neppi Modona 1992),[7] lie in the investigative and legal innovations prosecutors and instructing judges adopted to build their case. In other words, the maxi trial was a test of the learning process that Palermo judicial authorities had undergone through their participation in the judicial network.

Through the latter, Palermo prosecutors and instructing judges had learned how to handle confidential informants' testimonies and how to legally hold accountable those individuals who provided "external support" for the mafia without directly participating in this criminal organization (Spataro 2016). Both sets of investigative and legal tools, however, called for some significant adaptation to mafia crimes. As I discussed in chapter 4, the legislation introducing plea bargains had specifically limited their use to terrorism cases within a set period of time (Spataro 2016). Legislation allowing for the use of plea bargains on mafia cases would only be introduced in 1991 (Spataro 2016). For this reason, while seeking to learn from their peers, Palermo judicial professionals also had to develop innovative ways to apply plea bargains to mafia crimes. The increased independence provided by egalitarian structures within the prosecutor's and instructing judge's office allowed instructing judge Giovanni Falcone to devise a way around legal constraints on plea bargaining.

In 1984, Falcone sought out a former member of the Sicilian mafia, Tommaso Buscetta, who was living in Brazil while the war among mafia families in Palermo was ongoing (Lodato 2012, 140–141). Buscetta was also being prosecuted by American authorities for his involvement in mafia activities in the United States. Buscetta's resentment toward the fellow mafiosi who had killed his family members convinced him to provide information about *Cosa Nostra*'s inner workings (Lodato 2012, 141–142). Therefore, Falcone made a deal with American authorities that would grant Buscetta the kind of protection Italian authorities could not guarantee (La Licata 1993, 107). By doing so, Falcone devised a creative way to promise leniency to Buscetta in exchange for his collaboration. Buscetta would provide information to judge Falcone and testify against the Sicilian mafia during the maxi trial. He would then also collaborate with the FBI on investigations into the activities of *Cosa Nostra* "branches" in the United States. In exchange, Buscetta would be allowed to live in the United States under witness protection (La Licata 1993, 107).

This informal plea-bargaining technique allowed members of the Palermo investigative units to achieve unprecedented results in the prosecutorial response to mafia organizations. Thanks to Buscetta's testimony, Palermo prosecutorial authorities acquired a detailed understanding of *Cosa Nostra*'s inner workings for the first time. Buscetta explained that each mafia family ruled over its own territory, but that a higher level with representatives from all mafia families held control over a narrower set of issues, including killings and other violent actions (Cerasa and Recanatesi 1984). Thus, Buscetta provided judicial actors with a key to the connections among all mafia activities.

At the same time, the introduction of informal plea bargains via a creative process (which involved international cooperation between legal actors in different jurisdictions and different legal systems) could be considered an instance of judicial activism (Kmiec 2004). This is because the informal plea-bargaining process Falcone devised did not find any explicit textual basis in Italian criminal procedure at the time. Rather, this informal plea bargaining was based on an original interpretation of extant rules, which was in turn meant to fill a legal vacuum (Kmiec 2004). While prosecutors working on left-wing terrorism had benefited from legislation on this specific issue in the past, Falcone and the other members of the Palermo special investigative unit did not enjoy the same legislative support. However, as I already argued in the previous chapters, judicial activism entails different normative implications depending on the reasons for its deployment and the results it seeks to achieve (Kmiec 2004). In the case of Buscetta's testimonies, an activist approach to mafia investigations yielded undeniably positive results in stark contrast with previous prosecutorial efforts on the same criminal issue.

Furthermore, the use of plea bargains in mafia cases before their formalization via law was not the only innovation that allowed Palermo special investigative units to succeed in the maxi trial. While plea bargaining was something Palermo judicial professionals learned from their colleagues in other jurisdictions, the prosecutors and instructing judges working on *Cosa Nostra* investigations also produced their own innovations, which would later have a huge effect on corruption cases. Specifically, judge Falcone (alongside Milanese instructing judge Turone[8]) elaborated a legal theory that could apply to complex criminal organizations, like the mafia, and that Milanese prosecutors would later apply to the corruption network. This new legal theory identified "means crimes" and "end crimes" as distinct types of criminal activities within the same complex criminal scheme (Falcone and Turone 2015). As opposed to informal plea bargains, the application of this new legal theory to mafia investigations did not constitute an instance of judicial activism (Kmiec 2004). This is because Falcone and Turone's legal theory entailed a different investigative procedure—in other words, a different series of steps prosecutors and instructing judges should follow when focusing on mafia investigations. Thus, this legal theory did not require a creative interpretation of existing legal procedure, but only a different sequence of actions in the application of current legal norms.

According to Falcone, mafia activities were structured along different levels with the lowest and most basic level being traditional mafia activities, such as extortion and illegal substance trade (Falcone and Turone 2015, 124–126). These were "first-level crimes" or "end crimes" (125)—the very reason behind the existence of mafia organizations. In order to achieve these "end crimes," however, mafiosi needed to form a bond of loyalty, the "means crime" or proper affiliation into a criminal organization with its own rules (125). In order to prove the occurrence of the "means crime," namely the affiliation of several individuals into a mafia, judges and prosecutors had to start with proving the occurrence and coordination of all those activities for which the organization had been formed in the first place, namely the end crimes (Falcone and Turone 2015, 124–126).

Furthermore, Falcone also identified second-level and third-level mafia crimes that inevitably accompanied extortion and other first-level mafia activities (128–129). These second-level and third-level crimes were, respectively, killings among members of different mafia groups competing for control over first-level activities (128), and the so-called "*terrorismo mafioso*," namely mafia violence against prominent public officials for the purpose of preserving the criminal organization from external attacks (128). According to Falcone, only by substantiating the individual responsibilities of mafia affiliates for first-level crimes, would it be possible to prosecute activities at the second and third levels (128–129). Thus, focusing on proving the mafia's end crimes would allow judicial authorities to also outline (1) the existence of the organization itself (the means crime) and (2) the mafia's involvement in the killing of its rivals and enemies.

This legal theory fundamentally subverted previous approaches to mafia investigations. The 1972 parliamentary committee report into mafia activities outlines the legal theory Sicilian prosecutors had been traditionally applying to mafia cases. The latter consisted of proving individual affiliation with mafia organizations, rather than ascertaining the criminal activities deriving from it (Commissione Parlamentare d'Inchiesta sul Fenomeno della Mafia in Sicilia 1974, 712–713). This legal approach inevitably led to a weak and ineffective prosecutorial response. Because prosecutors and judges were attempting to prove "affiliation" rather than the criminal activities for which this criminal bond was formed, the evidence collected almost exclusively concerned the type of relationships among defendants (Commissione Parlamentare d'Inchiesta sul Fenomeno della Mafia in Sicilia 1974, 712–713). As a result, rather than being based on actual participation in criminal deeds, the evidence was based on a series of attitudes and patterns of individual interactions, which were deemed typical of mafia affiliates (Falcone and Turone 2015, 120–121).

The flaws of this approach appear even more clearly in the conversation between Pio La Torre and Cesare Terranova, both members of Parliament and members of the bicameral committee on mafia activities, and the Palermo prosecutors bringing charges in the so-called trial of the 114, Nestore Pedone and Domenico Signorino. The latter explained their difficulty in finding conclusive evidence proving the bond of loyalty among mafia members (Commissione Parlamentare d'Inchiesta sul Fenomeno della Mafia in Sicilia 1974, 712–713). More importantly, they partially recognized that evidence based on the defendants' patterns of relationships, such as the times they used to meet and the number of times they used to call each other, offered itself to increasingly subjective judgments (Commissione Parlamentare d'Inchiesta sul Fenomeno della Mafia in Sicilia 1974, 712–713). As they explained:

> There were no clear and definitive elements of proof, but only relevant clues, to the point that another court in another jurisdiction would have probably offered even more surprising conclusions in terms of acquittals. (Commissione Parlamentare d'Inchiesta sul Fenomeno della Mafia in Sicilia 1974, 712–713)

The effects of this investigative approach were visible in the low number of convictions. As previously mentioned, the "trial of the 114" concluded with only thirty-three convictions (Commissione Parlamentare d'Inchiesta sul Fenomeno della Mafia in Sicilia 1974, 712–713). On the other hand, Falcone's approach proved to be effective in providing enough evidence of the defendants' role in mafia organizations, leading to the maxi trial's success. Thus, the introduction of egalitarian structures within the Palermo prosecutor's and instructing judge's offices afforded judicial professionals the freedom to pursue new investigative and legal techniques. In turn, the unprecedented success of the 1986 maxi trial proved these new prosecutorial techniques' incredible effectiveness in the fight against mafia organizations.

THE PUSHBACK AGAINST EGALITARIAN ORGANIZATIONAL STRUCTURES

Palermo judicial professionals' successes against *Cosa Nostra* did not elicit unanimous support. Instead, factionalism within the Palermo prosecutor's office increased after the maxi trial. As I previously showed, the chief prosecutors that followed Pajno in office, chief Curti Giardina and chief Giammanco, did not share the latter's enlightened views and reinstated a harshly hierarchical structure of professional relationships. Furthermore, these lingering hostilities within the prosecutor's office found favorable conditions in the divisions among judicial associations within the High Council. When members of the special investigative units called on the High Council to support them, the latter failed to do so. Overall, as I explain in this section, the failure of judicial associations to defend prosecutorial progress against mafia organizations relegated Palermo prosecutors and instructing judges to extreme marginalization. At the same time, left without institutional support, Palermo judicial professionals relied on their relationships with civil society to build a new model of judicial professionalism.

The pushback against the Palermo special investigative units materialized first with the appointment of Curti Giardina, in 1987. As I previously explained, Curti Giardina worked tirelessly to undermine the organizational structures supporting the special investigative unit in his office. However, Curti Giardina found a useful ally in the new chief instructing judge, Antonino Meli. His appointment embodied judicial associations' failure to support aggressive prosecutorial action against mafia organizations. In order to appoint Meli, who had no experience with mafia investigations, the High Council rejected judge Falcone's candidacy, based on Meli's longer years in service (Scottoni 1988*b*). Meli's appointment was so polarizing as to lead a few Council members to vote against their own association (Scottoni 1988*b*). For instance, both representatives of UniCost and representatives of MD, the former a center-leaning and the latter a left-leaning judicial association, split on Meli's appointment, with some members from each association supporting judge Falcone instead (Scottoni 1988*b*).[9]

The intra-associational nature of these divisions makes them particularly hard to explain. The opposition to Falcone's appointment did not seem to run along partisan lines, or even between traditional and enlightened conservatives. Rather, the nature of this divide might find an explanation in the Italian judiciary's powerful defense of its corporate interest (Nelken 1996*a*, 100). Falcone's appointment would have informally established the preeminent importance of merit over seniority to determine judicial advancements. This would have seriously put into question the set of institutional guarantees that provided judicial professionals with safe promotions based solely on the number of years in service. Therefore, the defense of the judiciary's corporate interest might explain the "bipartisan" rejection of Falcone's candidacy: judicial associations became united in protecting the institutional mechanisms that guaranteed their members' professional advancements regardless of merit.

Furthermore, Falcone's appointment over Meli's would have established a dangerous precedent against well-established practices like *lottizzazione correntizia*, which relied on the absence of formal requirements except seniority to grant judicial associations ample discretion over the distribution of judicial posts among them. Overturning the importance of the seniority requirement would have therefore diminished judicial associations' influence over judicial posts' assignment. On the other hand, the divisions surrounding Falcone's appointment once again dispel the explanatory potential of the attitudinal model (Segal and Spaeth 2002). Ideological attitudes are not enough to explain judicial associations' support for aggressive mafia prosecutions or lack thereof.

Immediately after his appointment, Meli started dismantling the special investigative units on mafia investigations. As Giuseppe Di Lello, one of the unit members, pointed out, the consequences were "the end of democratic decision-making with the special investigative unit and the latter's eventual dissolution" (Di Lello 1989, 714). Meli's hostility toward the special unit must be contextualized within his "hierarchical" attitude (Stille 1995, 238–239), which led judge Falcone to flee the instructing office for the prosecutor's office, only to find the same style of leadership under chief prosecutor Giammanco (Stille 1995, 329–330).

Meli's appointment, along with Curti Giardina and Giammanco's efforts to dismantle egalitarian organizational structures within the prosecutor's office, exacerbated Palermo prosecutors' isolation and increased awareness of their own marginalization. Palermo prosecutors and instructing judges were acutely aware that they had been left on their own to tackle mafia organizations. As judge Di Lello (1989) argued, political praise for the work of the Palermo special investigative units served two purposes: first, giving the appearance of official support for anti-mafia efforts; second, delegating the entire responsibility of an effective response against *Cosa Nostra* to judicial professionals (713–714). At the same time, this made judicial professional useful scapegoats that could be solely held responsible for the state's failure to defeat mafia organizations (713–714). This strategy created a deep sense of marginalization among Palermo judicial professionals. The latter were left to bear on their shoulders an overwhelming responsibility, tackling a criminal and societal problem that only a massive and coordinated response from all state sectors could have overcome.

At the same time, Palermo prosecutors' active role in the fight against *Cosa Nostra* established a "virtuous precedent," a new model of prosecutorial professionalism that both relied on a tight relationship with civil society and inspired several civil society organizations, even beyond the Sicilian region. The emergence of a relationship between judicial professionals and civil society was visible, for instance, in chief Chinnici's outreach to local schools, civil society organizations, and local activists. The growing extent of mafia activities, and their deep reach in different sectors of society, including local politics, warranted a response that could not be limited to the judicial prosecution of this criminal system. For this reason, Chinnici took upon himself an educational goal, namely, to inform young people about the risks of drug addiction and the connection between mafia organizations and the drug market (Chinnici 1990, 13).

As part of this educational commitment, Chinnici also cooperated with several civil society organizations, above all the civil society organization *Citta' per l'Uomo*, in order to share his knowledge and understanding of mafia organizations with the public. In 1982, with the help of *Citta' per l'Uomo*'s leadership, Chinnici founded the *Centro Studi Sociali e Giuridici Cesare Terranova.*[10] The purpose of this center was to study mafia organizations not solely from a legal, but also from a sociological standpoint, so as to raise public awareness about this criminal issue.

In this respect, Chinnici embodied a new model of judicial professionalism. Chinnici's "educational goal" in seeking a relationship with civil society stemmed out of the awareness that judicial professionals were called to confront a societal issue with deep roots. I outlined a similar emphasis on judicial action's educational purpose in chapter 4, when discussing a new civic commitment emerging among prosecutors engaged in terrorism investigations. In the same way, Chinnici's involvement in civil society organizations signaled the emergence of a new awareness of the judicial role, whose duty to tackle broad social issues called for its deep involvement with civil society.

After Chinnici's death, Palermo judicial professionals' involvement in civil society did not cease, in fact, it intensified. Members of the Palermo special investigative units, like prosecutor Ayala, took active part in events organized by *Societa' Civile* (Ravelli 1987), the Milanese civil society organization I discussed in the previous chapter. *Societa' Civile*, in particular, found deep inspiration in Palermo prosecutors' fight against *Cosa Nostra*. As I detailed in chapter 4, the knowledge of mafia organizations acquired by Palermo prosecutors and their expertise in the prosecution of these criminal organizations deeply affected *Societa' Civile*'s members. Palermo judicial professionals, therefore, provided both a sociological paradigm for understanding complex criminal organizations and a new model of judicial professionalism. Moreover, Palermo prosecutors' marginalized status vis-à-vis other state agents conformed with *Societa' Civile*'s "us v. them" rhetoric, which pitted honest civil society and judicial professionals against corrupt elected officials and other state bureaucrats.

Furthermore, the High Council's mistreatment of Falcone was one of the reasons behind the creation of the new judicial association *Movimento per la Giustizia*. As I explained in chapter 4, the new judicial association formed in response to *lottizzazione correntizia* and other unethical practices judicial associations had adopted, often mimicking political parties. *Movimento*'s fight against *lottizzazione correntizia* obviously resonated with Palermo judicial professionals. Indeed, most members among several Palermo prosecutors and instructing judges leading the fight against organized crime joined *Movimento per la Giustizia* at its founding (*I Magistrati Vogliono Rompere l'Accerchiamento dei Partiti* 1988).

PROSECUTORIAL EXPERTISE AND CORRUPTION CASES: CLEAN HANDS ARRIVES IN PALERMO

As I have shown so far, the Palermo prosecutor's office offers important insights into the effect of different organizational structures on the development of prosecutorial effectiveness. Traditional conservatives' pushback against egalitarian structures in the late 1980s not only slowed down the fight against mafia organizations but also derailed the development of effective criminal prosecution against other complex criminal issues, especially corruption. As I explain in this section, only with the return to egalitarian structures under a newly appointed progressive chief prosecutor would Palermo judicial professionals be able to direct their expertise against systemic corruption and therefore join the Clean Hands operation's campaign.

After the maxi trial, Palermo prosecutors and instructing judges began using insights from this criminal proceeding to investigate local public officials' involvement in mafia activities. For instance, judge Falcone pursued an investigation into former Palermo mayor Vito Ciancimino's intermediary role between mafia organizations and the Palermo municipality (*L'Inchiesta Ciancimino Passata da Falcone alla Procura* 1988). As a result, judge Falcone brought charges "spanning from mafia affiliation, to money laundering, to corruption" against Ciancimino (*L'Inchiesta Ciancimino Passata da Falcone alla Procura* 1988). Instructing judge Guarnotta, another former member of the Palermo investigative unit, brought similar charges against Ciancimino in relation to the assignment of public contracts (Bolzoni 1990*a*). These investigations could have led to greater exposure of the interactions between corrupt politicians and mafiosi, but judicial authorities' hostility toward egalitarian structures and legal innovations prevented further developments.

Nevertheless, this type of pushback could not completely erase the significant progress in the accumulation of expertise that had occurred in previous years. Even though reactionary chief prosecutors and chief instructing judges opposed the formation of special units, some collaboration still occurred. Judge Di Lello, for instance, sought the collaboration of a group of young prosecutors for his investigations into Ciancimino (*'Ciancimino Dica Qual E' il Suo Lavoro' Signore Giudice, Dall'84 Faccio l'Imputato'* 1990). This collaboration was far from representing a special investigative unit and resembled more closely a simple instance of inter-office collaboration between the instructing judge and the prosecutors. However, this collaboration might have allowed judge Di Lello to pass down his expertise.

Despite efforts to continue looking into the relationship between mafiosi and local corrupt politicians, Palermo prosecutors could not immediately join in the Clean Hands' massive anti-corruption efforts. As I previously mentioned, chief Giammanco resigned only after mounting outrage among his subordinates over Falcone's death (*'Via Giammanco, Ma Non Basta'* 1992). Before his resignation, chief Giammanco had managed to stall important corruption investigations. In 1991, an extensive collaboration among local police forces produced a hundred-page-long report on the relationship between mafia members, corrupt politicians, and civil servants in an attempt to control government bids in Palermo (*Il Rapporto, le Polemiche, I Pentiti, Cosi' l'Inchiesta e' Diventata Valanga* 1993). While the report did not persuade chief Giammanco to form a special investigative unit, it did however persuade a confidential informant to come forward.[11]

Giuseppe Li Pera, an employee of the company Rizzani de Eccher, who was aware of the informal rules regulating corrupt exchanges in Palermo, decided to shed light on this criminal system (Bolzoni 1992*a*; *Il Rapporto, le Polemiche, I Pentiti, Cosi' l'Inchiesta e' Diventata Valanga* 1993). This dynamic (the coming forward of confidential informants with knowledge of the corruption system) looked remarkably similar to the one underlying the Clean Hands investigation. However, the case of Palermo underscores how the presence of favorable conditions, such as individuals willing to provide information, was not enough to produce effective corruption prosecutions without the presence of egalitarian structures. Li Pera's testimonies were not welcomed in chief Giammanco's office due to an ongoing rift between law enforcement and prosecutorial authorities, which led Li Pera to turn to the prosecutor's office in Catania instead (Bolzoni 1992*a*). This was sufficient to stall the case, and it prevented the Palermo office from immediately joining the anti-corruption effort in the Clean Hands operation.

The reintroduction of egalitarian structures under new progressive leadership at the Palermo prosecutor's office brought back the use of previously developed prosecutorial innovations and, consequently, an almost immediate increase in prosecutorial effectiveness. In January 1993, during the transition into the new appointment, chief Caselli found himself handling the capture of wanted mafia boss Totó Riina (Bolzoni 1993*c*). Riina's capture had been made possible by former mafia member Baldassare Di Maggio's "betrayal." Di Maggio offered his collaboration in exchange for a safe haven against the impending death sentence issued by the mafia against him, and leniency in his sentencing (Boffano and Custodero 1993).

Di Maggio's collaboration highlights the importance of expertise in plea-bargaining techniques for prosecutorial effectiveness and the role of the judicial network in diffusing such expertise. The law enforcement official who arrested Di Maggio had a personal connection with the incoming chief prosecutor, Gian Carlo Caselli, thanks to their work against terrorist organizations in the 1970s (Boffano and Custodero 1993). As a result, chief Caselli had a chance to meet with Di Maggio and take his testimony before even taking office in Palermo (Boffano and Custodero 1993). Di Maggio's collaboration paved the way for a new aggressive phase of investigations into the Sicilian mafia. To this end, chief Caselli assembled a special investigative unit consisting mostly of young prosecutors, some of which had been collaborating with judge Di Lello in their investigations into Ciancimino (Bolzoni and D'Avanzo 1993).

Furthermore, Palermo prosecutors could now find textual support for the use of plea bargains in mafia investigations, thanks to the introduction of legislation with this specific purpose in 1991 (Fioriglio 2003, 5). This legislation built on the maxi trial's experience and introduced leniency in exchange for collaboration with former mafia affiliates (Fioriglio 2003, 5). This revolutionary change in criminal procedure (which was, however, explicitly limited to mafia crimes) formalized the Palermo investigative units' practices that had produced the maxi trial's historical success. Therefore, the use of plea bargains by Palermo prosecutors in their efforts to uncover the interaction between *Cosa Nostra* and the corruption system could now rely on new legislation supporting these efforts. This facilitated the deployment of a legal strategy based on defendants' cooperation, therefore similar to the legal strategy underlying the Clean Hands operation, without resorting to activist interpretations of criminal procedure. At the same time, Palermo prosecutors' reservoir of accumulated expertise in the use of plea bargaining provided them with the necessary knowledge to use this legal tool effectively.

Therefore, progressive leadership reintroduced in the Palermo office the use of investigative novelties and organizational structures that had enhanced prosecutorial effectiveness against mafia organizations in the past. This resulted in massive achievements against *Cosa Nostra* in the early 1990s. Building on Di Maggio's testimony, chief Caselli and the young members of his team, Guido Lo Forte, Roberto Scarpinato, and Gioacchino Natoli, drafted a report detailing senator Giulio Andreotti's long relationship with prominent mafia bosses (Bolzoni and D'Avanzo 1993). Caselli and his team accused Andreotti, one of the leaders of the Christian Democratic Party, of "collaboration with mafia organizations" (Bolzoni and D'Avanzo 1993).

More importantly, chief Caselli appeared eager to reconsider Li Pera's testimonies about corrupt exchanges in Palermo. Relying on both former boss Di Maggio and Li Pera's testimonies, and after careful investigative work, in May 1993, Caselli and his special investigative unit ordered the arrests of several local and national politicians, businessmen, and *Cosa Nostra* members (*Arriva in Sicilia il Ciclone Tangenti Retata di Politici e Imprenditori* 1993). The charges were mostly of affiliation with mafia organizations (Bolzoni 1993*d*). Li Pera's testimonies outlined the existence of a criminal system that extended beyond traditional mafia activities to include corrupt exchanges. According to Li Pera, *Cosa Nostra* affiliates, local public officials, and company managers had crafted an informal agreement to regulate and distribute illegal profits from the fraudulent assignment of government bids among each other (Bolzoni 1993*d*).

Thanks to their enhanced freedom and accumulated expertise, the Palermo investigative unit set in motion a chain of incriminating testimonies similar to the one that had exposed the corruption system in Milan. Moreover, expertise in the application of plea bargaining to mafia cases allowed Palermo prosecutors to adapt the investigative methods of the Clean Hands investigation to the specifics of Palermo's criminal context. In line with the Clean Hands investigation's investigation strategy, Palermo prosecutors targeted the "supply side" of corruption, namely businessmen and company managers offering bribes to corrupt politicians and local mafia members. As a result, local businessmen like Filippo Salamone, one of the most prominent Sicilian tycoons, offered to describe the dynamics regulating the corruption system in Palermo in exchange for a lighter sentence (Bolzoni 1993*a*). The testimonies offered by local Palermo businessmen like Salamone prompted further testimonies from other local actors, especially local politicians, in a chain that eventually exposed the features of the corruption system in Palermo.[12]

Salamone and other company managers explained the informal rules the Christian Democratic Party and the Socialist Party followed to divide bribes among Sicilian politicians and national party officials (Bolzoni 1993*a*). Similar to the corruption system in Milan, company managers working in Palermo would rig public contract bids by bribing civil servants. For instance, businessmen seeking to obtain a contract with the publicly owned company Sirap agreed to pay a bribe to the politically appointed civil servant heading the company, who would then redistribute these illegal profits among political parties (*Il Rapporto, le Polemiche, I Pentiti Cosi' l'Inchiesta e' Diventata Valanga* 1993).

However, differently from the corruption system in Milan, mafia personalities had infiltrated the Palermo corruption network. Mafia boss Totó Riina had personally chosen one of the civil servants working for Sirap, Angelo Siino, to supervise the assignment of contracts and bribes. Siino had to make sure that every company receiving the assignment of a public contract would deliver 2% of its profits to the local *Cosa Nostra* unit and another 2% to fund *Cosa Nostra*'s general activities.[13] Therefore, Palermo prosecutors' expertise in the use of plea bargains allowed Caselli's team to follow the same investigative route as the Clean Hands investigation, targeting corrupt economic actors and unleashing a chain of incriminating testimonies. Legal expertise also allowed Palermo prosecutors to uncover the specificities of this corruption system, which *Cosa Nostra* boss Riina had come to control at least since 1981 (Bolzoni 1993*b*).[14]

Finally, under chief Caselli, the Palermo prosecutor's office rejoined the judicial network. Palermo prosecutors and instructing judges had previously joined the network in the 1980s to learn from their peers working on terrorism cases. The appointment of Gian Carlo Caselli to chief prosecutor guaranteed that the Palermo office would fully be reintegrated in the judicial network. Chief Caselli, who had been a prominent member of the judicial network in the past, invited coordinated action between the Palermo investigative unit and the Clean Hands team (Di Pietro 2017). In June 1993, along with members of the special unit Guido Lo Forte and Luigi Patronaggio, chief Caselli joined Clean Hands prosecutors in Milan to interrogate businessman Vincenzo Lodigiani (*Quel Filo Che Lega Palermo e Milano* 1993). This collaboration between the two prosecutors' offices guaranteed the continuous and mutual exchange of information concerning Lodigiani and other businessmen's participation in the corruption system (Di Pietro 2017).

This coordination between special units partially reflected the nature of the corruption system itself: the same actors, like Lodigiani, had corrupt dealings across several jurisdictions (Di Pietro 2017). Therefore, an effective prosecutorial response to systemic corruption should also unfold across jurisdictional lines. However, as it will become clear in the case study of Reggio Calabria, interconnections between different parts of the corruption system were not enough to guarantee coordination among special units. Rather, it was Chief Caselli's previous experience with the judicial network and his openness to collegial decision-making that facilitated the Palermo office's reintegration into this inter-jurisdictional collaboration.

Overall, the Palermo case study shows that the effective prosecution of systemic corruption depends on the organization of professional relationships within a prosecutor's office. Egalitarian structures will guarantee enhanced freedom to lower-ranked prosecutors and will therefore facilitate the emergence of legal innovations and the accumulation of prosecutorial expertise. More importantly, the Palermo case shows that successive attempts to dismantle these egalitarian structures may ultimately fail to reverse prosecutorial progress in the prosecution of complex issues. As long as expert personnel remain in place to hand down their knowledge and train younger prosecutors, there is a chance that prosecutorial expertise may survive the temporary suppression of egalitarian structures. This may produce the effective prosecution of systemic corruption when these organizational structures are reinstated.

The prosecutor's office in Reggio Calabria represents almost the specular opposite of the Palermo case study. Despite a similar criminal environment, Reggio Calabria prosecutors failed to join in the Clean Hands anti-corruption effort. This partially resulted from the absence of previous prosecutorial progress in the fight against the local mafia organization, the *'Ndrangheta*. Despite the *'Ndrangheta*'s control over large swaths of the Calabrian territory, and despite this criminal organization's involvement in the corruption system, Reggio Calabria prosecutors did not develop a similar expertise as their Palermo counterparts. Consequently, efforts to uncover systemic corruption and the *'Ndrangheta*'s role in this system were overall ineffective. In the following sections of this chapter, I show that the persistence of hierarchical structures and a bureaucratic approach to criminal prosecution hindered the development of prosecutorial independence and effectiveness within the Reggio Calabria prosecutor's office. Thus, despite the efforts to join in the Clean Hands' wave of corruption prosecutions, the lack of prosecutorial expertise undermined this effort.

REGGIO CALABRIA CHIEF PROSECUTORS

As opposed to the Palermo prosecutor's office, Reggio Calabria did not attract the same amount of attention to the appointment of its local authorities. This was partially a result of the lack of changes and turmoil in this office's administration, which did not seem to experience the same evolution as Palermo in its internal organization and prosecutorial practices. For this reason, the information available from archival sources about Reggio Calabria chief prosecutors is severely limited. As a result, it was not possible to outline brief profiles of Reggio Calabria chief prosecutors from 1975 to 1995. However, it is at least possible to identify Reggio Calabria prosecutorial authorities from 1983 to 1995. Sebastiano Suraci held the office of Reggio Calabria chief prosecutors from 1983 to 1986, and Giuliano Gaeta succeeded him in office from 1986 to 1995.[15]

While it was not possible to outline these chief prosecutors' legal profiles in full, there is some information available about Suraci's associational affiliation. Suraci was elected to the High Council in 1986 as a member of UniCost, the centrist judicial association (Coppola 1986). The latter, as opposed to MI, had less of a tendency to endorse traditionally conservative principles, and often supported more progressive associations such as MD within the High Council. However, Suraci used particularly loaded words to oppose judge Falcone's appointment to Palermo chief instructing judge. In rejecting judge Falcone's candidacy, Suraci expressed in clear terms his hostility toward a judicial culture that promoted "attitudes of exasperated personalism" (Stille 1995, 221). As I previously mentioned, judicial associations internally split on Falcone's appointment. Therefore, Suraci's attitudes do not necessarily signal his adherence to either a conservative or progressive understanding of the legal profession. Rather, they demonstrate compliance with judicial association's hostility toward appointments based on a candidate's qualifications besides seniority or a concern with the Italian judiciary's general corporate interest (Nelken 1996*a*, 100).

Gaeta succeeded Suraci in office in Reggio Calabria and his tenure was remarkably stable. Unfortunately, given the lack of information, it was not possible to fully test the effect of legal ideology on prosecutorial authorities' choice of organizational structure within the Reggio Calabria office. While Suraci's affiliation with UniCost offers some interesting counterintuitive observations about this relationship, there is not enough information to test legal ideology's effect on chief prosecutors' predilection for hierarchy or egalitarianism in this case. Nevertheless, in the following section, I show how the Reggio Calabria prosecutor's office's internal organization remained remarkably stable in its hierarchical structure for the whole period under consideration, with significant implications for prosecutorial independence and effectiveness against complex criminal issues.

THE REGGIO CALABRIA PROSECUTOR'S OFFICE'S ORGANIZATIONAL STRUCTURE

Similar to the situation in Palermo in the late 1970s, judicial posts in Reggio Calabria presented significant challenges. The presence of deeply rooted and well-organized criminal organizations, along with a constant lack of resources, made the Reggio Calabria prosecutor's office a challenging post, especially for young prosecutors. However, as opposed to Palermo, the working environment in Reggio Calabria did not show significant signs of improvement over the years under consideration in this analysis.[16] While enlightened prosecutorial and judicial authorities in Palermo created space for their subordinates' innovations in the fight against mafia organizations, no similar development is clearly visible in Reggio Calabria. Rather, the working environment in the Reggio Calabria office remained hostile so as to cause an impressively high personnel turnover over the years, especially among young trainees.

In a 1988 High Council report on the state of mafia prosecutions in Calabria, High Council representatives described a situation in which "even judicial trainees, despite being committed and well-prepared, request a transfer after only two years" (Coppola 1988). Furthermore, the lack of expert personnel was compounded by the impossibility for the High Council to order senior personnel's transfer to the Reggio Calabria office. Therefore, the High Council started discussing ways to reward young prosecutors who decided to prolong their stay in this jurisdiction (Coppola 1988). However, three years after this first report, the High Council was still debating how to do this (Coppola 1991).

The hostile working environment and high turnover clearly created adverse conditions to the development of prosecutorial effectiveness, especially against mafia organizations. Despite facing a similar criminal context as their Palermo counterparts, Reggio Calabria prosecutors did not develop similar investigative and legal innovations in the fight against the *'Ndrangheta*. *'Ndrangheta* families went to war with each other between 1975 and 1979 and would be at war again in 1983–1985 (Gratteri and Nicaso 2010). *Cosa Nostra* mafia wars had produced favorable conditions that Palermo judicial professionals had exploited, thanks to the increasing expertise they developed via their participation in the judicial network. On the other hand, the mafia wars between *'Ndrangheta* factions did not lead to similar prosecutorial successes in Reggio Calabria. Thus, this similar criminal context highlights the lack of investigative and legal innovations among Reggio Calabria prosecutors.

Even more interestingly, the relative geographical proximity[17] between the Reggio Calabria and Palermo prosecutors' offices did not lead to the diffusion of the investigative and legal innovations the latter deployed against mafia organizations. Reggio Calabria prosecutors continued with a bureaucratic and traditional approach against mafia organizations, which was awfully inadequate and ineffective. This approach is visible in the 1979 trial against *'Ndrangheta* boss De Stefano, which took place in Reggio Calabria. The trial, which counted 8,760 defendants, appeared as a massive prosecutorial effort against the local mafia. However, out of these thousands of defendants, only twenty-eight were eventually convicted (Falcone and Turone 2015, 121). This was due to the prosecutorial approach to these cases: much like the "trial of the 114," the trial against boss De Stefano also relied on an investigative method based on proving individual affiliation to the *'Ndrangheta* via behavioral clues, such as individual habits and patterns of interactions (Falcone and Turone 2015, 121). Therefore, similar to the "trial of the 114," the trial against boss De Stefano also resulted in an astonishing failure.

In the years following the 1979 De Stefano trial, Reggio Calabria prosecutors continued approaching mafia investigations with the same method. The persistence of this traditional approach and the lack of legal innovations in the prosecution of mafia organizations are due to chief Gaeta's lasting preference for a hierarchical approach to the relationship with his subordinates. The latter manifested especially in the absence of special investigative units within the Reggio Calabria prosecutor's office. Even external interventions were not enough to prompt the institutional change in organizational structures that would have set the Reggio Calabria office on a trajectory toward increased prosecutorial effectiveness.

In 1987, for instance, the Parliamentary bicameral committee on mafia activities visited Reggio Calabria. This visit seemed to mobilize prosecutorial authorities against *'Ndrangheta* influence on local public agencies, particularly in the healthcare sector (*Reggio Calabria, Sull'Unita' Sanitaria la Magistratura Ha Aperto un'Inchiesta* 1987). Consequently, chief prosecutor Giuliano Gaeta established a special law enforcement unit so that different police corps could coordinate investigations into *'Ndrangheta* interferences in the assignment of government bids (P.S. 1987). The suspicion was that mafia-directed companies were often the beneficiaries of public funds. Although the creation of a special law enforcement unit might remind of innovations first adopted by Palermo prosecutors, the way chief Gaeta set up this investigative effort fit well within a hierarchical organization of professional relationships and a bureaucratic approach to criminal investigations.

First of all, chief Gaeta created this special law enforcement unit after the parliamentary committee's visit, therefore as a result of external pressure from Parliament. There were no collegial consultations between Gaeta and his subordinates on the creation of this special law enforcement task force. In addition, there was no attempt to create a similar special investigative unit within the prosecutor's office. The absence of collegiality within the Reggio Calabria prosecutor's office is also visible in the fact that the law enforcement task force had to report to just one prosecutor, Fulvio Rizzo (P.S. 1987). In line with the hierarchical nature of professional relationships within the Reggio Calabria office, only one prosecutor would oversee the special police unit's efforts. This organizational structure also clearly reflected the bureaucratic approach to criminal investigations, which relied on a single prosecutor in charge of most cases.

Prosecutor Rizzo's investigation, based on the special task force's investigative work, concluded with several charges of "fraud, corruption and mafia affiliation" (*Per lo Scandalo della USL di Reggio Finiscono in Carcere 12 Persone* 1987). However, the hierarchical and bureaucratic approach to criminal investigations once again undermined their effectiveness. At the same time as Rizzo's investigation, the Reggio Calabria instructing judge's office had been looking into mafia activities in a way that resembled, at least on a very superficial level, the work of Palermo instructing judges. Prosecutor Rizzo and his superior, chief Gaeta, did not make significant efforts to coordinate investigations with the team of Reggio Calabria instructing judges that had been leading similar investigations into *'Ndrangheta* activities. Furthermore, a more in-depth analysis reveals that hierarchical relationships also dominated the instructing judge's office. Despite appearances, Reggio Calabria instructing judges had also not deviated from the traditional investigative approach to mafia crimes.

From 1985 to 1992, a new mafia war hit Reggio Calabria. The competition between the De Stefano and Imerti clans, which also revolved around control over new government bids in the infrastructure sector, brought about hundreds of casualties (Gratteri and Nicaso 2010, 61–64). Within this context, chief instructing judge Vincenzo Macrí decided to set up an enduring collaboration with his subordinate, Antonio Lombardo. Macrí and Lombardo focused their investigative efforts on the events spanning from boss De Stefano's death in 1985 to the ongoing conflict between mafia clans in 1988 (Veltri 1988*a*). The two instructing judges were able to issue 107 indictments, ninety-one of which were for mafia affiliation (Veltri 1988*b*).

Despite the superficial resemblance to the Palermo investigative unit, the collaboration between chief judge Macrí and judge Lombardo did not represent a true adoption of this method of work. First of all, the hierarchical relationship between chief Macrí and his subordinate emptied the formation of this special unit of significant resemblance to the ones in Palermo. The latter had included several lower-ranked prosecutors or instructing judges, working together as peers under their chief's supervision. The Reggio Calabria special unit, on the other hand, consisted essentially of the hierarchical relationship between its two members.

One alternative explanation for its structure could be the lack of sufficient instructing judges to form a larger unit of peers. However, a small Calabrian jurisdiction like Locri had created a "mini" investigative unit, with two prosecutors working together as peers on mafia cases (Mazzocchi 1988). Furthermore, the Locri special investigative unit's aggressive investigative efforts against the *'Ndrangheta* created significant turmoil within this small office, leading to a High Council's inquiry into the relationship between the local chief prosecutor and his subordinates (Mazzocchi 1988). Thus, this brief comparison between Reggio Calabria and Locri further illustrates that the lack of special investigative units in the former jurisdiction was more likely the result of the local leadership's choices, rather than scarce resources' inevitable consequence.

Second, clear differences were visible between the Reggio Calabria instructing judges' unit and the Palermo investigative unit in their investigative methods. The latter considered all potentially related mafia cases, due to a new understanding of the relationship between "means crimes" and "end crimes" (Falcone and Turone 2015). On the other hand, chief judge Macrí and judge Lombardo narrowed their work to all cases directly deriving from the chain of murders in the ongoing *'Ndrangheta* war. As a result, Macrí and Lombardo excluded those criminal cases that might concern mafia activities other than violence among rival clans (Sentenza della Suprema Corte di Cassazione, Prima Sezione Penale, 8042/1992). Thus, although judge Macrí and judge Lombardo's investigation provided a thorough description of the *'Ndrangheta*'s internal organization (Sentenza della Suprema Corte di Cassazione, Prima Sezione Penale, 8042/1992, 18–19), its scope was limited to the families currently involved in the ongoing conflict.

Furthermore, chief judge Macrí and judge Lombardo applied the traditional legal approach to mafia investigations that had dominated the "trial of the 114" and the 1979 De Stefano trial. The Court of Cassation's ruling outlines the two Reggio Calabria instructing judges' legal approach. The chief judge and his subordinate used four types of considerations to bring charges of mafia affiliations against the defendants, which relied on highly circumstantial evidence. First, the circumstances and features of the killings resonated strongly with a violent conflict between rival criminal factions (Sentenza della Suprema Corte di Cassazione, Prima Sezione Penale, 8042/1992, 18–19). Second, they noted that the relationships among the individuals involved, such as their family affiliation, their business relationships, and similar, represented strong clues of the defendants' mafia affiliation (Sentenza della Suprema Corte di Cassazione, Prima Sezione Penale, 8042/1992, 18–19). Third, the defendants' typical behaviors and habits, along with their criminal background, fit with the defendants' plausible affiliation with the mafia. Finally, information from confidential informants also substantiated the defendants' direct involvement in the mafia killings (Sentenza della Suprema Corte di Cassazione, Prima Sezione Penale, 8042/1992, 18–19).

The Court of Cassation's final ruling clearly shows that the Reggio Calabria instructing judges remained loyal to the traditional approach to mafia investigations, which determined one's mafia affiliation based on behavioral patterns and habits. This stood in stark contrast with Palermo judicial professionals' new approach, which instead relied on tracing the factual connections between means crimes and end crimes to outline mafia activities' overall structure. Moreover, Macrí and Lombardo's choice to apply a legal approach based on circumstantial evidence excluded the use of plea bargaining. The latter's absence did not imply the complete lack of confidential informants. Macrí and Lombardo partially built their case on tips provided by individuals with some relationship to the mafia families at war (Sentenza della Suprema Corte di Cassazione, Prima Sezione Penale, 8042/1992, 15).

Nevertheless, confidential informants' contributions also revolved around confirming one's mafia affiliation through personal habits and relationships. In other words, the two judges did not use confidential informant's tips as a window into mafia activities' structure, but as confessions about individuals belonging to the *'Ndrangheta*. It is also clear from the nature of these contributions that the two judges did not work to foster favorable conditions to the emergence of confidential informants, as the Palermo investigative units had done. Thus, reliance on spontaneous tips from confidential informants reinforced judge Macrí and judge Lombardo's perception that the *'Ndrangheta* was by its nature "impenetrable" (Veltri 1988*b*).[18] This determination set a dangerous precedent for Reggio Calabria prosecutorial authorities, who would come to distrust the use of confidential informants in mafia investigations for years.

Despite the inherent weaknesses in Macrí and Lombardo's legal approach, the two judges' efforts produced at least modest results: of the 107 defendants, sixty-eight were convicted of mafia affiliation and related crimes.[19] However, the Reggio Calabria instructing judges' work did not create that reservoir of expertise that could have set this office on a path toward increased effectiveness. Hierarchical structures and traditional methods of investigations continued dominating both the work of Reggio Calabria instructing judges and prosecutors. As a result, even after the disbandment of the instructing office at the end of the 1980s, and the likely influx of personnel into the local prosecutor's office, local judicial professionals continued lacking expertise in new legal tools, such as plea bargaining, and new investigative approaches, such as the concept of means and end crimes. Reggio Calabria prosecutors also held an incomplete understanding of mafia organizations and their activities. This created adverse conditions to the effective prosecution of systemic corruption. As I explain in the following section, the lack of expertise and the persistence of hierarchical structures undermined local efforts to join the Clean Hands operation's wave of corruption investigations.

CLEAN HANDS AND REGGIO CALABRIA: THE FAILURE OF CORRUPTION PROSECUTIONS

In 1992, a series of investigations into the relationships between corrupt politicians and mafia organizations brought political upheaval within the city of Reggio Calabria. The investigations came while the Clean Hands operation was gaining steam and, therefore, appeared as a possible attempt by Reggio Calabria prosecutors to emulate their Milanese peers. Nevertheless, the persistence of hierarchical structures within the Reggio Calabria prosecutor's office had created such a dearth of expertise that the latter inevitably undermined these investigations' effectiveness. Thus, the Reggio Calabria prosecutor's office was incapable of holding participants in the corruption network accountable for their crimes.

The best picture of the state of professional relationships within the Reggio Calabria prosecutor's office at the time of the Clean Hands investigation comes from a young prosecutor's account in 1994. According to prosecutor Squillace Greco (1994), prosecutorial authorities in Reggio Calabria held either a "bureaucratic understanding of their profession" (893) or an overly assertive understanding of their role (893). Both conceptions compromised prosecutorial work's "efficiency" (893). Oftentimes, superiors (including chief prosecutor Giuliano Gaeta) were not "a credible point of reference for the organization of judicial work, nor for facilitating coordinated prosecutorial action" (893). Furthermore, the high ratio of young prosecutorial trainees in Reggio Calabria rendered the consequences of a lack of leadership even more acute (893).

In July 1992, prosecutor Roberto Pennisi brought charges against some of Reggio Calabria's most prominent politicians and local administrators, "decimating" the city administration (Sergi 1992*a*). It is plausible that the Clean Hands operation's findings might have prompted Reggio Calabria prosecutorial authorities to investigate the existence of a similar corruption system locally. Indeed, the alleged bribery scheme in Pennisi's investigation bore a striking resemblance to the ones uncovered by Milanese prosecutors.[20] However, long-standing hierarchical structures and local prosecutors' lack of expertise had created adverse conditions to the effective prosecution of systemic corruption.

For instance, Pennisi's investigation did not in any way build on findings from previous investigative efforts, such as prosecutor Rizzo's or judge Macri and judge Lombardo's work. It is also noticeable that prosecutor Pennisi, who took the lead in trying to emulate his colleagues in the Clean Hands operation, was new to the Reggio Calabria prosecutor's office (Bonsanti 1992). As previously explained, the persistence of a hostile working environment had created high turnover among Reggio Calabria prosecutors. Pennisi immediately demonstrated an unusual fervor in his investigations into the local political class. When asked if he felt uncomfortable about putting under investigation the whole city council, Pennisi answered:

> It would be better to have no political class at all, rather than a political class of this kind.[21]

Pennisi's words echo that understanding of the judicial profession as an inherent "substitution role" (Della Porta 2001, 4) in the face of other branches' systemic failure to tackle corruption, which I explored in chapter 4. As I argued there, this conception of the judicial mission represents one possible aspect of judicial activism. However, Pennisi's words take this idea to an extreme, as they present the absence of politics as a better alternative than corrupt politics. At the same time, Pennisi's convictions elude attitudinal explanations of prosecutorial behavior (Segal and Spaeth 2002), given the manifest hostility to (corrupt) politics regardless of its leaning.

Interestingly, in his effort to emulate the Clean Hands team's work, prosecutor Pennisi established an enduring collaboration with another prosecutor, Giuseppe Verzera (Bonsanti 1992). This might have been a genuine attempt to emulate Milanese prosecutors' special investigative unit. However, the adoption of this investigative structure was without a real precedent to support it within the Reggio Calabria office. Initially, Pennisi seemed to follow the same investigation route as the Clean Hands operation: one of the corrupt businessmen under investigation, Giuseppe Multari, decided to provide information about bribes exchanges for the local airport (*Reggio, Interrogatorio - Fiume per l'Ex Sindaco DC* 1992). Multari offered prosecutors Pennisi and Verzera a clear picture of the informal rules regulating illicit exchanges between himself and prominent politicians in the Reggio Calabria city council (*Reggio, Interrogatorio - Fiume per l'Ex Sindaco DC* 1992). Moreover, Multari's willingness to provide information convinced former Reggio Calabria mayor Agatino Licandro to confess as well (*Reggio, Interrogatorio – Fiume per l'Ex Sindaco DC* 1992).

Licandro offered additional information about the corruption system in Reggio Calabria, describing not just his role in bribe exchanges but also other politicians' and businessmen's involvement (Licandro and Varano 1993). Nevertheless, this plentiful information did not set in motion the same chain reaction sparked by confessions and testimonies in the Clean Hands operation. Prosecutors Pennisi and Verzera did follow up on Licandro's revelations, which led to corruption charges and even pretrial detention for several prominent politicians (Sergi 1992*b*). Among those charged with corruption, three names stood out: Paolo Battaglia, Giovanni Palamara, and Luigi Aliquó, who had all overseen the city administration in the past

(Sergi 1992*b*). Nevertheless, prosecutors Pennisi and Verzera had a hard time obtaining more confessions from the public officials they charged with corruption. Even more noticeable was the lack of collaboration from the economic actors involved in bribe exchanges. After Multari's confession, few, if any, other businessmen came forward with information.

This lack of collaboration partially resulted from long-standing hierarchical structures and lack of expertise among Reggio Calabria prosecutors. In order to emulate the work of the Clean Hands team, Reggio Calabria prosecutors targeted the "supply side" of corruption, namely the economic actors willing to pay bribes in exchange for public contracts, like Multari. However, the *'Ndrangheta* had deeply infiltrated the local supply side. On the other hand, as I showed before, Reggio Calabria prosecutors had not developed expertise in those legal tools, such as plea bargaining, that would have allowed to break the bond of loyalty between mafia members and their accomplices. Instead, prosecutorial work became dependent on confidential informants' voluntary information proffers. In addition, prosecutors seemed to lack the leadership qualities necessary to take charge of investigative efforts (Squillace Greco 1994, 895). This often turned into an inability to collect solid evidence to confirm confidential informants' contributions (Squillace Greco 1994, 895). This is visible in Pennisi and Verzera's investigation into the local corruption system.

Despite the overall lack of further testimonies, Pennisi and Verzera built a case against the alleged existence of an elite group including members of various political parties and *'Ndrangheta* affiliates, which ruled over bribe exchanges for government bids in Reggio Calabria (Gerino 1992). According to the investigation, *'Ndrangheta* clans would receive between 4% and 5% of these bribes in exchange for "overseeing" these public works (Gerino 1992). Most of Pennisi and Verzera's investigative work in this case relied on other evidence than personal testimonies. The only testimonies that seemed to directly confirm the existence of a collaboration between politicians and *'Ndrangheta* members came from former *'Ndrangheta* affiliates (Sergi 1993*a*).

These testimonies concerned the killing of another prominent Calabrian public official, Lodovico Ligato, who was executed by the *'Ndrangheta* because of his interference with the established rules of the corruption system (Sergi 1993*a*). Based on these testimonies, Pennisi argued that this elite group's political members had ordered Ligato's killing. However, the Court of Cassation found the evidence insufficient to substantiate the existence of a "principal-agent" relationship between corrupt politicians and the *'Ndrangheta* (Sergi 1993*a*).

These developments in the Ligato trial speak to the lack of expertise in handling confidential informants' contributions among Reggio Calabria prosecutors. Instead of developing the use of plea bargaining on mafia cases, prosecutors and judges in Reggio Calabria relied on the spontaneous collaboration of mafia affiliates. This meant that informants' contributions often did not come as the result of a comprehensive investigative effort, but instead as its starting point. Pennisi's investigation into the Ligato's murder relied heavily on former *'Ndrangheta* affiliates' spontaneous testimonies, which were not enough to substantiate the prosecution's case. Thus, Reggio Calabria prosecutors' continued reliance on voluntary contributions rather than plea bargaining weakened their investigative efforts into systemic corruption.

Furthermore, it also reinforced the assumption that the *'Ndrangheta* was an impenetrable criminal organization that would never produce reliable confidential informants. This distrust was visible in the statements made by local judicial actors at the capture of one of the *'Ndrangheta*'s most feared bosses, Antonino Imerti, in 1993. On this occasion, law enforcement authorities stated:

> capture is the result of intelligence work, of purely technical investigative work without any form of external collaboration, without confidential informants' contributions, without any kind of tips or hints from anyone.[22]

It would take ten years for significant prosecutorial expertise to develop within the Reggio Calabria office, partially as a result of personnel migration from other jurisdictions.[23] The emergence of prosecutorial expertise would eventually pierce this misperception about the '*Ndrangheta*'s "impenetrability (Pignatone, Prestipino and Savatteri 2012).

Moreover, the persistence of hierarchical structures within the Reggio Calabria prosecutor's office had insulated the latter from the judicial network. The results are visible in the lack of networking efforts between Reggio Calabria prosecutors and the Clean Hands team. Pennisi and Verzera's investigation also involved businessman Vincenzo Lodigiani, among others (Sergi 1992*c*). Lodigiani's company had carried out public works allover Italy, including Milan and Palermo. Investigations into Lodigiani's business transactions in both jurisdictions gave rise to significant cooperation between the Clean Hands team and Palermo prosecutors (*Quei Soldi in Odor di Mafia 'Consulto' Borrelli—Caselli* 1993). However, the same did not happen in Reggio Calabria (*Quei Soldi in Odor di Mafia 'Consulto' Borrelli—Caselli* 1993).

Despite Pennisi and Verzera's investigations into Lodigiani, there is no evidence that the two prosecutors ever sought or received offers of cooperation from other offices investigating the same defendant. The Clean Hands team had been exchanging legal documents with Palermo (Di Pietro 2017) and had even traveled to this jurisdiction to coordinate investigations (*Quei Soldi in Odor di Mafia 'Consulto' Borrelli—Caselli* 1993). On the contrary, there is no evidence that any of these forms of collaboration occurred between the Clean Hands team and Reggio Calabria prosecutors. The reason for this difference between Reggio Calabria and Palermo lies in the appointment of Gian Carlo Caselli. Chief Caselli had been an active participant in the judicial network during the 1980s. Collaboration between the Clean Hands team and Palermo prosecutors started after Caselli's appointment to the Sicilian office (Di Pietro 2017). On the other hand, none of the prosecutors working in Reggio Calabria had previously taken part in the judicial network. Thus, another legacy of hierarchical structures within the Reggio Calabria prosecutor's office was enduring insulation from networking efforts, even during the Clean Hands operation.

The latter further undermined Reggio Calabria prosecutors' investigative efforts. Pennisi and Verzera seemed to have built an effective case against the members of the city and regional administrations alleged to be part of an elite group of politicians and mafiosi overseeing bribe exchanges. The case concluded with eighteen convictions and seven acquittals (Sergi 1994). The acquittals concerned all the politicians accused of ordering the killing of Ligato (*Per L'Assassinio di Ligato Prosciolti I Politici Calabresi* 1994). Overall, the wave of investigations into the Reggio Calabria corruption system resulted in only one conviction that stood the Reggio Calabria Court of Appeals' test.[24]

Therefore, the case of Reggio Calabria shows that even the presence of a driven and highly motivated prosecutor like Pennisi could not overcome the enduring lack of expertise that decades of hierarchical control had produced within this office. Furthermore, even the introduction of new institutions created specifically to empower prosecutors against organized crime could not overcome this dearth of expertise. Prosecutor Pennisi was a member of a new special branch within the Reggio Calabria prosecutor's office, called *direzione distrettuale antimafia* (Sergi 1992*d*). A new law had established these special branches to encourage the presence of qualified personnel focusing only on mafia investigations in each prosecutor's office (Vigna 2006, 524). However, the creation of this new institution was not enough to promote the emergence of effective prosecutorial action against mafia and corruption crimes in Reggio Calabria. Thus, this case study demonstrates that even institutional reforms are not enough to promote effective corruption prosecutions without a reservoir of legal expertise resulting from long-lasting egalitarian relationships among prosecutors.

CONCLUSION

The case studies of the prosecutors' offices in Palermo and Reggio Calabria offer important insights into the role of organizational structures in facilitating the accumulation of legal expertise necessary to the effective prosecution of corruption. The Palermo prosecutor's office shows that the early restructuring of professional relationships along egalitarian lines can lay the foundations for the development of prosecutorial effectiveness, despite possible setbacks in later years. When the progressive faction took control of the Palermo prosecutor's office in 1993, early investments in egalitarian structures and legal expertise significantly paid off. Palermo prosecutors could rely on their previously accumulated expertise in mafia investigations to join the anti-corruption effort in the Clean Hands operation and produce effective results in the fight against systemic corruption. On the other hand, the persistence of hierarchical structures in the Reggio Calabria office created a hostile working environment, which led to high personnel turnover. These conditions resulted in an enduring dearth of prosecutorial expertise and the ineffective prosecution of organized crime first and systemic corruption later.

Furthermore, these two case studies demonstrate that organized crime's involvement in the corruption network does not explain differences in prosecutorial effectiveness against this criminal phenomenon. Both Palermo and Reggio Calabria share the presence of powerful mafia organizations within their territory. However, the accumulation of significant expertise in mafia investigations among Palermo prosecutors was enough to overcome possible obstacles to effective corruption prosecutions resulting from *Cosa Nostra*'s participation in the latter. On the other hand, the lack of legal expertise in mafia investigations among Reggio Calabria prosecutors also hindered the effective prosecution of systemic corruption within this jurisdiction. Thus, egalitarian structures of professional relationships and the resulting accumulation of expertise hold more explanatory power over the outcome of corruption prosecutions than the type of criminal actors involved in this phenomenon.

NOTES

1. Nando Dalla Chiesa, founder of the civil society organization *Società Civile*, argued that the High Council would "come to regret appointing somebody so close to former governor D'Acquisto" (Mazzocchi 1990).
2. Quote in La Licata (1993, 61), author's translation.
3. Quote in Chinnici (1990, 12), author's translation.
4. Indro Montanelli was a renowned Italian journalist at the time.
5. *Autonomia Operaia* was one of several left-wing terrorist groups.
6. As I explained in chapter 4, "*Cultura del coordinamento*" came to identify the networking of judges and prosecutors working in coordination with each other on the same criminal issue.

7. Although the Palermo Court of Appeals partially overruled the findings in the maxi trial, the Court of Cassation eventually intervened to confirm the special investigative units' charges in the case. The Court of Cassation's decision, in turn, bestowed legitimacy onto the special teams' legal approach and investigative methods (Neppi Modona 1992).

8. In chapter 4, I explained that instructing judge Turone had worked alongside instructing judge Colombo on the P2 investigation.

9. Noticeably, the only member of *Magistratura Democratica* to support Falcone's appointment on the basis of his exceptional qualifications was Gian Carlo Caselli (Scottoni 1988*b*).

10. Ennio Pintacuda, audio recording of a conference on Rocco Chinnici, April 21, 1995. Accessible at https://www.radioradicale.it/scheda/72190/72260-rocco-chinnici-luomo-e-il-giudice-org-dal-centro-terranova-e-dalla-rivista.

11. Chief prosecutor Giammanco did not consider the findings in the report particularly relevant, and for this reason the prosecutorial response was limited: only seven local businessmen were put under arrest, to the police's dismay (*Il Rapporto, le Polemiche, I Pentiti, Cosi' l'Inchiesta e' Diventata Valanga* 1993).

12. For instance, in August, following Salamone and other businessmen's testimonies, a local politician whose name remained confidential started collaborating with the prosecutorial team, providing information about more than seventy people, including businessmen, civil servants, politicians and others, involved in corruption (R.F. 1993).

13. Among these activities, Di Maggio revealed that a conspicuous part of these bribes to Cosa Nostra served to fund boss Riina's legal counsel in his trials. Riina had become so demanding and controlling over this system to request in one case that, out of a bribe of one billion lire, only 300 million would be distributed among party officials, and the rest be used to contribute to Cosa Nostra's financial needs. (*Le Mani della Mafia sugli Appalti Di Maggio: Ecco Come I Boss Gestivano le Opere Pubbliche* 1993; *I Pentiti: Negli Uffici della Regione le Riunioni per Pilotare gli Appalti* 1993).

14. As a result of the 1981 mafia war, *Cosa Nostra* had gone from being internally "democratic" to being "a dictatorship" (Bolzoni 1993*b*). Having become the new ruler of Cosa Nostra, boss Toto' Riina had established his absolute control over Cosa Nostra's activities. At this point, Riina also moved to "centralize" the local corruption system (Bolzoni 1993*b*). Under Riina's leadership, Cosa Nostra's central committee negotiated public contracts directly with politicians, and then proceeded to redistribute some of the profits to local mafia families and the elected officials involved in the exchange (Bolzoni 1993*b*). This was a decisive step toward the mafia becoming an "internal actor" in the corruption system (Bolzoni 1993*b*).

15. It was not possible to fully reconstruct how long each chief prosecutor's tenure was. 1983 is the first year when I could find clear information about Suraci, while Gaeta appears as the chief prosecutor still in 1995. These conclusions are based on information from journalistic accounts available in *La Repubblica*'s online archive.

16. The Reggio Calabria prosecutor's office would show massive improvements in the prosecution of local mafia organizations in the late 2000s (Pignatone, Prestipino

and Savatteri 2012), subverting previous trends, which instead are at the center of this analysis due to the latter's time frame.

17. The diffusion of investigative innovations from Milan to Palermo, despite the geographical distance between these two jurisdictions, highlights the absence of a similar diffusion between relatively close Southern jurisdictions like Palermo and Reggio Calabria.

18. Macrí and Lombardo's assumptions would eventually turn out to be wrong, when years later a new group of judicial professionals would conduct the most comprehensive investigation into *'Ndrangheta* crimes in Reggio Calabria based on confidential informants' testimonies (Pignatone, Prestipino and Savatteri 2012).

19. This number can be deduced from the defendants appealing to the Court of Cassation (Sentenza della Suprema Corte di Cassazione, Prima Sezione Penale, 8042/1992).

20. The then mayor of Reggio Calabria, Agatino Licandro, was repeatedly warned by his party peers that local prosecutors might start looking into bribe exchanges, that they might want "to do in Calabria what is being done in Milan" (Licandro and Varano 1993, 54).

21. Quote in Bonsanti (1992). Author's translation.

22. Quote in Sergi (1993*b*). Author's translation.

23. Pignatone, who would later lead the Reggio Calabria prosecutor's office, was a young prosecutor in the Palermo office at the time of the Clean Hands investigation. In his book with Prestipino and Savatteri (2012), Pignatone explains how prosecutorial work can create the conditions for confidential informants to come forward.

24. This is visible in the data about appellate corruption convictions for the Reggio Calabria jurisdiction in figure 1.6.

Conclusion

Lessons for Prosecutorial Success against Corruption

The purpose of my analysis in this book has been to draw some important lessons about the root causes of prosecutorial independence and effectiveness against systemic corruption from the Clean Hands operation's unprecedented success. The latter had a profound and lasting impact on the Italian political system. The main political protagonists of the so-called "First Republic," namely the Christian Democratic Party and the Socialist Party, have all but disappeared as a result of electoral backlash to their deep involvement in the corruption system (Fisman and Golden 2017, 222–223). This led several commentators to paint the Clean Hands operation as a politically motivated judicial effort to target specific political forces. However, there is little evidence to support the argument that this was a coordinated effort (Nelken 1996*a*, 105–106) or a judicial coup against government actors (Nelken 2002*b*, 57). Furthermore, as I showed in my empirical analysis, the expectations of the attitudinal model (Segal and Spaeth 2002) do not seem to explain prosecutorial behavior in the Clean Hands operation.

Nevertheless, the Clean Hands operation did in fact deeply impact the Italian political system, in some cases producing long-sought political effects for left-wing political forces, such as the former Italian Communist Party. The latter had been excluded from active participation in government coalitions during the First Republic and could now aspire to a government role after rebranding itself (Nelken 1996*a*, 107). Similar observations also apply to right-wing political forces that had been excluded from government coalitions during the First Republic due to their deep ties with the country's Fascist past. The *Movimento Sociale Italiano* (Italian Social Movement), which formed after World War II and had deep ties to the former Fascist regime, also rebranded itself in the years following the Clean Hands operation, taking on a more moderate and reformist appearance and a new name, *Alleanza Nazionale* (National Alliance).

As a result, since the Clean Hands operation, the Italian party system has experienced a process of deinstitutionalization visible in its increased levels of electoral volatility (Emanuele and Chiaramonte 2020). More importantly, the rise of new political forces, which exploited the political vacuum following the Clean Hands operation, paved the way for ruling coalitions which included political actors previously excluded from government. In addition, the new political protagonists of the so-called Second Republic offered countervailing narratives about the Clean Hands operation's causes and meaning and have often used the latter to argue in favor or against reforms to the Italian judicial branch (Nelken 2002*a*).

Interestingly, in the three decades following the Clean Hands operation, Italian politics has witnessed the emergence of new populist political forces on both sides of the political spectrum (Verbeek and Zaslove 2016). On the one hand, Silvio Berlusconi's *Forza Italia* Party (Go Italy) filled the political vacuum left by previous center-right forces and replaced them with a new right-wing populist political party. *Forza Italia*'s electoral strength revolved around Berlusconi's political outsider status and "self-made man" narrative, which embodied typical populist themes. *Forza Italia*'s rise to prominence offered inclusion into a ruling coalition for both *Alleanza Nazionale* and another political party, the *Lega Nord* (Northern League). The latter represents another right-wing variation on populist themes (Verbeek and Zaslove 2016, 306–307) due to its ideological attitudes shifting over time from secessionist aspirations to extreme xenophobia.

Berlusconi's alternate tenures as prime minister clearly represent instances of democratic backsliding in Italian politics (Ziblatt and Levitsky 2018). At the same time, they might also offer interesting insights into how to overcome right-wing populism, especially via a strong judiciary (Weyland 2022, 15–16). Having soon become himself the target of corruption investigations, Berlusconi adopted a narrative that painted the Clean Hands operation as a politically motivated campaign by "communist judges" to destroy their political rivals. This created an atmosphere of open conflict between Berlusconi's government and the Italian judiciary (Nelken 2002*a*, 121), which, on the other hand, dismissed its internal divisions to protect itself against attacks from the political class (Nelken 2002*a*, 120). At the same time, Berlusconi's government passed legislation that would create new obstacles to corruption prosecutions (Nelken 2002*a*, 126).

More populist parties have formed over the years on different sides of the ideological spectrum than *Forza Italia* and *Lega Nord*. After resigning from the bench, prosecutor Di Pietro established *Italia dei Valori* (Italy of Values) as a single-issue party focused on anti-corruption policy. Years later, *Movimento Cinque Stelle* (Five Stars Movement) also formed with a similar focus. These political forces are harder to define in terms of the typical left-right spectrum. As Verbeek and Zaslove (2016) explain, *Movimento Cinque Stelle* presents itself as a "populist left-libertarian movement" (307). Both parties adopted a political rhetoric that unambiguously praises judicial efforts in the Clean Hands operation for their results against corruption.

The Five Star Movement, in particular, drew a distinction between ethically minded civil society, which it claims to represent and corrupt political elites (Verbeek and Zaslove 2016, 307). The new populist party took this dichotomy to new extremes by choosing to build its infrastructure solely online to avoid falling into the same pitfalls and traps as conventional political forces. In the party's view, this would have prevented *Movimento* members from developing corrupt behavior and practices. Therefore, one of the most relevant political consequences of the Clean Hands operation has been to introduce a new cleavage in Italian politics around anti-corruption policies and attitudes (Sberna and Vannucci 2013), which populist movements on both sides of the political spectrum built upon.

Therefore, the Clean Hands operation represents a critical juncture in recent Italian history due not only to its unprecedented success in the prosecution of systemic corruption but also to its deep, though unintended, effects on the political context. In this book, I proposed an argument about the Clean Hands operation's causes that rejects attitudinal explanations (Segal and Spaeth 2002; Ceron and Mainenti 2015) and instead builds on the legal and institutionalist literature on Italian judicial and prosecutorial institutions' evolution (Della Porta 2001; Nelken 1996*a*, 1996*b*, 2002*b*; Guarnieri 2003). My argument contributes to this literature by further articulating the concept of decentralization (Nelken 1996*a*, 99–100) not just at the national but also at the local level, thanks to an examination of organizational structures within local prosecutor's offices.

In chapter 1, I presented my argument as a general theory of prosecutorial independence and effectiveness. My analysis traces back the roots of prosecutorial independence and effectiveness to the decentralization of power over prosecutorial work, coupled with the introduction of egalitarian organizational structures within local prosecutors' offices. These massive institutional transformations may lead to increase in prosecutorial independence from both higher ranks and local prosecutorial authorities, therefore allowing lower-ranked prosecutors to experiment with varied investigative and legal approaches. Increased prosecutorial independence, in turn, may promote the accumulation of an unprecedented reservoir of expertise among prosecutorial actors. These conditions, along with the emergence of judicial activism among local prosecutors, explain the Clean Hands operation's unprecedented success.

When applied to the specifics of the Italian context, my argument points first and foremost to the Italian prosecutorial system's radical transformation after the return to democracy following the end of World War II. In the years from 1945 to 1975, judicial associations fought to restructure Italian judicial and prosecutorial institutions and implement the decentralization of appointment and promotion powers from a select judicial elite to the greater body of all judicial professionals (inclusive of prosecutors). As I explained in chapter 2, this massive institutional transformation freed lower judicial ranks from the constraints imposed on them by hierarchical control of judicial careers. More importantly, this decentralization process created significant room for local prosecutorial authorities to choose their preferred organizational model for regulating the relationships with their subordinates. For this reason, chapters 3–5 focus on the structure of professional relationships within local prosecutors' offices in Rome, Milan, Palermo, and Reggio Calabria.

Through these case studies, I showed that local chief prosecutors' decision to adopt egalitarian organizational structures set their offices, particularly Milan and Palermo, on a trajectory to increased prosecutorial independence and effectiveness. As I showed in chapters 4 and 5, the adoption of this collegial organizational method allowed lower-ranked prosecutors to pursue new investigative and legal approaches out of their own initiative and even facilitated inter-jurisdictional collaboration between prosecutorial offices. Thanks to the Milan prosecutor's office collegial decision-making, Milanese prosecutors were able to develop new approaches to the investigation of terrorist groups, which resulted in several trials and convictions against these organizations. Furthermore, these prosecutorial successes attracted the attention of Palermo instructing judges and prosecutors, who would adopt similar prosecutorial methods as a result of their collaboration with their Milanese counterparts, thanks to the collegial environment within their offices.

On the other hand, as I showed in chapters 3 and 5, the persistence of hierarchical structures regulating the relationship between local chief prosecutors and their subordinates in Rome and Reggio Calabria severely compressed prosecutorial independence, and with it, local prosecutors' ability to develop more effective approaches to complex criminal issues over time. The tight hierarchical control of Roman chief prosecutors over their subordinates severely limited the latter's ability to adopt aggressive investigative approaches against terrorist organizations and corruption. Furthermore, the Roman prosecutor's office often appropriated corruption investigations from other jurisdictions via a process I defined as "prosecutorial gatekeeping." Similarly, Reggio Calabria chief prosecutors' hierarchical control of their office produced the continued flight of young prosecutors and a dearth of local qualified personnel in the long run. These conditions severely undermined investigations into local mafia organizations and their relationships with corrupt politicians.

Furthermore, changes to local organizational structures within these prosecutors' offices also introduce interesting longitudinal variation. The latter highlights the importance of timing in the introduction of specific organizational structures. While the introduction of egalitarian structures may immediately increase prosecutorial independence, this is not enough to produce prosecutorial effectiveness in the short term. This is visible in the Roman prosecutor's office, whose introduction of egalitarian structures at the time of the Clean Hands operation could not compensate for the dearth of expertise in corruption prosecutions from the long-lasting presence of hierarchical control. Rather, prosecutorial effectiveness derives from the stability of these egalitarian structures, which can increase prosecutorial effectiveness in the long run despite temporary reversals to hierarchy.

In other words, prosecutorial independence via the introduction of egalitarian decision-making will eventually produce prosecutorial effectiveness in the long run if local prosecutorial authorities allow egalitarian structures to remain in place for enough time unencumbered. This is particularly the case of Palermo, where organizational structures were temporarily discontinued in the late 1980s. Nevertheless, individual efforts to pass down accumulated prosecutorial expertise facilitated the return of effective prosecution with the reintroduction of egalitarian structures at the time of the Clean Hands operation.

Furthermore, the case studies show how the adoption of different organizational structures mostly followed from chief prosecutors' legal preferences and understanding of their professional mission. Traditionally conservative chief prosecutors adopted hierarchical structures in line with the anti-democratic instincts deriving from reactionary legal conservatism. On the other hand, both enlightened conservative chief prosecutors and progressive chief prosecutors, who wished to uphold the democratic principles in the new Constitution, opted for egalitarian structures that "democratized" the relationship with their subordinates. Thus, the alternation of specific organizational structures reflects the ideological battle between different legal factions within the Italian judiciary and the profound relationship between institutions and legal ideology.

Therefore, the Clean Hands operation was the culmination of long historical trends, particularly the accumulation of prosecutorial expertise resulting from the presence of egalitarian organizational structure in key prosecutors' offices, such as the ones in Milan and Palermo, and the suspension of prosecutorial gatekeeping by the prosecutor's office in Rome, which also resulted from the introduction of egalitarian organizational structures within that office. Furthermore, these egalitarian structures and accumulation of expertise allowed Milanese prosecutors to develop new investigative and legal approaches to corruption prosecutions. These new approaches, which embodied a more activist understanding of the judicial profession, or "role substitution," as Della Porta (2001, 6) defines it, produced incredibly effective results in breaking up a corruption system that had survived several previous attempts to do the same. While these methods created inevitable tensions with extant defendants' rights, as Nelken points out, the application of legal rules against corruption was the actual "revolution" in the Clean Hands operation (1996*a*, 96; 1996*c*, 188).

LESSONS FROM THE CLEAN HANDS OPERATION: PROSECUTING CORRUPTION AROUND THE WORLD

Although my analysis focuses on the Italian prosecutorial system and its anti-corruption efforts, the theory I developed in this book can travel well beyond the Italian case. In fact, practitioners have long looked at the Clean Hands operation as a source of inspiration (Moro 2004). Since corruption remains a salient issue for several democracies, it is worth briefly exploring how my theory may apply to a few other cases. In chapter 1, I addressed the structure of the prosecutorial system both at the national and local levels. In the following sections, I briefly explore the implications of my theory for the prosecution of corruption in Brazil and Japan. I illustrate how my theory can help make sense of recent developments in the prosecution of corruption in each of these two cases. However, this brief analysis is mostly limited to the application of my theoretical framework to prosecutorial institutions at the national level. I leave the empirical and theoretical works on local prosecutorial institutions to future researchers.

Brazil

The Brazilian prosecutorial system has garnered much public and scholarly attention since the start of the Car Wash Operation in 2014. The latter, which started as a routine investigation into local money laundering efforts via a car wash business, soon turned into a massive anti-corruption campaign involving two Brazilian presidents and hundreds of elected officials. While the Car Wash operation has formally concluded, questions remain over its unprecedented success in exposing systemic corruption. As I mentioned before, Brazilian judicial professionals quite explicitly recognized the Italian Clean Hands operation as a model for their own actions (Moro 2004). However, it is worth exploring whether Brazilian judicial professionals also enjoyed institutional conditions that would allow them to act independently enough to imitate Clean Hands prosecutors and to accumulate the necessary expertise to deploy Clean Hands operation strategy and tactics. Based on the theory I offered in this book, those favorable institutional conditions would amount to a decentralized prosecutorial system and egalitarian institutions at the level of local prosecutorial offices.

The 1988 Brazilian Constitution establishes the Brazilian prosecutorial system's main features. In particular, the Constitution granted Brazilian prosecutors an unprecedented level of autonomy from other government branches (Sadek and Cavalcanti 2003, 203). As a result, the Public Prosecution today consists of an independent institution distinct from the rest of the judicial profession (Sadek and Cavalcanti 2003, 203–204, 206). Furthermore, prosecutors enjoy extensive institutional and economic guarantees of their autonomous status: the constitutional text grants Brazilian prosecutors "due benefits" (Sadek and Cavalcanti 2003, 206) and establishes "lifetime tenure" (206), along with setting up severe constraints on removal of prosecutors by other authorities (206). More importantly, lower-ranked prosecutors enjoy a safe pathway to professional advancement that essentially frees them from any need to appease their superiors in the prosecutorial hierarchy.

The Brazilian Constitution goes to great lengths to outline the rules regulating professional advancements for both judges and prosecutors. Even though these groups are distinct, the same rules apply (Carvalho and Leitão 2019, 99). At a superficial look, the Brazilian prosecutorial system would appear to represent an internally directed elitist justice system, according to the classification I offered in chapter 1. This is because higher-ranked judicial professionals fill vacancies at their level by drawing from the justice system's lower ranks (Jardim de Santa Cruz Oliveira and Garoupa 2011, 536). Therefore, this institutional design would seem to leave the professional fate of lower-ranked prosecutors in the hands of their higher-ranked colleagues. If this were the case, we should expect Brazilian prosecutors to enjoy little to no *de facto* independence within such a strictly hierarchical system. However, a few constitutional guarantees intervene to enhance prosecutorial independence.

First of all, the Constitution states that appointments to higher posts must be based either on a judicial professional's years in service or on the latter's qualifications (Jardim de Santa Cruz Oliveira and Garoupa 2011, 536). The application of seniority as a principle for professional advancement empties higher-ranked judicial professionals of any discretion. Seniority is an objective criterion that is hardly open to manipulation. Merit, on the other hand, might reintroduce significant discretion, by giving higher-ranked judicial professionals the ability to impose their own views on the lower ranks via an evaluation system. However, once again, the Brazilian Constitution intervenes to remove such discretionary powers from higher-ranked prosecutors. According to the Brazilian constitution, "merit-based promotion requires two years in office at the respective level and that the judge should be in the top fifth of the seniority list of such level" (Jardim de Santa Cruz Oliveira and

Garoupa 2011, 537). Thus, merit-based appointments do not seem to entail a broadly subjective evaluation. Rather, these objective criteria limit higher ranks' control over lower-ranked colleagues' careers.

These rules make the Brazilian system remarkably similar to the Italian one. As I explained in chapter 2, starting in the 1970s, Italian judicial professionals also enjoyed a safe pathway to professional advancement based on seniority. Therefore, it is inaccurate to describe the Brazilian justice system as an elitist system. Rather, the presence of significant constitutional guarantees that afford lower-ranked prosecutors a safe pathway to professional advancement is a clear sign of decentralization.

For this reason, when describing the Public Prosecutor in Brazil, Sadek and Cavalcanti (2003) argued that the latter is "decentralized, lacking a functional hierarchy and therefore giving substantial autonomy to each prosecutor" (208). Even though lower-ranked prosecutors may not be able to affect the selection of officials in charge of promotions and appointments, extant constitutional guarantees eliminate any need for them to do so. This is because the Brazilian constitution affords every Brazilian prosecutor with a safe professional trajectory and frees them from higher-ranked officials' control over their professional fate. Thus, the Brazilian prosecutorial system is closer to a decentralized justice system than a hierarchical one.

Finally, while evidence of organizational structures at the local level is not readily available, current laws seem to leave a lot of room for lower-ranked prosecutors' independence vis-à-vis their local authorities. This is because "according to legal norms, each prosecutor has a right to select his own cases" (Sadek 2001, 72). Furthermore, the Brazilian constitution explicitly establishes that prosecutorial action should solely follow a prosecutor's own initiative rather than other individuals' preferences or commands. Therefore, these constitutional provisions void local hierarchical structures of their coercive powers. As Carvalho and Leitão (2019) argue:

> members of the PPO [Public Prosecutor's Office] do not have to follow an institutional line adopted by the organization's leadership [. . .] for instance, prosecutors cannot be ordered to bring suit, or not to bring suit, or to support a certain legal thesis over another. (96)

Thus, local hierarchical structures appear incompatible with these legal provisions, and lower-ranked prosecutors enjoy significant freedom from their immediate superiors.

Based on these considerations, it should not come as a surprise that Brazilian prosecutors managed to achieve astonishing successes against systemic corruption in the Car Wash operation. While there are several aspects of the latter's anti-corruption campaign that deserve further examination due to their "illiberal" tendencies (De Sá e Silva 2020), Brazilian prosecutors and judges' ability to conduct such a massive anti-corruption effort fit within the predictions of my theory in this book: a decentralized national prosecutorial system and increasing egalitarianism within local prosecutorial institutions lead to increases in prosecutorial independence and effective corruption prosecutions in the long run. It took Brazil less than thirty years from the enactment of the 1988 Constitution to witness massive prosecutorial achievements against systemic corruption, which have also inspired similar efforts across Latin American countries with more limited success (González-Ocantos and Hidalgo 2019). Thus, at a superficial look, the Brazilian case and the Lava Jato Operation seem to confirm my theory and represent an interesting venue of future research.

Japan

While Brazil represents a positive case of prosecutorial independence and effectiveness against systemic corruption, Japan, on the other hand, clearly represents a negative case. Interestingly, Japan also seems to confirm the basic predictions of my theory. Scholars have often pointed at the similarities between the Japanese party system and the Italian party system (at least in the post–World War II era until 1992, the so-called Italian "First Republic"). Both systems revolved around one party's electoral dominance—the Liberal Party in Japan and the Christian Democratic Party in Italy, which were in turn marred by internal factionalism (Bettcher 2005). Scholars also highlighted similarities in the level and features of political corruption across these two countries (Johnson 2003, 257).

However, to this day, Japan has not experienced an anti-corruption effort of similar scope as the Car Wash or the Clean Hands operation. Therefore, the lack of similarly extensive and effective prosecutorial efforts against corruption within the Japanese context warrants an explanation. Although a thorough examination of the Japanese case is beyond the goals of this book, a brief review of the Japanese prosecutorial system's structure provides an initial confirmation of my theory. Japanese prosecutorial institutions show clear hierarchical features at the national level and a dire lack of egalitarianism at lower levels. These conditions might help explain the absence of significant prosecutorial effectiveness against systemic corruption in Japan.

When analyzing the Japanese prosecutorial system, a good starting point is to ask whether the latter is internally or externally directed. Japanese prosecutors seem to be under the control of the Minister of Justice, at least formally. However, in his study of Japanese prosecutors, Johnson (2002) finds that, under normal circumstances, the Minister of Justice's influence over the prosecution is not felt by this institution's members, who barely even remember who the current Minister is (120). The only significant exception to the Minister's extraneity seems to be corruption investigations against elected officials (120). In those instances, Johnson highlights the Minister's inclination to intervene in prosecutorial work (120). Therefore, even though the Japanese prosecutorial system finds itself formally under the executive branch's control, it would be inaccurate to describe this institution as externally directed. Rather, as Johnson (2002) argues, "the Minister reigns, while the prosecutors rule" (120).

Furthermore, a brief analysis of prosecutorial careers and their trajectory provides even more evidence that the Japanese prosecutorial system is internally directed. Within this system, promotions and appointments seem to depend on higher-ranking prosecutorial authorities, the so-called prosecutor executives (Johnson 2012, 48). In making these decisions, prosecutor executives take into account lower-ranked prosecutors' "college of origin, ideology, age and seniority [. . .] and previous job performance" (Johnson 2012, 48).

Based on this evidence, the Japanese prosecutorial system clearly appears to be hierarchical and internally directed, because higher-ranked officials control the careers of young and lower-ranking professionals. Furthermore, appointments appear to depend considerably on performance evaluations and an ideological assessment of prosecutors' political views (Johnson 2012, 48). Both of these evaluative criteria tend to repress prosecutorial independence by encouraging ideological conformity with higher-ranked prosecutors' ideology across all levels of this institution (Johnson 2012, 48).

In addition to a clearly hierarchical and internally directed structure, the Japanese prosecutorial system also seems to enforce a strict hierarchical organization of its professional relationships at all levels. In other words, Japanese prosecutorial institutions' organizational structure and informal rules of conduct seem to leave little to no room at all for egalitarian decision-making. This is mostly due to "the principle of prosecutor unity" (Johnson 2002, 121), which implies that the prosecutorial system's hierarchical structure is meant to hold it together as a single body working in unison (Johnson 2002, 121). This results in the Prosecutor General's ability to issue binding directives for all members of the institution at any level (Johnson 2002, 121). More importantly, this hierarchical principle of internal organization "gives the various office heads, and all prosecutor managers, authority to direct their subordinates in any work-related area" (Johnson 2002, 121).

Further reinforcing this highly hierarchical internal organization are the detailed instructions that manager prosecutors impose on their subordinates, along with "the *kessai* system of consultation and review" (Johnson 2002, 118, 130). The former traps lower-ranked prosecutors into a web of regulations that deprive them of any initiative when making key decisions (Johnson 2002, 129–130). This leads Johnson to argue that "Japanese prosecutors work in an organization saturated with policy directives" (Johnson 2002, 131). The *kessai* system requires lower-ranked prosecutors to seek their immediate superior's opinion, especially when they wish to stray away from the guidelines (Johnson 2002, 129, 130–131). Prosecutors consider these policies "indispensable guides to action" (Johnson 2002, 128). As a result, Japanese prosecutors enjoy almost no discretion in their decision-making, which instead follows strict guidelines from their immediate superiors.

Both the presence of thorough guidelines and the practice of *kessai* strengthen the already-hierarchical organizational structure of the Japanese prosecutorial system. Thus, the hierarchical environment in which Japanese prosecutors find themselves severely reduces their independence at all levels of this institution. Consequently, lower-ranked Japanese prosecutors do not enjoy the freedom to develop legal and investigative approaches outside of established guidelines. These conditions explain the lack of effective prosecutorial efforts against systemic corruption in Japan. As previously mentioned, Japanese Ministers of Justice seem to have demonstrated a certain propensity to use their formal oversight powers to interfere with corruption investigations in the past (Johnson 2002, 120). On top of this, the Japanese prosecutorial system suffers from institutional arrangements that severely diminish prosecutorial independence and undermine the development of prosecutorial expertise in the long run. For instance, the *kessai* system creates significant incentives for prosecutors to drop corruption cases involving elected officials (Johnson 2002, 131).

These features of the Japanese prosecutorial system are visible at work in the Shipbuilding Scandal, which involved illicit exchanges between companies and elected officials for legislation benefiting the maritime transport and construction industry (Johnson 2000, 64). While Japanese prosecutors did in fact arrest and convict several politicians and businessmen involved in this corruption scheme, the most prominent political figures, like MP Eisaku Sato, escaped (65). Johnson illustrates particularly well how the hierarchical structure of professional relationships among Japanese prosecutors hindered prosecutorial effectiveness in this case. As previously explained, Japanese prosecutors have to participate in incessant consultations with their superiors (66). This produces an endless flow of information, detailing an investigation's trajectory and prosecutors' decisions in the case (66). More importantly, this hierarchical structure facilitates the transmission of these reports to the highest prosecutorial authority in the system, which includes both the Prosecutor General and the Minister of Justice (66).

As Johnson (2000) recounts, during the Shipbuilding Scandal investigation, the Prosecutor General called a meeting between the prosecutors leading the case and a few officials from the Ministry of Justice, among others (66). This meeting was the beginning of the end for prosecutorial efforts to hold politicians accountable in the Shipbuilding Scandal. After the meeting, the Minister of Justice invoked his formal power over the Prosecutor General and put an end to the effort to arrest MP Eisaku Sato (67). While partially shedding light on a significant corruption scheme, the investigation concluded without achieving accountability against the most powerful defendants in the case.

The Japanese case, therefore, falls squarely within the predictions of the theory I offered in this book. As the Shipbuilding Scandal shows, the Japanese prosecutorial system's hierarchical structure and lack of internal egalitarianism profoundly undermine prosecutorial independence and effectiveness against corruption. In addition, this system's internal hierarchy facilitates interventions by external actors such as the Minister of Justice, which also contribute to the weakening of prosecutorial independence and effectiveness. Unfortunately, unless the Japanese prosecutorial system's institutional design changes toward an attenuation of its hierarchical features, the latter will continue to pose serious obstacles to the development of effective corruption prosecutions.

BROADER IMPLICATIONS AND FUTURE VENUES OF RESEARCH

In this book, I offered a theoretical framework for understanding prosecutorial independence and effectiveness against systemic corruption and applied it to Italian context and the Clean Hands operation. My analysis provides several broad implications that can help inform scholarly research into similar topics in the future. First of all, one of the broader implications in my analysis is the importance of prosecutorial institutions' internal organization for understanding prosecutorial behavior and, as a result, the outcome of corruption investigations. The necessary question we need to ask in order to determine the level of prosecutorial independence is a simple, but often neglected one: who do prosecutors work for? Hierarchy and decentralization clearly help provide answers to this question. Within a hierarchical system, prosecutors' behavior will necessarily follow the constraints imposed on them by the institutional structure. Consequently, they will tend to act in accordance with the preferences of the institution or individual who controls their professional fate. On the other hand, decentralization will free these actors from concerns about the consequences of their choices for their professional trajectory. Therefore, decentralization fuels prosecutorial independence, allowing prosecutorial actors to explore a variety of legal and investigative approaches and lean into increasingly assertive behavior.

Similar observations apply to the nature of local organizational structures. Hierarchy and egalitarianism among prosecutors in the same office mimic at the local level the dynamics inherent in the principal-agent dilemma inherent in hierarchy and decentralization at the national level. Local hierarchical structures constrain prosecutorial initiative where it is most important: in the pursuit of legal and investigative novelties that might produce more effective outcomes. On the other hand, egalitarian structures foster prosecutorial initiatives, creating increasing room for creativity and innovation in the pursuit of effective prosecution.

The focus of my book on prosecutorial institutions opens several venues of future research in the same vein. First of all, my book offers a systematic classification of prosecutorial systems, both at the national and local levels. The inclusion of local institutions in my analysis fills a vacuum in the extant literature on prosecutorial systems. Furthermore, the brief application of my theoretical framework to Brazil and Japan in this chapter suggests its explanatory potential for other prosecutorial systems than Italy. Therefore, future research could test the application of this theoretical framework to other domestic contexts to explain the success of corruption prosecutions (or lack thereof) in other countries. Moreover, classifying prosecutorial systems as either hierarchical or decentralized may raise interesting empirical puzzles about the diffusion of such structures and the reason behind this process. As Nelken points out (2010), politicians and policy-makers often intentionally engage in systemic comparison of criminal justice structures when pursuing reform in their own country (3). Therefore, by providing a classification of prosecutorial systems, this book may also facilitate an empirical inquiry into the diffusion of similar institutions across countries and the reason behind this phenomenon. Finally, in this book, I focused on both formal and informal institutions. The theoretical framework I proposed includes both types, and its application to other contexts may help further shed light on the informal organizational structures regulating prosecutorial offices and prosecutorial systems.

As new institutionalism suggests (Smith 1988), while institutions affect behavior, at the same time, institutional structures do not form or change in a vacuum. Actors' legal preferences and understanding of their professional mission affect their organizational choices. Therefore, another broad implication of my analysis in this book is the importance of legal ideologies. In this book, I thoroughly explored the effects of legal conservatism and progressivism on prosecutorial behavior. In my analysis, I showed how legal philosophy profoundly affects prosecutorial behavior more than political preferences. Thus, my analysis suggests the importance of a renewed focus on legal ideology to understand not just judicial but also prosecutorial behavior, specifically in relation to corruption prosecutions.

Bibliography

"A Roma I Documenti di Gladio." *La Repubblica*, November 14, 1990.

"Anas, Una Nuova 'Bomba' Scoppia su Tangentopoli." *La Repubblica*, January 21, 1993. http://ricerca.repubblica.it/repubblica/archivio/repubblica/1993/01/21/anas-una-nuova-bomba-scoppia-su.html

"Arriva in Sicilia il Ciclone Tangenti Retata di Politici e Imprenditori." *Il Giornale di Sicilia*, May 27, 1993.

"Da Ieri Di Pietro Indaga a Roma." *La Repubblica*, October 1, 1992. http://ricerca.repubblica.it/repubblica/archivio/repubblica/1992/10/01/di-pietro-da-ieri-indaga-roma.html?ref=search

"'Ciancimino Dica Qual E' il Suo Lavoro' Signore Giudice, Dall'84 Faccio l'Imputato'." *Il Giornale di Sicilia*, June 8, 1990.

"De Michelis e Bernini Roma Non Avochera'." *La Repubblica*, August 19, 1992. http://ricerca.repubblica.it/repubblica/archivio/repubblica/1992/08/19/de-michelis-bernini-roma-non-avochera.html?ref=search

"Dopo 40 Anni la Procura E' Diretta da un Milanese." *Corriere della Sera*, September 19, 1976.

"Fumata Nera per il PM di Palermo." *La Repubblica*, May 23, 1987. https://ricerca.repubblica.it/repubblica/archivio/repubblica/1987/05/23/fumata-nera-per-il-pm-di-palermo.html?ref=search

"Giudici, I Pentiti Non Sono Credibili." *La Repubblica*, May 22, 1984. http://ricerca.repubblica.it/repubblica/archivio/repubblica/1984/05/22/giudici-pentiti-non-sono-credibili.html?ref=search

"I Magistrati Accusano il Procuratore Micale." *Corriere della Sera*, February 22, 1974.

"I Magistrati Vogliono Rompere l'Accerchiamento dei Partiti." *La Repubblica*, November 5, 1988. http://ricerca.repubblica.it/repubblica/archivio/repubblica/1988/11/05/magistrati-vogliono-rompere-accerchiamento-dei.html

"I Pentiti: Negli Uffici della Regione le Riunioni per Pilotare gli Appalti." *Il Giornale di Sicilia*, May 27, 1993.

"Il Consiglio Superiore Decide Oggi il Trasferimento del Procuratore Capo Micale." *Corriere della Sera*, April 21, 1975.

"Il Dottor Mauro Gresti Nominato Procuratore Capo della Repubblica." *Corriere della Sera*, July 17, 1976.

"Il Rapporto, le Polemiche, I Pentiti, Cosi' l'Inchiesta e' Diventata Valanga." *Il Giornale di Sicilia*, May 27, 1993.

"'Il Super Pool Necessario alle Indagini'." *La Repubblica*, December 21, 1990. http://ricerca.repubblica.it/repubblica/archivio/repubblica/1990/12/21/il-super-pool-necessario-all-indagine.html?ref=search

"L'Inchiesta Ciancimino Passata da Falcone alla Procura." *La Repubblica*, April 21, 1988. http://ricerca.repubblica.it/repubblica/archivio/repubblica/1988/04/21/inchiesta-ciancimino-passata-da-falcone-alla.html?ref=search

"La 'Guerra' tra Micale e i Suoi Sostituti." *Corriere della Sera*, March 8, 1975.

"La Scelta del CSM." *La Repubblica*, May 22, 1996. http://ricerca.repubblica.it/repubblica/archivio/repubblica/1996/05/22/la-scelta-del-csm.html

"Le Mani della Mafia sugli Appalti Di Maggio: Ecco Come I Boss Gestivano le Opere Pubbliche." *Il Giornale di Sicilia*, May 4, 1993.

"Milano, Borrelli E' da Ieri il Nuovo Procuratore Capo." *La Repubblica*, March 18, 1988. https://ricerca.repubblica.it/repubblica/archivio/repubblica/1988/03/18/milano-borrelli-da-ieri-il-nuovo.html?ref=search

"Per Gallucci Critiche e Riconoscimenti dei Magistrati Romani." *Corriere della Sera*, November 19, 1980.

"Per L'Assassinio di Ligato Prosciolti I Politici Calabresi." *La Repubblica*, May 28, 1994. https://ricerca.repubblica.it/repubblica/archivio/repubblica/1994/05/28/per-assassinio-di-ligato-prosciolti-politici.html?ref=search

"Per l'Omicidio Saronio Dovete Assolvere Negri con la Formula Piena." *La Repubblica*, May 18, 1984. http://ricerca.repubblica.it/repubblica/archivio/repubblica/1984/05/18/per-omicidio-saronio-dovete-assolvere-negri.html?ref=search

"Per lo Scandalo della USL di Reggio Finiscono in Carcere 12 Persone." *La Repubblica*, May 20, 1987. http://ricerca.repubblica.it/repubblica/archivio/repubblica/1987/05/20/per-lo-scandalo-della-usl-di-reggio.html?ref=search

"Quei Soldi in Odor di Mafia 'Consulto' Borrelli – Caselli." *La Repubblica*, June 2, 1993. https://ricerca.repubblica.it/repubblica/archivio/repubblica/1993/06/02/quei-soldi-in-odor-di-mafia.html?ref=search

"Quel Filo Che Lega Palermo e Milano." *La Repubblica*, June 3, 1993. http://ricerca.repubblica.it/repubblica/archivio/repubblica/1993/06/03/quel-filo-che-lega-palermo-milano.html

"Reggio Calabria, Sull'Unita' Sanitaria la Magistratura Ha Aperto un'Inchiesta." *La Repubblica*, February 6, 1987. https://ricerca.repubblica.it/repubblica/archivio/repubblica/1987/02/06/reggio-calabria-sull-unita-sanitaria-la-magistratura.html?ref=search

"Reggio, Interrogatorio - Fiume per l'Ex Sindaco DC." *La Repubblica*, July 26, 1992. https://ricerca.repubblica.it/repubblica/archivio/repubblica/1992/07/26/reggio-interrogatorio-fiume-per-ex.html?ref=search

"Savia nei Guai per Trecento Milioni della Tangente Enimont." *La Repubblica*, June 1, 1997. http://ricerca.repubblica.it/repubblica/archivio/repubblica/1997/06/01/savia-nei-guai-per-300-milioni-della.html

"Sono Irrevocabili le Dimissioni del Procuratore Capo De Matteo." *Corriere della Sera*, June 28, 1980.

"Sulle Mazzette Romane Non Deve Indagare Di Pietro." *La Repubblica*, September 29, 1992. http://ricerca.repubblica.it/repubblica/archivio/repubblica/1992/09/29/sulle-mazzette-romane-non-deve-indagare.html?ref=search

"Un Pool di Giudici a Consulto sulle Maxitangente a Milano." *La Repubblica*, March 23, 1988. https://ricerca.repubblica.it/repubblica/archivio/repubblica/1988/03/23/un-pool-di-giudici-consulto-sulle-maxitangenti.html?ref=search

"Un Pool per Affittopoli." *La Repubblica*, September 15, 1995. https://ricerca.repubblica.it/repubblica/archivio/repubblica/1995/09/15/un-pool-per-affittopoli.html?ref=search

"'Via Giammanco, Ma Non Basta'." *La Repubblica*, August 12, 1992.

Albini, Rita, and Livio Colombo. 1987. "Le Otto Aziende della Nomenklatura." *Società Civile*, 2(February): 3–5.

Alexander, A. Lawrence. 2015. "Judicial Activism: Clearing the Air and the Head." In *Judicial Activism: An Interdisciplinary Approach to the American and European Experiences*, edited by Coutinho, Luís Pereira, Massimo La Torre, and Steven D. Smith, 15–20. New York: Springer.

Almerighi, Mario. 1993. "Vi Ricordate lo Scandlo Petroli?" *La Repubblica*, March 14. https://ricerca.repubblica.it/repubblica/archivio/repubblica/1993/03/14/vi-ricordate-lo-scandalo-petroli.html

Balzanelli, Aldo. 1988. "Signorelli Istigo' I Killer." *La Repubblica*, July 3. http://ricerca.repubblica.it/repubblica/archivio/repubblica/1988/07/03/signorelli-istigo-killer.html.

Barbacetto, Gianni. 1987. "Scandalo delle Aree d'Oro Ma il Caso Non É Chiuso." *Società Civile*, 2(1): 9.

Barbacetto, Gianni, Peter Gomez, and Marco Travaglio. 2012. *Mani Pulite La Vera Storia 20 Anni Dopo*. Milano: Chiarelettere.

Barsotti, Vittoria, Paolo G. Carozza, Marta Cartabia, and Andrea Simoncini. 2015. *Italian Constitutional Justice in Global Context*. New York: Oxford University Press.

Bartoli Costa, Rita. 2001. *Una Storia Vera a Palermo*. Caltanissetta: Sciascia.

Bellu, Giovanni Maria. 1996. "Coiro Lascia la Procura di Roma." *La Repubblica*, September 5. https://ricerca.repubblica.it/repubblica/archivio/repubblica/1996/09/05/coiro-lascia-la-procura-di-roma.html

Benson, Michael L., et al. 1988. "District Attorneys and Corporate Crime: Surveying the Prosecutorial Gatekeepers." *Criminology*, 26(3): 505–518.

Bettcher, Kim Eric. 2005. "Factions of Interest in Japan and Italy: The Organizational and Motivational Dimensions of Factionalism." *Party Politics*, 11(3): 339–358.

Bianconi, Giovanni. 2015. "Pignatone, La Toga Prudente Arbitro dei Destini del Comune." *Corriere della Sera*, June 19. http://roma.corriere.it/notizie/politica/15

_giugno_19/pignatone-toga-prudente-arbitro-destini-comune-16f8e4bc-1652-11e5-9531-d169a57fe795.shtml

Boffano, Ettore. 2009. "Storia del Giudice Coraggioso Che Smantello' Prima Linea." *La Repubblica*, September 24.

Boffano, Ettore, and Alberto Custodero. 1993. "Generale Parleró...Sono l'Autista di Riina'." *La Repubblica*, January 17. http://ricerca.repubblica.it/repubblica/archivio/repubblica/1993/01/17/generale-parlero-sono-autista.html?ref=search

Bolzoni, Attilio. 1985. "Affare Sme Martinazzoli Accusa." *La Repubblica*, September 1. http://ricerca.repubblica.it/repubblica/archivio/repubblica/1985/09/01/affare-sme-martinazzoli-accusa.html?ref=search

Bolzoni, Attilio. 1988. "Meli Torna da Vincitore." *La Repubblica*, August 3. https://ricerca.repubblica.it/repubblica/archivio/repubblica/1988/08/03/meli-torna-da-vincitore.html?ref=search

Bolzoni, Attilio. 1989. "Chi Mi Ha Accusato Paghera'." *La Repubblica*, July 26. https://ricerca.repubblica.it/repubblica/archivio/repubblica/1989/07/26/chi-mi-ha-accusato-paghera.html?ref=search

Bolzoni, Attilio. 1990*a*. "Ciancimino Incastrato dagli 007 di Bankitalia." *La Repubblica*, July 3. https://ricerca.repubblica.it/repubblica/archivio/repubblica/1990/07/03/ciancimino-incastrato-dagli-007-di-bankitalia.html?ref=search

Bolzoni, Attilio. 1990*b*. "Palermo, Falcone Da' il Benvenuto al Nuovo Procuratore Giammanco." *La Repubblica*, June 20. https://ricerca.repubblica.it/repubblica/archivio/repubblica/1990/06/20/palermo-falcone-da-il-benvenuto-al-nuovo.html

Bolzoni, Attilio. 1992*a*. "Catania, in Carcere gli Intoccabili." *La Repubblica*, November 20. https://ricerca.repubblica.it/repubblica/archivio/repubblica/1992/11/20/catania-in-carcere-gli-intoccabili.html

Bolzoni, Attilio. 1993*a*. "Appalti, Sotto Tiro I Big della Sicilia." *La Repubblica*, August 7. http://ricerca.repubblica.it/repubblica/archivio/repubblica/1993/08/07/appalti-sotto-tiro-big-della-sicilia.html?ref=search

Bolzoni, Attilio. 1993*b*. "Appalti alla Siciliana: Era Riina il Capofila." *La Repubblica*, May 27. http://ricerca.repubblica.it/repubblica/archivio/repubblica/1993/05/27/appalti-alla-siciliana-era-riina-il.html?ref=search.

Bolzoni, Attilio. 1993*c*. "La Caduta del Boss dei Boss." *La Repubblica*, January 16. https://ricerca.repubblica.it/repubblica/archivio/repubblica/1993/01/16/la-caduta-del-boss-dei-boss.html?ref=search

Bolzoni, Attilio. 1993*d*. "Appalti alla Siciliana 'Era Riina il Capofila'." *La Repubblica*, May 27. https://ricerca.repubblica.it/repubblica/archivio/repubblica/1993/05/27/appalti-alla-siciliana-era-riina-il.html?ref=search

Bolzoni, Attilio, and Giuseppe D'Avanzo. 1993. "Da Caselli un Dossier – Bomba." *La Repubblica*, April 21. http://ricerca.repubblica.it/repubblica/archivio/repubblica/1993/04/21/da-caselli-un-dossier-bomba.html?ref=search

Bonsanti, Sandra. 1992. "Un Anno da Giudice sul Vulcano di Reggio." *La Repubblica*, September 9. https://ricerca.repubblica.it/repubblica/archivio/repubblica/1992/09/09/un-anno-da-giudice-sul-vulcano-di.html?ref=search

Borgna, Paolo. 2017. "Ricostruire la Giustizia Penale nel Dopoguerra. I Nuovi Valori Costituzionali e l'Indipendenza del Giudice." *Questione Giustizia* (online).

http://questionegiustizia.it/articolo/ricostruire-la-giustizia-penale-nel-dopoguerra_i-nuovi-valori-costituzionali-e-l-indipendenza-del-giudice_10-10-2017.php (Accessed on October 10, 2017)

Brinks, Daniel M. 2007. *The Judicial Response to Police Killings in Latin America: Inequality and the Rule of Law*. New York: Cambridge University Press.

Caroli, Paolo. 2015. "The Role of the Judiciary within the Construction of Collective Memory. The Italian Transition." *Wroclaw Review of Law, Administration & Economics*, 5(1): 162–179.

Carrubba, Clifford J., et al. 2015. "When Parchment Barriers Matter: De Jure Judicial Independence and the Concentration of Power." Unpublished manuscript. https://www.gretchenhelmke.com/uploads/7/0/3/2/70329843/parchment.pdf

Carvalho, Ernani, and Natália Leitão. 2019. "Operationalizing and Measuring Prosecutorial Independence: The Brazilian Case." In *Beyond Higher Courts the Justice Complex in Latin America*, edited by M. C. Ingram and D. Kapiszewski. Notre Dame: University of Notre Dame Press.

Caselli, Gian Carlo. 2009. *Le Due Guerre*. Milano: Melampo Editore.

Cazzola, Franco, and Massimo Morisi. 1996. *La Mutua Diffidenza: Il Reciproco Controllo tra Magistrati e Politici nella Prima Repubblica*. Milano: Feltrinelli.

Cecchetti, Giorgio. 1991. "I Giudici di Gladio Scrivono 'Roma Blocca le Indagini'." *La Repubblica*, April 2.

Cerasa, Giuseppe, and France Recanatesi. 1984. "Ecco I Comandamenti della Mafia." *La Repubblica*, October 2. https://ricerca.repubblica.it/repubblica/archivio/repubblica/1984/10/02/ecco-comandamenti-della-mafia.html

Ceron, Andrea, and Marco Mainenti. 2015. "Toga Party: The Political Basis of Judicial Investigations against MPs in Italy (1983–2013)." *South European Society and Politics* 20(2): 223–242.

Chang, Eric C. C., Miriam A. Golden, and Seth J. Hill. 2010. "Legislative Malfeasance and Political Accountability." *World Politics* 62(2): 177–220.

Chinnici, Rocco. 1990. *L'Illegalita' Protetta*. Palermo: La Zisa.

Colaprico, Piero, and Luca Fazzo. 1992. "Altri Dieci Politici Sotto Inchiesta E Tabacci Va Processato." *La Repubblica*, October 10, 1992. http://ricerca.repubblica.it/repubblica/archivio/repubblica/1992/10/10/altri-dieci-politici-sott-inchiesta-tabacci.html

Colaprico, Piero, and Luca Fazzo. 1993. "Larini Inguaia Craxi." *La Repubblica*, February 10.

Collier, David. 1991. "The Comparative Method: Two Decades of Change." In *Comparative Political Dynamics: Global Research Perspectives*, edited by Dankwart Rustow and Kenneth Paul Erickson, 7–31. New York: Harper Collins Publishers.

Colombo Livio. 1990. "Le Mille e una Stecca." *Società Civile*, 5(6): 24.

Colombo, Gherardo. 1994. "Le Indagini della Magistratura Italiana nei Reati contro la Pubblica Amministrazione il Danno Conseguente alla Corruzione." *Questione Giustizia*, 2–3: 467–478.

Colombo, Gherardo. 2010. *Il Vizio della Memoria*. Milano: Feltrinelli Editore.

Coppola, Franco. 1986. "La Piccola Svolta al CSM." *La Repubblica*, February 5. https://ricerca.repubblica.it/repubblica/archivio/repubblica/1986/02/05/la-piccola-svolta-al-csm.html?ref=search

Coppola, Franco. 1988. "Nella Trincea Chiamata Calabria." *La Repubblica*, February 23. http://ricerca.repubblica.it/repubblica/archivio/repubblica/1988/02/23/nella-trincea-chiamata-calabria.html?ref=search

Coppola, Franco. 1991. "L'Accusa del CSM 'Stato in Agonia'." *La Repubblica*, May 9. https://ricerca.repubblica.it/repubblica/archivio/repubblica/1991/05/09/accusa-del-csm-stato-in-agonia.html

Coppola, Franco. 1992*a*. "Mele alla Procura di Roma." *La Repubblica*, July 2.

Coppola, Franco. 1992*b*. "Misteri, Scivoloni, Trabocchetti Questo E' il Porto delle Nebbie." *La Repubblica*, June 23.

Coppola, Franco. 1992*c*. "Caselli a Palermo." *La Repubblica*, December 18. http://ricerca.repubblica.it/repubblica/archivio/repubblica/1992/12/18/caselli-palermo.html

Corbet, Sylvie. 2021. "France's Sarkozy Convicted of Corruption, Sentenced to Jail." Associated Press, March 1. https://apnews.com/article/nicolas-sarkozy-convincted-corruption-france-6ee89cb03ba8f3888ac64447ebf61f28

Corte di Assise di Appello di Roma March 14, 1985.

Corte di Assise di Roma, October 12, 1988.

Couso, Javier, and Lisa Hilbink. 2011. "From Quietism to Incipient Activism." In *Courts in Latin America*, edited by Gretchen Helmke and Julio Rios-Figueroa, 99–127. New York: Cambridge University Press.

Couso, Javier, Alexandra Huneeus, and Rachel Sieder. 2010. *Cultures of Legality: Judicialization and Political Activism in Latin America*. New York: Cambridge University Press.

D'Avanzo, Giuseppe. 1992. "E il Procuratore delle Polemiche Decide di Non Andare in Pensione." *La Repubblica*, February 11.

D'Avanzo, Giuseppe. 1993. "Roma Procura delle Nebbie? No, Capitale delle Inchieste." *La Repubblica*, July 23. http://ricerca.repubblica.it/repubblica/archivio/repubblica/1993/07/23/roma-procura-delle-nebbie-no-capitale.html?ref=search

Dalla Chiesa, Nando. 1986. "Il Caffe' di Mottini e il Segretario." *Società Civile*, 1(4): 3.

Dalla Chiesa, Nando. Interview by author. Milan, Italy. March 31.

Davigo, Piercamillo, and Grazia Mannozzi. 2007. *La Corruzione in Italia: Percezione Sociale e Controllo Penale*. Roma: Laterza.

De Sá e Silva, Fábio. 2020. "From Car Wash to Bolsonaro: Law and Lawyers in Brazil's Illiberal Turn (2014–2018)." *Journal of Law and Society*, 47(1): 90–110.

De Vito, Riccardo. 2017. "Soggetti Soltanto alla Legge. I Magistrati e le Carriere." *Questione Giustizia*, 4: 58–65.

Del Mastro, Azzurra. 2014. *La Magistratura e il CSM nel Sistema Costituzionale Italiano. Il Fenomeno della Politicizzazione delle Correnti*. PhD diss., Università degli Studi "Roma Tre."

Della Porta, Donatella. 2001. "A Judges' Revolution? Political Corruption and the Judiciary in Italy." *European Journal of Political Research*, 39(1): 1–21.

Della Porta, Donatella, and Alberto Vannucci. 2007. *Mani Impunite. Vecchia e Nuova Corruzione in Italia.* Roma: Laterza.

Della Porta, Donatella, and Alberto Vannucci. 2012. *Corrupt Exchanges: Actors, Resources, and Mechanisms of Political Corruption.* New York: Walter de Gruyter, Inc.

Della Porta, Donatella, and Alberto Vannucci. 2016. *The Hidden Order of Corruption: An Institutional Approach.* New York: Routledge.

Della Porta, Donatella, Salvatore Sberna, and Alberto Vannucci. 2015. "Centripetal and Centrifugal Corruption in Post-democratic Italy." *Italian Politics*, 30(1): 198–217.

Di Federico, Giuseppe. 1978. "La Professione Giudiziaria ed il Suo Contesto Burocratico." *Rivista Trimestrale di Diritto e Procedura Civile*, 2: 798–781.

Di Federico, Giuseppe. 1981. "Saggio Introduttivo." In *Le Attività Extragiudiziarie dei Magistrati Ordinarie*, edited by Francesca Zanotti, xi–lxxvi. Padova: CEDAM.

Di Federico, Giuseppe. 1990. "'Lottizzazioni Correntizie' e 'Politicizzazione' del CSM: Quali Rimedi?" *Quaderni costituzionali*, 2: 279–297.

Di Federico, Giuseppe. 2012. "Il Contributo del Csm alla Crisi della Giustizia." Paper presented at the workshop Le Novità in Materia di Ordinamento Giudiziario, October 19.

Di Lello, Giuseppe. 1989. "Cronache Istituzionali. Trappole per Giudici a Palermo." *Questione Giustizia*, 3: 711–716.

Di Nicola, Andrea. 2003. "Dieci Anni di Lotta alla Corruzione in Italia. Cosa Non Ha Funzionato e Cosa Puó Ancora Funzionare." In *Rapporto sulla criminalità in Italia*, edited by M. Barbagli , 109–133. Bologna: Il Mulino.

Di Pietro, Antonio. 1991. "La Tangente Moderna." *Società Civile*, May: 8–9.

Di Pietro, Antonio. Interview by author. Phone. July 30.

E.V. 1995. "Pensioni Facili un Pool di Giudici Indaga a Roma." *La Repubblica*, November. https://ricerca.repubblica.it/repubblica/archivio/repubblica/1995/11/09/pensioni-facili-un-pool-di-giudici.html?ref=search

Edmondo Bruti Liberati. 2017. "Magistratura e Società nell'Italia Repubblicana. Esperiena Storica e Problemi Aperti." Lecture, Scuola Superiore della Magistratura, Italy, June 14.

Emanuele, Vincenzo, and Alessandro Chiaramonte. 2020. "Going Out of the Ordinary. The De-Institutionalization of the Italian Party System in Comparative Perspective." *Contemporary Italian Politics*, 12(1): 4–22.

Falcone, Giovanni, and Giuliano Turone. 2015. "Tecniche di indagine in materia di mafia." *Rivista di Studi e Ricerche sulla criminalitàorganizzata*, 1(1): 116–153.

Fazzo, Luca. "Il PM Escluso dal Pool Vuol Uscire dal Processo 'Duomo Connection'." *La Repubblica*, October 1, 1991. https://ricerca.repubblica.it/repubblica/archivio/repubblica/1991/10/01/il-pm-escluso-dal-pool-vuol-uscire.html

Fioriglio, Gianluigi. 2003. "Brevi Riflessioni in Tema di Premialità, Dissociazione e Collaboratori di Giustizia." *Trimestre*, 1–2: 171–186.

Fisman, Raymond, and Miriam A. Golden. 2017. *Corruption: What Everyone Needs To Know*. New York: Oxford University Press.

Fracanzani, Edoardo Maria. 2014. *Le Origini del Conflitto: I Partiti Politici, la Magistratura e il Principio di Legalità nella Prima Repubblica (1974 – 1983)*. Soveria Mannelli: Rubbettino Editore.

Freddi, Giorgio. 1978. *Tensioni e Conflitto nella Magistratura: Un'Analisi Istituzionale dal Dopoguerra al 1968*. Roma: Laterza.

Garoupa, Nuno, and Tom Ginsburg. 2009. "Guarding the Guardians: Judicial Councils and Judicial Independence." *The American Journal of Comparative Law*, 57(1): 103–134.

Georgakopoulos, Nicholas L. 2000. "Discretion in the Career and Recognition Judiciary." *The University of Chicago Law School Roundtable*, 7(1): 205–225.

Gerino, Claudio. 1992. "La Super-Cupola di Politici e Mafiosi." *La Repubblica*, December 3. http://ricerca.repubblica.it/repubblica/archivio/repubblica/1992/12/03/la-super-cupola-di-politici-mafiosi.html?ref=search

Giglioli, Pier Paolo. 1996. "Political Corruption and the Media: The Tangentopoli Affair." *International Social Science Journal*, 48(3): 381–394.

Golden, Miriam, and Lucio Picci. 2006. "Corruption and the Management of Public Works in Italy." In *International Handbook on the Economics of Corruption*, edited by Susan Rose-Ackerman, 457–483. Cheltenham and Northampton: Edward Elgar.

Golden, Miriam A. 2003. "Electoral Connections: The Effects of the Personal Vote on Political Patronage, Bureaucracy and Legislation in Postwar Italy." *British Journal of Political Science*, 33(2): 189–212.

Golden, Miriam A., and Eric C. C. Chang. 2001. "Competitive Corruption: Factional Conflict and Political Malfeasance in Postwar Italian Christian Democracy." *World Politics*, 53(4): 588–622.

González-Ocantos, Ezequiel, and Viviana Baraybar Hidalgo. 2019. "Lava Jato Beyond Borders." *Taiwan Journal of Democracy*, 15(1): 63–89.

González-Ocantos, Ezequiel. 2014. "Persuade Them or Oust Them: Crafting Judicial Change and Transitional Justice in Argentina." *Comparative Politics*, 46(4): 479–498.

González-Ocantos, Ezequiel A. 2016. *Shifting Legal Visions: Judicial Change and Human Rights Trials in Latin America*. New York: Cambridge University Press.

Gratteri, Nicola, and Antonio Nicaso. 2010. *Fratelli di Sangue*. Milano: Edizioni Mondadori.

Guarnieri, Carlo. 2003. *Giustizia e Politica: I Nodi della Seconda Repubblica*. Bologna: Il Mulino.

Guarnieri, Carlo. 2004. "Appointment and Career of Judges in Continental Europe: The Rise of Judicial Self-government." *Legal Studies*, 24(1–2): 169–187.

Guarnieri, Carlo. 2007. "Lawyers and Statist Liberalism in Italy." In *Fighting for Political Freedom: Comparative Studies of the Legal Complex and Political Liberalism*, edited by Terence C. Halliday, Lucien Karpik, and Malcolm Feeley, 439–463. Oxford and Portland: Hart Publishing.

Hav, F. 1992. "Via ai 'Pool,' l'Inchiesta Si Specializza." *Corriere della Sera*, December 30.

Hav. F. 1996. "Salvi: Grave Perdita, E' un Punto di Riferimento." *Corriere della Sera*, September 5.

Hawkins, Derek. 2019. "Progressive Lawyer Wins San Francisco District Attorney Race, Continuing National Reform Trend." *Washington Post*, November 10. https://www.washingtonpost.com/nation/2019/11/10/progressive-lawyer-wins-san-francisco-district-attorney-race-continuing-national-reform-trend/

Hilbink, Lisa. 2007. *Judges beyond Politics in Democracy and Dictatorship: Lessons from Chile*. New York: Cambridge University Press.

Hilbink, Lisa. 2012. "The Origins of Positive Judicial Independence." *World Politics*, 64(4): 587–621.

Hirschl, Ran. 2008. "The Judicialization of Mega-Politics and the Rise of Political Courts." *Annual Review of Political Science*, 11: 93–118.

Hirschl, Ran. 2009. *Towards Juristocracy: The Origins and Consequences of the New Constitutionalism*. Cambridge, MA: Harvard University Press.

Holland, Kenneth M. 1991. *Judicial Activism in Comparative Perspective*. New York: Springer.

Iaryczower, Matias, Pablo T. Spiller, and Mariano Tommasi. 2002. "Judicial Independence in Unstable Environments, Argentina 1935-1998." *American Journal of Political Science*, 46(4): 699–716.

Imposimato, Ferdinando, and Sandro Provvisionato. 2018. *Doveva Morire Chi Ha Ucciso Aldo Moro Il Giudice dell'Inchiesta Racconta*. Milano: Chiarelettere.

Ingram, Matthew C. 2012. "Crafting Courts in New Democracies: Ideology and Judicial Council Reforms in Three Mexican States." *Comparative Politics*, 44(4): 439–458.

Ingram, Matthew C. 2015. *Crafting Courts in New Democracies: The Politics of Subnational Judicial Reform in Brazil and Mexico*. Cambridge: Cambridge University Press, 2015.

Ingram, Matthew C. 2016. "Networked Justice: Judges, the Diffusion of Ideas, and Legal Reform Movements in Mexico." *Journal of Latin American Studies*, 48(4): 739–768.

Interview with former prosecutor Antonio Di Pietro, phone, July 30, 2017.

Interview with prosecutor Armando Spataro, Milan, April 23, 2016.

Italian Parliament. Commissione Parlamentare d'Inchiesta sul Fenomeno della Mafia in Sicilia on December 17, 1974. *Testo delle Dichiarazione del Dottor Nestore Pedone e del Dottor Domenico Signorino, Sostituti Procuratori della Repubblica presso il Tribunale di Palermo*. VI Legislature.

Italian Parliament. Commissione Parlamentare d'Inchiesta sul Fenomeno della Mafia in Sicilia. February 4, 1976. *Relazione Conclusiva*. VI Legislature.

Italian Parliament. Commissione Parlamentare d'Inchiesta sulla Strage di Via Fani, sul Sequestro e l'Assassinio di aldo Moro, e sul Terrorismo in Italia. 1990. *Allegato alla Relazione. Volume LII*. Eighth Legislature. https://www.senato.it/service/PDF/PDFServer/BGT/908833.pdf (Accessed on June 14, 2023).

Italian Parliament. Commissione Parlamentare di Inchiesta sul Rapimento e la Morte di Aldo Moro. 2015*a*. *Resoconto stenografico*. Seventeenth Legislature, seduta n. 35, May 6. http://documenti.camera.it/leg17/resoconti/commissioni/stenografici/html/68/audiz2/audizione/2015/05/06/indice_stenografico.0035.html (Accessed on June 14, 2023).

Italian Parliament. Relazione alla Commissione parlamentare di indagine sul caso Moro. 2015*b*. *Resoconto Stenografico della Relazione alla Comissione*. Seventeenth Legislature, seduta n. 29, March 25. http://documenti.camera.it/leg17/resoconti/commissioni/stenografici/html/68/audiz2/audizione/2015/03/25/indice_stenografico.0029.html (Accessed on June 14, 2023).

Jardim De Santa Cruz Oliveira, Maria Angela, and Nuno Garoupa. 2011. "Choosing Judges in Brazil: Reassessing Legal Transplants from the United States." *The American Journal of Comparative Law*, 59(2): 529–561.

Johnson, David. 2003. "A Tale of Two Systems: Prosecuting Corruption in Japan and Italy." In *The State of Civil Society in Japan*, edited by Frank J. Schwartz and Susan J. Parr, 257–280. New York: Cambridge University Press.

Johnson, David T. 2000. "Why the Wicked Sleep: The Prosecution of Political Corruption in Postwar Japan." *Asian Perspective*, 24(4): 59–77.

Johnson, David T. 2002. *The Japanese Way of Justice: Prosecuting Crime in Japan*. New York: Oxford University Press.

Johnson, David T. 2012. "Japan's Prosecution System." *Crime and Justice*, 41(1): 35–74.

Kapiszewski, Diana. 2012. *High Courts and Economic Governance in Argentina and Brazil*. New York: Cambridge University Press.

Kmiec, Keenan D. 2004. "The Origin and Current Meanings of 'Judicial Activism'." *California Law Review*, 92(5): 1441–1477.

La Licata, Francesco. 1993. *Storia di Giovanni Falcone*. Milano: Rizzoli.

La Torre, Massimo. 2015. "Between Nightmare and Noble Dream: Judicial Activism and Legal Theory." In *Judicial Activism: An Interdisciplinary Approach to the American and European Experiences*, edited by Coutinho, Luís Pereira, Massimo La Torre, and Steven D. Smith, 3–14. New York: Springer.

LaPalombara, Joseph. 1989. *Democracy, Italian Style*. New Haven: Yale University Press.

Lentini, Fabrizio. 2011. *La Primavera Breve Quando Palermo Sognava una Citta' per l'Uomo*. Milano: Paoline.

Levitsky, Steven, and Daniel Ziblatt. 2018. *How Democracies Die*. New York: Penguin Random House.

Licandro, Agatino, and Aldo Varano. 1993. *La Citta' Dolente: Confessione di un Sindaco Corrotto*. Torino: Einaudi.

Lijphart, Arend. 1975. "The Comparable-Cases Strategy in Comparative Research." *Comparative Political Studies*, 8(2): 158–177.

Lindqquist, Stefanie, and Frank Cross. 2009. *Measuring Judicial Activism*. New York: Oxford University Press.

Lodato, Saverio. 2012. *Quarant'Anni di Mafia: Storia di una Guerra Infinita*. BUR Rizzoli: Milano.

Lutz, Ellen L., and Kathryn Sikkink. 2000. "International Human Rights Law and Practice in Latin America." *International Organization*, 54(3): 633–659.

M. Ne. 1987. "Delle Chiaie-Infelisi, il Caso Finisce al CSM." *Corriere della Sera*, April 6.

Maddow, Rachel, and Michael Yarvitz. 2020. *Bag Man: The Wild Crimes, Audacious Cover-Up, and Spectacular Downfall of a Brazen Crook in the White House*. New York: Crown Publishing Group.

Madeo, Alfonso. 1971. "Il Procuratore Capo di Palermo Ucciso a Raffiche di Mitra con il Suo Autista." *Il Corriere della Sera*, May 6.

Marroni, Stefano. 1988. "Un Arresto Che Offende Anche la Nostra Liberta'." *La Repubblica*, March 18. https://ricerca.repubblica.it/repubblica/archivio/repubblica/1988/03/18/un-arresto-che-offende-anche-la-nostra.html?ref=search

Mastrogiacomo, Daniele. 1993. "Palazzaccio alla Riscossa." *La Repubblica*, January 22. PALAZZACCIO ALLA RISCOSSA - la Repubblica.it

Mastrogiacomo, Daniele. 1994. "I Sostituti di Roma 'Mele Siamo con Te'." *La Repubblica,* January 13.

Mastrogiacomo, Daniele. 1996*a*. "'Non E' il Porto delle Nebbie'." *La Repubblica*, March 14. https://ricerca.repubblica.it/repubblica/archivio/repubblica/1996/03/14/non-il-porto-delle-nebbie.html?ref=search

Mastrogiacomo, Daniele. 1996*b*. "Coiro Sotto Processo al CSM." *La Repubblica*, June 7. https://ricerca.repubblica.it/repubblica/archivio/repubblica/1996/06/07/coiro-sotto-processo-al-csm.html

Mastrogiacomo, Daniele. 1998. "Inchiesta Bis sui Palazzi d'Oro." *La Repubblica*, March 6.

Mazzocchi, Silvana. 1985. "Le Battaglie del Grande Inquisitore." *La Repubblica*, September 4. http://ricerca.repubblica.it/repubblica/archivio/repubblica/1985/09/04/le-battaglie-del-grande-inquisitore.html

Mazzocchi, Silvana. 1987. "E Cosi' Infelisi, il PM- Superstar Imbocco' il Viale del Tramonto." *La Repubblica*, April 16. http://ricerca.repubblica.it/repubblica/archivio/repubblica/1987/04/16/cosi-infelisi-il-pm-superstar.html

Mazzocchi, Silvana. 1988. "Scontro nel CSM sul Caso dei Giudici Anti 'Ndrangheta." *La Repubblica*, October 19. https://ricerca.repubblica.it/repubblica/archivio/repubblica/1988/10/19/scontro-nel-csm-sul-caso-dei-giudici.html

Mazzocchi, Silvana. 1990. "Il CSM Elegge tra le Polemiche il Procuratore Capo di Palermo." *La Repubblica*, June 8. https://ricerca.repubblica.it/repubblica/archivio/repubblica/1990/06/08/il-csm-elegge-tra-le-polemiche-il.html?ref=search

Melton, James, and Tom Ginsburg. 2014. "Does De Jure Judicial Independence Really Matter? A Reevaluation of Explanations for Judicial Independence." *Journal of Law and Courts*, 2(2): 187–217.

Meniconi, Antonella. 2015. "La Storia dell'Associazionismo Giudiziario: Alcune Annotazioni." *Questione Giustizia*, 4: 220–226.

Merryman, John Henry, and Vincenzo Vigoriti. 1967. "When Courts Collide: Constitution and Cassation in Italy." *The American Journal of Comparative Law*, 15(4): 665–686.

Mershon, Carol. 1996. "The Costs of Coalition: Coalition Theories and Italian Governments." *American Political Science Review*, 90(3): 534–554.

Michel, Verónica. 2017. "The Role of Prosecutorial Independence and Prosecutorial Accountability in Domestic Human Rights Trials." *Journal of Human Rights*, 16(2): 193–219.

Milella, Liana. 1998*a*. "Milano Roma, Non Esistono Due Giustizie." *La Repubblica*, March 16. http://ricerca.repubblica.it/repubblica/archivio/repubblica/1998/03/16/milano-roma-non-esistono-due-giustizie.html?ref=search

Milella, Liana. 1998*b*. "Caltagirone Pago' I Giudici." *La Repubblica*, December 16. http://ricerca.repubblica.it/repubblica/archivio/repubblica/1998/12/16/caltagirone-pago-giudici.html?ref=search

Milella, Liana. 2016. "Magistratura al Voto per l'ANM, Davigo Grande Favorito." *La Repubblica*, March 6. Magistratura al voto per l'Anm, Davigo grande favorito - la Repubblica.

Ministerio Fiscal. N.d. "El Consejo Fiscal." https://www.fiscal.es/el-consejo-fiscal (Accessed on June 11, 2023).

Montana, Riccardo, and David Nelken. 2011. "The Ambivalent Role of Italian Prosecutors and their Resistance to 'Moral Panics' about Crime." In *Routledge Handbook of International Criminology*, edited by Cindy J. Smith, Sheldon X. Zhang, and Rosemary Barberet, 286–297. New York: Routledge.

Montoro Luigi. 1990. "Ancora della Progressione in Carriera del Magistrato." *Magistratura Indipendente*, 2(1): 15–16.

Moriondo, Ezio. 1967. *L'Ideologia della Magistratura Italiana*. Roma: Laterza.

Moro, Sergio Fernando. 2004. "Considerações Sobre a Operação Mani Pulite." *Revista Cej*, 8(26): 56–62.

Moro, Sérgio Fernando. 2018. "Preventing Systemic Corruption in Brazil." *Daedalus*, 147(3): 157–168.

Mulé, Giorgio. 1990. "Ciancimino Torna in Carcere." *Il Giornale di Sicilia*, June 6.

Munck, Gerardo L. 2004. "Tools for Qualitative Research." In *Rethinking Social Inquiry: Diverse Tools, Shared Standards*, edited by Henry E. Brady and David Collier, 105–121. New York: Rowman & Littlefield Publishers, Inc.

Nelken, David. 1996*a*. "The Judges and Political Corruption in Italy." *Journal of Law & Society* 23(1): 95–112.

Nelken, David. 1996*b*. "A Legal Revolution? The Judges and Tangentopoli." In *The New Italian Republic: From the Fall of the Berlin Wall to Berlusconi*, edited by Stephen Gundle and Simon Parker, 191–205. New York: Routledge.

Nelken, David. 1996*c*. "Stopping the Judges." *Italian Politics*, 11: 187–204.

Nelken, David. 1997. "Il Significato di Tangentopoli: La Risposta Giudiziaria alla Corruzione e I Suoi Limiti." In *Storia d'Italia. Annali 14. Legge Diritto Giustizia*, edited by Violante, Luciano and Livia Minervini, 597–627. Torino: Einaudi.

Nelken, David. 2002. *Tangentopoli*. In *La Criminalità in Italia*, edited by M. Barbagli and U. Prismi Gatti, 55–67. Bologna: Le edizioni del Mulino.

Nelken, David. 2002*a*. "Legitimate Suspicions? Berlusconi and the Judges." *Italian Politics*, 18: 112–128.

Nelken, David. 2002*b*. *Tangentopoli*. In *La Criminalità in Italia*, edited by M. Barbagli and U. Prismi Gatti, 55–67. Bologna: Le edizioni del Mulino.

Nelken, David. 2010. *Comparative Criminal Justice Making Sense of Difference*. Thousand Oaks: Sage Publications Inc.

Nelken, David. 2013. "Can Prosecutors Be Too Independent? An Italian Case-Study." In *European Penology*, edited by Tom Daems, Dirk van Zyl Smit, and Sonja Snacken, 249–270. Portland: Hart Publishing.

Nelken, David, and Maria Letizia Zanier. 2006. "Tra Norme e Prassi: Durata del Processo Penale e Strategie degli Operatori del Diritto." *Sociologia del diritto*, 33(1): 143–166.

Neppi Modona, Guido. 1992. "Giustizia in Cassazione." *La Repubblica*, February 2. http://ricerca.repubblica.it/repubblica/archivio/repubblica/1992/02/01/giustizia-in-cassazione.html?ref=search

Neppi Modona, Guido. 1993. "Le Indagini di Milano." *La Repubblica*, February 21. http://ricerca.repubblica.it/repubblica/archivio/repubblica/1993/02/21/le-indagini-di-milano.html?ref=search

Nese, Marco. 1984. "Come al CSM Si E' Raggiunta l'Unanimità nella Votazione per la Scelta di Boschi." *Corriere della Sera*, March 15.

Olson, Susan M. 1984. "Challenges to the Gatekeeper: The Debate over Federal Litigation Authority." *Judicature*, 68: 71–86.

Orlando, Leoluca. 1989. "Palermo Il Consenso Governante." *Società Civile*, 5(May): 31.

P.S. 1987. "Sessanta Avvisi di Reato a Reggio Calabria." *La Repubblica*, April 25. http://ricerca.repubblica.it/repubblica/archivio/repubblica/1987/04/25/sessanta-avvisi-di-reato-reggio-calabria.html

Pederzoli, Patrizia, and Carlo Guarnieri. 1997. "The Judicialization of Politics, Italian Style." *Journal of Modern Italian studies*, 2(3): 321–336.

Pelizzari, Mario. 1976. "Niente Circolari Indigeste, Ma un'Allegra Bicchierata." *Corriere della Sera*, September 23, 1976: 8.

Peruzzotti, Enrique, and Catalina Smulovitz. 2003. "Societal and Horizontal Controls: Two Cases of a Fruitful Relationship." In *Democratic Accountability in Latin America*, edited by Scott Mainwaring and Christopher Welna, 309–331. New York: Oxford University Press.

Pignatone, Giuseppe, Michele Prestipino, and Gaetano Savatteri. 2012. *Il Contagio: Come la'Ndrangheta Ha Infettato l'Italia*. Roma: Laterza.

Pintacuda Ennio. 1986. "Palermo e l'Italia delle Citta'." *Società Civile*, 1(March): 11.

Pizzi, William T., and Luca Marafioti. 1992. "The New Italian Code of Criminal Procedure: The Difficulties of Building an Adversarial Trial System on a Civil Law Foundation." *The Yale Journal of International Law*, 17: 1.

Pizzorno, Alessandro. 1992. "La Corruzione nel Sistema Politico." Introduction to *Lo Scambio Occulto,* by Donatella Della Porta, 13–43. Bologna: Il Mulino.

R.F. 1993. "Tangenti, Politico Siciliano Avrebbe Gia' Fatto 70 Nomi." *Il Giornale di Sicilia*, August 11.

Ravelli, Fabrizio. 1987. "'Ma Chi Ha Fatto Piu' Carriera in Sicilia I Giudici Antimafia o gli In'." *La Repubblica*, January 24. https://ricerca.repubblica.it/repubblica/archivio/repubblica/1987/01/24/ma-chi-ha-fatto-piu-carriera-in.html?ref=search

Ravelli, Fabrizio. 1989. "Tangenti, Ligato Imputato." *La Repubblica*, May 31. https://ricerca.repubblica.it/repubblica/archivio/repubblica/1989/05/31/tangenti-ligato-imputato.html?ref=search

Ravelli, Fabrizio. 1993. "E' Armistizio tra Roma e Milano." *La Repubblica*, February 20. http://ricerca.repubblica.it/repubblica/archivio/repubblica/1993/02/20/armistizio-tra-roma-milano.html?ref=search

Reale, Federica. 2018. "Il Giudice per le Indagini Preliminari: un Distacco Reale o Apparente dal Giudice Istruttore?" *Italian Review of Legal History*, 4(7): 1–23.

Recanatesi, Franco. 1986. "Uccidendo Chinnici la Mafia Ci Ha Sfidato e Ora Dovra' Pagare." *La Repubblica*, February 8. https://ricerca.repubblica.it/repubblica/archivio/repubblica/1986/02/08/uccidendo-chinnici-la-mafia-ci-ha-sfidato.html?ref=search

Roberto, Suro. 1987. "338 Guilty in Sicily in Mafia Trial; 19 Get Life Terms." *The New York Times*, December 17. http://www.nytimes.com/1987/12/17/world/338-guilty-in-sicily-in-a-mafia-trial-19-get-life-terms.html.

Riker, William H. 1962. *The Theory of Political Coalitions*. New Haven: Yale University Press.

Ríos-Figueroa, Julio. 2007. "Fragmentation of Power and the Emergence of an Effective Judiciary in Mexico, 1994–2002." *Latin American Politics and Society*, 49(1): 31–57.

Ríos-Figueroa, Julio. 2012. "Justice System Institutions and Corruption Control: Evidence from Latin America." *Justice System Journal*, 33(2): 195–214.

Rodríguez-Garavito, César. 2011. "Ethnicity. gov: Global Governance, Indigenous Peoples, and the Right to Prior Consultation in Social Minefields." *Indiana Journal of Global Legal Studies*, 18(1): 263–305.

Rosa, Riccardo, and Matteo Zilocchi. 2021. *Il Corvo di Palermo. Le Lettere Anonime Che Spaccarono l'Antimafia e Infettarono la Giustizia Italiana*. Palermo: Glifo Edizioni.

Rosso, Umberto. 1987. "Palermo, Nuovo Procuratore." *La Repubblica*, July 16. https://ricerca.repubblica.it/repubblica/archivio/repubblica/1987/07/16/palermo-nuovo-procuratore.html?ref=search

Rosso, Umberto. 1992. "Le Condizioni dei Giudici 'Ribelli'." La Repubblica, July 27. http://ricerca.repubblica.it/repubblica/archivio/repubblica/1992/07/25/le-condizioni-dei-giudici-ribelli.html.

Sadek, Maria Tereza. 2001. "The Public Prosecutor's Office and Legal Change in Brazil." *IDS Bulletin*, 32(1): 65–73.

Sadek, Maria Tereza, and Rosângela Batista Cavalcanti. 2003. "The New Brazilian Public Prosecutor: An Agent of Accountability." In *Democratic Accountability in Latin America*, edited by Scott Mainwaring and Cristopher Welna, 201–227. New York: Oxford University Press.

Sarzanini, Lorenza. 1992. "'Roma Non E' il Porto delle Nebbie.' Il Procuratore Mele: Le Inchieste su Tangenti e SAFIM Non Si Fermano." *Il Messaggero*, November 11.

Sberna, Salvatore, and Alberto Vannucci. 2013. "'It's the Politics, Stupid!'. The Politicization of Anti-Corruption in Italy." *Crime, Law and Social Change*, 60(5): 565–593.

Scottoni, Franco. 1985. "Una Giornata per la Giustizia, Manifestazione in 23 Città." *La Repubblica*, June 16.

Scottoni, Franco. 1988*a*. "Moro-Ter Chiesti 29 Ergastoli." *La Repubblica*, February 5. http://ricerca.repubblica.it/repubblica/archivio/repubblica/1988/02/05/moro-ter-chiesti-29-ergastoli.html

Scottoni, Franco. 1988*b*. "Il CSM Ha 'Bocciato' Falcone." *La Repubblica*, January 20. https://ricerca.repubblica.it/repubblica/archivio/repubblica/1988/01/20/il-csm-ha-bocciato-falcone.html?ref=search

Scottoni, Franco. 1992*a*. "Chiudete il Caso Gladio." *La Repubblica*, February 4. 'CHIUDETE IL CASO GLADIO' - la Repubblica.it

Scottoni, Franco. 1992*b*. "Safim Sotto Inchiesta." *La Repubblica*, June 10. http://ricerca.repubblica.it/repubblica/archivio/repubblica/1992/06/10/safim-sotto-inchiesta.html?ref=search

Scottoni, Franco. 1993. "Voglia di Pace tra Roma e Milano." *La Repubblica*, February 19. http://ricerca.repubblica.it/repubblica/archivio/repubblica/1993/02/19/voglia-di-pace-tra-roma-milano.html?ref=search

Scuteri, Antonio. 1992. "Il Nuovo Catasto Nato a Tangentopoli." *La Repubblica*, August 13. http://ricerca.repubblica.it/repubblica/archivio/repubblica/1992/08/13/il-nuovo-catasto-nato-tangentopoli.html?ref=search.

Segal, Jeffrey A., and Harold J. Spaeth. 1996. "The Influence of Stare Decisis on the Votes of United States Supreme Court Justices." *American Journal of Political Science*, 40(4): 971–1003.

Segal, Jeffrey A., and Harold J. Spaeth. 2002. *The Supreme Court and the Attitudinal Model Revisited*. New York: Cambridge University Press.

Sentenza della Suprema Corte di Cassazione, Prima Sezione Penale, 8042/1992.

Sergi, Pantaleone. 1992*a*. "In Manette Tutta la Giunta." *La Repubblica*, July 18. http://ricerca.repubblica.it/repubblica/archivio/repubblica/1992/07/18/in-manette-tutta-la-giunta.html?ref=search

Sergi, Pantaleone. 1992*b*. "Manette ai Potenti di Reggio." *La Repubblica*, September 8. http://ricerca.repubblica.it/repubblica/archivio/repubblica/1992/09/08/manette-ai-potenti-di-reggio.html?ref=search.

Sergi, Pantaleone. 1992*c*. "Se Quello Canta' Cosí Franó il Sistema." *La Repubblica*, September 9. http://ricerca.repubblica.it/repubblica/archivio/repubblica/1992/09/09/se-quello-canta-cosi-frano-il.html.

Sergi, Pantaleone. 1992*d*. "Reggio, Appalti e 'Ndrangheta." *La Repubblica*, May 19. https://ricerca.repubblica.it/repubblica/archivio/repubblica/1992/05/19/reggio-appalti-ndrangheta.html?ref=search

Sergi, Pantaleone. 1993*a*. "I Giudici sul Delitto Ligato 'Nessuna Sconfessione'." *La Repubblica,* April 8. http://ricerca.repubblica.it/repubblica/archivio/repubblica/1993/04/08/giudici-sul-delitto-ligato-nessuna.html?ref=search

Sergi, Pantaleone. 1993*b*. "Preso Imerti, Re della 'Ndrangheta." *La Repubblica*, March 24. http://ricerca.repubblica.it/repubblica/archivio/repubblica/1993/03/24/preso-imerti-re-della-ndrangheta.html?ref=search.

Sergi, Pantaleone. 1994. "Gli Onorevoli Condannati." *La Repubblica*, February 23. http://ricerca.repubblica.it/repubblica/archivio/repubblica/1994/02/23/gli-onorevoli-condannati.html?ref=search.

Severisio Anna. "Le Mani sull'Ospedale." *Società Civile*, 1(March): 3.

Shin, Gi-Wook, and Rennie J. Moon. 2017. "South Korea after Impeachment." *Journal of Democracy*, 28(4): 117–131.

Skaar, Elin. 2011. *Judicial Independence and Human Rights in Latin America: Violations, Politics, and Prosecution*. New York: Palgrave Macmillan.

Smith, Jamil. 2021. "'Progressive Prosecutors' Are Working within the System To Change It. How Is That Going?" *Vox*, July 30, 2021. https://www.vox.com/2021/7/30/22600669/larry-krasner-philadelphia-reform-prosecutors-crime

Smith, Rogers M. 1988. "Political Jurisprudence, the 'New Institutionalism', and the Future of Public Law." *American Political Science Review*, 82(1): 89–108.

Smulovitz, Catalina, and Enrique Peruzzotti. 2000. "Societal Accountability in Latin America." *Journal of Democracy*, 11(4): 147–158.

Società Civile. 1986. "Sottogovernare Milano." 4(December).

Società Civile. 1987. "Ma Questi Cosa Vogliono Un Oggetto Misterioso nel Cielo di Milano." 8(September).

Solazzo, Adriano. 1976. "Sette Uditori di Fresca Nomina Sostituiranno i 13 Giudici Trasferiti." *Corriere della Sera*, September 2.

Spataro, Armando. 2011. *Ne Valeva la Pena: Storie di Terrorismi e Mafie, di Segreti di Stato e di Giustizia Offesa*. Roma: Laterza.

Spataro, Armando. Interview by author. Milan, Italy. April 23.

Squillace Greco, Ettore. 1994. "Tangentopoli e Processo Penale in Reggio Calabria." *Questione Giustizia*, 4: 890–896.

Stajano Corrado. 1986. "Le Vecchie Rughe della Capitale Morale." *Società Civile*, 1(4): 4.

Stille, Alexander. 1995. *Excellent Cadavers: The Mafia and the Death of the First Italian Republic*. New York: Vintage Books.

Tony, Piero. 2015. *Io Non Posso Tacere. Confessioni di un Giudice di Sinistra*. Torino: Einaudi. Kindle.

Van Aaken, Anne, Lars P. Feld, and Stefan Voigt. 2010. "Do Independent Prosecutors Deter Political Corruption? An Empirical Evaluation across Seventy-Eight Countries." *American Law and Economics Review*, 12(1): 204–244.

Vauchez, Antoine. 2004. *L'institution Judiciaire Remotivée. Le Processus d'Institutionnalisation d'une Nouvelle justice en Italie (1960-2000)*. Paris: LGDJ.

Veltri, Filippo. 1988*a*. "Guerra di Mafia in 141 a Giudizio." *La Repubblica*, June 26. http://ricerca.repubblica.it/repubblica/archivio/repubblica/1988/06/26/guerra-di-mafia-in-141-giudizio.html?ref=search

Veltri, Filippo. 1988*b*. "Nuova 'Ndrangheta a Giudizio in 107." *La Repubblica*, June 28. http://ricerca.repubblica.it/repubblica/archivio/repubblica/1988/06/28/nuova-ndrangheta-giudizio-in-107.html?ref=search

Veltri, Filippo. 1992. "Carnevale: Colpo di Spugna su Quattro Ergastoli di Mafia." *La Repubblica*, March 20. http://ricerca.repubblica.it/repubblica/archivio/repubblica/1992/03/20/carnevale-colpo-di-spugna-su-quattro-ergastoli.html?ref=search

Verbeek, Bertjan, and Andrej Zaslove. 2016. "Italy: A Case of Mutating Populism?" *Democratization*, 23(2): 304–323.

Vigna, Piero Luigi. 2006. "Fighting Organized Crime, with Particular Reference to Mafia Crimes in Italy." *Journal of International Criminal Justice*, 4: 522–527.

Violante, Luciano. 2018. "Torino, Quarant'Anni Fa Iniziava il Processo alle BR Che Segnava l'Inizio della Fine." *Corriere della Sera*, March 9. https://torino.corriere.it/cultura/18_marzo_09/processo-brigate-rosse-l-inizio-fine-566eb4c2-237f-11e8-a79f-45565073a066.shtml

Voigt, Stefan, and Alexander J. Wulf. 2019. "What Makes Prosecutors Independent? Analysing the Institutional Determinants of Prosecutorial Independence." *Journal of Institutional Economics*, 15(1): 99–120.

Volcansek, Mary L. 1999. *Constitutional Politics in Italy: The Constitutional Court.* New York: St. Martin's Press.

Weyland, Kurt. 2005*a*. "Theories of Policy Diffusion Lessons from Latin American Pension Reform." *World Politics*, 57(2): 262–295.

Weyland, Kurt. 2005*b*. "The Diffusion of Innovations: How Cognitive Heuristics Shaped Bolivia's Pension Reform." *Comparative Politics*, 38(1): 21–42.

Weyland, Kurt. 2022. "How Populism Dies: Political Weaknesses of Personalistic Plebiscitarian Leadership." *Political Science Quarterly*, 137(1): 9–42.

Winter, Brian. 2017. "Brazil's Never-Ending Corruption Crisis: Why Radical Transparency Is the Only Fix." *Foreign Affairs*, 96(3): 87–94.

Woods, Patricia J. 2008. *Judicial Power and National Politics: Courts and Gender in the Religious-Secular Conflict in Israel.* Albany: Suny Press.

Index

Note: Page numbers followed by "n" denote endnotes.

About the Author

Dr. Lucia Manzi holds a PhD in political science from the University of Notre Dame. She is currently an assistant professor of political science at SUNY Plattsburgh. Dr. Manzi's research focuses on the prosecution of systemic corruption, prosecutorial behavior, and prosecutorial institutions, with a special focus on Italian politics. Her work has appeared in the *Law and Society Review* and the *Justice System Journal*.

www.ingramcontent.com/pod-product-compliance
Lightning Source LLC
LaVergne TN
LVHW010719210926
848485LV00002B/79
* 9 7 8 1 6 6 6 9 3 8 4 8 7 *